TRUMPET AFTER TRUMPET

TRUMPET AFTER TRUMPET

ERWIN R. GANE

Pacific Press® Publishing Association
Nampa, Idaho
Oshawa, Ontario, Canada
www.pacificpress.com

Cover design resources from iStockphoto.com
Inside design by Aaron Troia

Copyright © 2012 by Pacific Press® Publishing Association
Printed in the United States of America
All rights reserved

Library of Congress Cataloging-in-Publication Data:

Gane, Erwin R.
    Trumpet after trumpet : will Revelation's seven trumpets sound again? / Erwin R. Gane.
      p. cm.
    ISBN 13: 978-0-8163-2622-8 (pbk.)
    ISBN 10: 0-8163-2622-3 (pbk.)
  1. Bible. N.T. Revelation—Criticism, interpretation, etc. 2. Seventh-day Adventists—Doctrines. I. Title.

    BS2825.52.G36 2012
    228'. 06—dc23

                                                                              2011050395

You can obtain additional copies of this book by calling toll-free 1-800-765-6955 or by visiting www.adventistbookcenter.com.

12 13 14 15 16 • 5 4 3 2 1

Dedication

I dedicate this book to my beloved wife, Winsome, who for long years has patiently and lovingly encouraged me to speak and write the truths of God's Word. She has studied with me and offered helpful suggestions. But more importantly, her life has consistently demonstrated the love and tender concern of the Lord Jesus Christ for every individual within the orbit of her influence.

CONTENTS

CHARTS

PREFACE

My study of Revelation's trumpets began, in earnest, years ago when I was asked to teach the upper division Daniel and Revelation course at Pacific Union College. I was surprised that there was so little consensus among scholars on this section of Scripture. So much of what has been written is confusing, even contradictory. In this book I have tried to explain, as simply as possible, the meaning of the trumpets without attempting to relate my interpretation to the many and various interpretations that have already been offered.

My method allows the Bible to be its own expositor. We can grasp the symbolism of the trumpets only when we compare it with similar symbolism throughout Scripture. By tracing the symbols through both Old and New Testaments, the student can arrive at solid conclusions as to the meaning of Revelation's symbols.

I have also made considerable use of Ellen G. White's writings, not because I have departed from the Protestant principle that the Bible and the Bible only is the rule of our faith and practice, but because I am thoroughly convinced that God gave Ellen White insights into future events that are remarkably consistent with scriptural forecasts. My purpose is to establish interpretations from the Bible and then to use Ellen White's writings as corroboration.

The interpretive method that I favor is the philosophy of history approach. As I will explain in the first chapter, this method is an expansion of the continuous-historical recapitulationist interpretation, which regards the sections of Revelation as providing parallel coverage of Christian history from the time of Christ to the Second Advent.

The philosophy of history interpretation adds to this approach by recognizing history as cyclical and repetitive. Thus a historical application of an apocalyptic prophecy can reveal the type or kind of events that will occur in the end time.

This approach is opposed by those who think that apocalyptic prophecy can have only one application. Yet Jesus said the events surrounding the destruction of Jerusalem would typify events in the Middle Ages and events surrounding His second advent (see Matt. 24). Moreover, many interpreters have recognized a dual application of the little horn power of Daniel 8, regarding it as referring to both pagan and papal Rome. Furthermore, the prophecy of the seven churches (Rev. 2; 3) is generally recognized as having three applications: to the churches in Asia Minor in John's day; to the universal Christian church at any single stage of history; and to seven periods of church history.

By applying the philosophy of history approach to the trumpets, I have identified a dual interpretation of the prophecy. Without ignoring the validity of the historical application, I have recognized that the historical events often typify end-time events. I am convinced that the time prophecies were given to establish our confidence in historical interpretations. But these time prophecies are not intended to enable us to set times for end-time events. Rather, the type or kind of historical events enables us to foresee similar events in the end time. Such end-time applications must be entirely consistent with the specifications of each prophecy; they should not be the product of the interpreter's imagination.

I pray that readers will prayerfully consider the contents of this book, but more important, that they will commit themselves to seeking the Lord earnestly in preparation for the challenging events about to burst upon our world.

Chapter 1

The Theme and Structure of Revelation

The book of Revelation shows Christ, our heavenly High Priest, caring for the spiritual interests of His church throughout the Christian era. The theme of the book is simply stated in Revelation 1:1: "The revelation of Jesus Christ, which God gave him to show to his servants what must soon take place. He made it known by sending his angel to his servant John."

Revelation depicts Christ as fostering the spiritual life of His church during the period extending from His ascension until the Second Advent. He sends messages at every stage of Christian history—messages designed to encourage His beleaguered people, who are being attacked by Satan, the great adversary. These attacks come in the form of temptations to veer away from Christ by conforming to the mores of ungodly societies, and they come in the form of physical attacks upon Christ's faithful ones by those who wish to eliminate the influence of their testimony.

Christ's revelation of Himself necessarily involves His attempts to counteract Satan's destructive work. Hence the book of Revelation dwells, to a considerable degree, on the great controversy between Christ and Satan throughout the Christian era. Christ's revelation to

John, which is John's testimony to the church, involves an outline of Satan's work through religious and political powers designed to destroy Christ's church. It also involves Christ's counteracting influence by which He deals with those who cooperate with Satan, withdrawing His guiding and protecting influence from them and punishing them for their unfaithfulness.

The book of Revelation provides the encouraging assurance that Christ functions as our heavenly Mediator until the time shortly before His second advent that is often called "the close of probation." Revelation also encourages us by depicting Christ as our heavenly Judge and Advocate, who, prior to His second advent, investigates whether His professed people have received and are continually appropriating the power of His grace by the indwelling of the Holy Spirit. Revelation indicates that this pre-Advent judgment ends at the close of probation, shortly before the Second Advent. Then events occur that, inspired and spurred on by Satan, are designed to destroy the faithful people of God. But Christ is ever at hand to control the furnace of affliction lest it consume them.

Revelation guides our minds to the time at which Jesus will return in glory, raining retribution on those who have declared themselves His enemies and the enemies of His people. Then follows a graphic account of the triumph of His people in the heavenly kingdom, followed by the raising of the wicked at the end of one thousand years, the descent to this earth of the saved of all ages within the New Jerusalem, the final destruction of the wicked, the re-creation of the earth, and the eternal rejoicing of the people of God, who associate joyfully with Him and with one another forever.

The book of Revelation is meant to be understood; it was never a closed book. Much of the book of Daniel was closed until "the time of the end" (Dan. 12:9), when its vital messages would be revealed.

But Revelation has always been an open book, written for the edification and consolation of Christ's people. There's no question, however, that parts of Revelation have been understood only since the end-time unfolding of Daniel's prophecies.

The fact that Revelation is to be understood by Christ's followers is underlined by the blessing pronounced upon those who read it and who practice its teachings: "Blessed is he who reads and those who hear the words of this prophecy, and keep those things which are written in it; for the time is near" (Rev. 1:3, NKJV).

Ellen White urged Christian believers to give special attention to the book of Revelation.

> The solemn messages that have been given in their order in the Revelation are to occupy the first place in the minds of God's people. Nothing else is to be allowed to engross our attention.
>
> Precious time is rapidly passing, and there is danger that many will be robbed of the time which should be given to the proclamation of the messages that God has sent to a fallen world. Satan is pleased to see the diversion of minds that should be engaged in a study of the truths which have to do with eternal realities.
>
> The testimony of Christ, a testimony of the most solemn character, is to be borne to the world. All through the book of Revelation there are the most precious, elevating promises, and there are also warnings of the most fearfully solemn import. Will not those who profess to have a knowledge of the truth read the testimony given to John by Christ? Here is no guesswork, no scientific deception. Here are the truths that concern our present and future welfare. What is the chaff to the wheat?[1]

When the books of Daniel and Revelation are better understood, believers will have an entirely different religious experience. They will be given such glimpses of the open gates of heaven that heart and mind will be impressed with the character that all must develop in order to realize the blessedness which is to be the reward of the pure in heart.

The Lord will bless all who will seek humbly and meekly to understand that which is revealed in the Revelation. This book contains so much that is large with immortality and full of glory that all who read and search it earnestly receive the blessing to those "that hear the words of this prophecy, and keep those things which are written therein."[2]

As we near the close of this world's history, the prophecies relating to the last days especially demand our study. The last book of the New Testament scriptures is full of truth that we need to understand. Satan has blinded the minds of many, so that they have been glad of any excuse for not making the Revelation their study. But Christ through His servant John has here declared what shall be in the last days, and He says, "Blessed is he that readeth, and they that hear the words of this prophecy, and keep those things which are written therein." Rev. 1:3.[3]

INTERPRETATIONS OF REVELATION

Many commentaries on Revelation have been written over the centuries. (A list appears in the bibliography; see pages 313–320.) Few commentaries agree on major points of interpretation. The confusion is especially notable in the attempted interpretations of the seven trumpets. Such is the diversity of opinion that the average reader becomes immersed in a quagmire of confused detail and contradiction.

My purpose in writing this book is not to attempt to relate my understanding to the many different views of the trumpets, but simply to present the results of my own prayerful Bible study. Occasional endnotes will identify some points of agreement or disagreement. No approach to the book of Revelation will be productive unless the inquirer has constant recourse to the teaching ministry of the Holy Spirit. Jesus' promise is paramount: "But the Counselor, the Holy Spirit, whom the Father will send in my name, he will teach you all things, and bring to your remembrance all that I have said to you" (John 14:26). "When the Spirit of truth comes, he will guide you into all the truth, for he will not speak on his own authority, but whatever he hears he will speak, and he will declare to you the things that are to come" (John 16:13). I certainly do not claim that I am the only one whose mind is guided by the Spirit in the study of the book of Revelation. Even so, I have sought His teaching ministry as I have studied and written.

Commentators have used five main approaches to Revelation: (1) the preterist interpretation; (2) the futurist interpretation; (3) the continuous-historical straight line interpretation; (4) the continuous-historical recapitulationist interpretation; and (5) the philosophy-of-history interpretation.

The preterist interpretation confines the fulfillment of Revelation's messages mostly to the past, especially to the era of the early Christian church. Interpreters who adopt this approach ignore Revelation's cosmic sweep of history and its special focus on the end time.

The futurist interpretation says that for the most part, Revelation's prophecies will be fulfilled in what, from our perspective, is still the future. Dispensationalists and pre-Tribulationists employ this method of interpretation. They believe the events of Revelation 4 through 19 will occur within a seven-year period shortly before Christ's second advent, and they propound the idea of the secret rapture, the teaching that seven years before Christ's glorious appearing, faithful believers will be taken secretly to heaven.[4]

The continuous-historical straight line interpretation identifies the fulfillment of Revelation's prophecies in the period of history from Jesus' day to His second coming. Interpreters who follow this approach see the successive sections of Revelation as comprising a continuous line of events occurring in order throughout the Christian era.

The continuous-historical recapitulationist interpreters, Uriah Smith among them, see the sections of Revelation as paralleling each other, each of them reaching from the time of Christ to His second advent. In other words, they believe the seven churches, the seven seals, and the seven trumpets cover essentially the same periods of history from different perspectives.

Much can be said in favor of this view, but attempting to find too close a parallel between the churches, seals, and trumpets results in distortion. For example, the sixth *church* is Philadelphia (Rev. 3:7–13), regarded as representing the period of church history from 1798–1844, but the sixth *seal* is the Second Coming (Rev. 6:12–17). And while the seventh *church* is Laodicea, regarded as symbolizing the historical period of the church from 1844 to the second coming of Jesus, the seventh *seal* refers to events immediately *after* the Second Coming.

A more recent approach to Revelation is the philosophy-of-history interpretation. This view finds that Revelation portrays history as being cyclical. For example, the white horse of the first seal (Rev. 6:1, 2) is not seen as referring exclusively to the proclamation of righteousness by faith in the apostolic era; rather, it pictures the proclamation of this gospel truth in *every* era of Christian history—our era being portrayed as the time of the first angel's message of Revelation 14:6, 7.

In the philosophy-of-history approach, the prophecies of Revelation are seen as having applications at various stages of history. But the applications are not left to the imagination of the interpreter; they grow out of the detailed specifications of the prophecy itself. For example, the initial events that occur when the sixth seal is opened (Rev. 6:12, 13)—the great earthquake, the darkening of the sun, and the falling of the stars—may refer to events in history that were types or examples of similar events that will take place immediately prior to the second coming of Jesus. Such events are presented in the Old Testament as occurring in connection with the "day of the Lord" at the end of the world (see Isa. 29:5, 6; 13:9–11; 34:1–4). That all the events of Revelation 6:12–17 occur immediately prior to and at the Second Advent is clear from the context.

Kenneth Strand wrote of the application of the philosophy-of-history method in interpreting Revelation:

> Instead of treating the many variations, I would simply call attention here to one somewhat embracive approach which might loosely be called "philosophy of history." The particular type of "philosophy of history" which I have in mind correlates in a certain sense with both preterist and continuous-historical interpretation, but it does so in a way that allows for repeated historical fulfillments beyond the writer's own time or beyond any other specific time in history. From a certain viewpoint, this approach may be considered essentially a variation of the continuous-historical mode of

interpreting the book of Revelation. As a striking example of the approach I quote a few paragraphs from Ellen G. White, *Acts of the Apostles* (Mountain View, Calif., 1911), pp. 585–589:

"The names of the seven churches are symbolic of the church in different periods of the Christian era. The number seven indicates completeness, and is symbolic of the fact that the messages extend to the end of time, while the symbols used reveal the condition of the church at different periods in the history of the world. . . .

"At the time when John was given this revelation, many had lost their first love of gospel truth. But in His mercy God did not leave the church to continue in a backslidden state. In a message of infinite tenderness He revealed His love for them, and His desire that they should make sure work for eternity. 'Remember,' He pleaded, 'from whence thou are fallen, and repent, and do the first works.'

"The church was defective, and in need of stern reproof and chastisement; and John was inspired to record messages of warning and reproof and entreaty to those who, losing sight of the fundamental principles of the gospel, should imperil their hope of salvation. But always the words of rebuke that God finds it necessary to send are spoken in tender love, and with the promise of peace to every penitent believer. 'Behold, I stand at the door, and knock,' the Lord declares; 'if any man hear My voice, and open the door, I will come in to him, and will sup with him, and he with Me.'

"And for those who in the midst of conflict should maintain their faith in God, the prophet was given the words of commendation and promise: 'I know thy works: behold, I have set before thee an open door, and no man can shut it:

for thou hast a little strength, and hast kept My word, and hast not denied My name. . . . Because thou hast kept the word of My patience, I also will keep thee from the hour of temptation, which shall come upon all the world, to try them that dwell on the earth.' The believers were admonished: 'Be watchful, and strengthen the things which remain, that are ready to die.' 'Behold, I come quickly: hold that fast which thou hast, that no man take thy crown.'

"It was through one who declared himself to be a 'brother in tribulation,' that Christ revealed to His church the things that they must suffer for His sake. Looking down through long centuries of darkness and superstition, the aged exile saw multitudes suffering martyrdom because of their love for the truth. But he saw also that He who sustained His early witnesses would not forsake His faithful followers during the centuries of persecution that they must pass through before the close of time. 'Fear none of those things which thou shalt suffer,' the Lord declared; 'behold, the devil shall cast some of you into prison, that ye may be tried, and ye shall have tribulation: . . . be thou faithful unto death, and I will give thee a crown of life.'

"And to all the faithful ones who were striving against evil, John heard the promises made: 'To him that overcometh will I give to eat of the tree of life, which is in the midst of the paradise of God.' 'He that overcometh, the same shall be clothed in white raiment; and I will not blot out his name out of the book of life, but I will confess his name before My Father, and before his angels.' 'To him that overcometh will I grant to sit with Me in My throne, even as I also overcame, and am set down with My Father in His throne.' "[5]

Strand's discussion and his use of Ellen White illustrate the philosophy-of-history approach to the seven churches (Rev. 2; 3). This approach suggests that the prophecy of the seven churches has three fulfillments or applications:

1. The messages apply to the seven churches of Asia Minor in John's day that are named in the prophecy.
2. All of these messages apply to churches in every era of history since the time of Christ. For example, the message to Ephesus is relevant to the church at every stage of history, including the Christian church of the twenty-first century.
3. Each of the messages applies to a specific historical era of the church: the message addressed to Ephesus applies to the apostolic era; the message addressed to Smyrna applies to the immediate post-apostolic era, and so on. The message to Laodicea, then, applies to the period of the church shortly before the Second Coming.

The validity of this third application is confirmed by a comparison of the messages to the condition of the church and the world in each of the seven periods of history. John was told that his messages focused not only on the church of his day but also on the church of the future. His messages were a revelation of what "must soon take place" (Rev. 1:1); "the time is near" (verse 3). John was instructed to "write what you see, what is and *what is to take place hereafter*" (verse 19; italics added). So, the symbolism in each of the seven messages to the churches is relevant to seven periods of the church's and the world's history.

The seven seals

In my book *Heaven's Open Door*,[6] I have pointed out the validity of the philosophy-of-history interpretation for the seven seals. Church members in John's day who had read Revelation 4 and 5 would understand the symbolism of the Lamb (Christ) before the throne of the Father to be a depiction of Christ's intercessory ministry for believers. They would have interpreted John's symbolism in the light of the Epistle to the Hebrews, chapters 7–10.

But since the opening of the book of Daniel, with a new awareness of the significance of the pre-Advent judgment message of Daniel 7:9–14 and 8:14, many understood that the opening of the door between the two apartments of the sanctuary (Rev. 4:1) symbolizes the beginning of the antitypical day of atonement, the background to which was the opening of the door of the Most Holy Place of the earthly sanctuary on the tenth day of the seventh month of the Israelite religious year (Lev. 16). Thus, Revelation 4 and 5 may validly be regarded as the pre-Advent judgment scene portrayed by Daniel in chapters 7 and 8 of his book.[7]

This being the case, the seven seals (Rev. 6:1–8:1) symbolize God's messages not only to the church through Christian history but also to the church in the period of the pre-Advent judgment, that is, from 1844 to the coming of Jesus. As pointed out above, the message of the white horse (Rev. 6:2), the righteousness by faith message, applies to the church at every stage of history, not only in the apostolic era. This message in our era is the first angel's message of Revelation 14:6, 7, which is the "everlasting gospel."

The second seal, the red horse (Rev. 6:3, 4), symbolizes God's warnings and judgments for those who have rejected the message of the first seal, the righteousness by faith message. The third seal, the black horse (Rev. 6:5, 6), represents final warnings and judgments for those who have rejected the first message. The second and third seals in our era parallel the warnings and judgments of the second and third angels' messages of Revelation 14:8–11.

The fourth seal (Rev. 6:7, 8) represents the retribution meted out upon those who have rejected the previous three messages. According to Scripture, God's punishment of evildoers is ongoing (see Rom. 1:18). In every era of history, including ours, peoples and nations that have rejected God's loving entreaties suffer the withdrawal of His protection and are obliged to endure the inevitable consequences of their wrongdoing. This retribution will be especially intense when the seven last plagues are poured out after the close of probation (Rev. 16).

The fifth seal symbolizes the vindication in the pre-Advent judgment of those who have accepted the first three messages, the "saints" of Revelation 14:12, those "who keep the commandments of God, and the faith of Jesus" (KJV). Those among them who die before Jesus' coming are pronounced "blessed" (Rev. 14:13) because "they . . . rest from their labors, for their deeds follow them."

The sixth seal (Rev. 6:12–17) represents the coming of Christ, who executes the decisions of the pre-Advent judgment court. This passage is paralleled by Revelation 14:17–20, which describes the destruction of unbelievers at Christ's second advent.

The seventh seal (Rev. 8:1) portrays the final opening of the book of destiny at the Second Coming. This book (Rev. 5) cannot be opened until every seal is broken. The book is a scroll sealed with seven seals. The scroll cannot be unraveled and read until all the seals are broken, and they are not finally broken until the Second Coming.

So, the little book that appears in Revelation 5 doesn't outline the events described in the rest of Revelation. It is the verdict of the heavenly court condemning unbelievers to death and finally and irrevocably vindicating the people of God. The "silence in heaven" is a symbol of the peace and rejoicing of God's people after the tumultuous events through which they have passed. This "silence" is spoken of in Isaiah 62:1–3:

> For Zion's sake I will not keep silent, and for Jerusalem's sake I will not rest, *until her vindication goes forth as brightness, and her salvation as a burning torch.* The nations shall see your vindication, and all the kings your glory; and you shall be called by a new name which the mouth of the Lord will give. You shall be a crown of beauty in the hand of the Lord, and a royal diadem in the hand of your God (italics added).[8]

In what follows in this book I shall apply the philosophy-of-history approach to the seven trumpets (Rev. 8:2–11:19). The continuous-historical recapitulationist interpreters suggest the only fulfillment of the prophecy of the trumpets is in a succession of historical events from Jesus' day until His second coming.[9] However, Revelation 8:5 pictures the trumpets as sounding *after the close of probation.* But, as we shall demonstrate, there was a close of probation for Israel as the chosen nation, and there is a close of probation for the world a short time before the Second Coming. Therefore, the trumpets may be viewed as applying both historically and eschatologically. History repeats itself. The historical events depicted in the seven trumpets are types or examples of similar events that will occur shortly before Jesus' appearing.

THE NATURE OF APOCALYPTIC PROPHECY

The book of Revelation, like the book of Daniel, is apocalyptic literature, and as such, it has three major characteristics. First, it is based on visions and dreams. Of course, general Bible prophecy is also based on visions and dreams that God gave to the prophets. The Lord Himself declared, "If there is a prophet among you, I the LORD make myself known to him in a vision, I speak with him in a dream" (Num. 12:6). But biblical apocalyptic prophecy refers to visions and dreams more frequently than does general prophecy. For instance, the prophecies in Daniel 2, 7, 8, 9, and 11 all came through visions and dreams that God gave Daniel. Like the book of Daniel, Revelation is the record of visions that God gave to John. Revelation 1:9, 10 says that when he was a prisoner on the island of Patmos, the Lord appeared to him. John writes, "I was in the Spirit [i.e., in vision] on the Lord's day" (Rev. 1:10), and a description of his first vision follows. In fact, the entire book of Revelation is composed of visions Christ gave to John. He told the apostle: "Now write what you see, what is and what is to take place hereafter" (Rev. 1:19). John obeyed, and the result is the book of Revelation.

Second, apocalyptic literature makes a large use of symbolism. Consider the great image of Daniel 2 and the unusual beasts of Daniel 7 and 8, and note the extensive use of symbolism in the book of Revelation. We may cite the Lamb and the little book of Revelation 5, the four horses of chapter 6, the souls under the altar (Rev. 6:9–11), the difficult symbols of the first six trumpets, the dragon of chapter 12, and the two beasts of chapter 13.

The problem for the Bible student is to interpret these symbols in the manner intended by the Holy Spirit. It is possible to read into the symbolism all kinds of meanings that God didn't intend. It is easy to find historical events that seem to fulfill the symbolism and thus to assign meanings to the symbolism that are quite foreign to Scripture.

The only valid approach to interpreting the symbolism in Revelation is to allow the Bible to be its own expositor. To discover what the Holy Spirit meant a symbol to represent, we must search Scripture for prior uses of that symbol. Of course, symbols may be used in a number of different ways, but we can find an application of the symbol that matches the manner in which John uses it. This rather arduous process results in an interpretation of the trumpets consistent with Scripture rather than one that grows out of our fertile imagination.

Some scholars point out that there is a similarity between the symbolism in Revelation and that employed in non-canonical apocalypses such as 1 Enoch. But Jon Paulien comments: "Although there are many parallels of language and imagery between Revelation and Jewish apocalypses such as 1 Enoch, the theological differences are very significant. Far more apocalyptic ideas and themes are missing in Revelation than are used."[10] That is to say, 1 Enoch contains a great deal of apocalyptic imagery, as does Revelation, but only a small portion of Revelation's apocalyptic imagery resembles that of 1 Enoch.

Because John's messages were originally sent to the seven churches in Asia Minor, it is possible that he used symbolism familiar to the Gentiles of that time. We must remember that John was a prisoner on Patmos, which likely had extremely limited library facilities, if any at all. We can only guess the extent of his knowledge of non-canonical apocalypses, and we don't know how familiar the Gentile Christians of Asia Minor were with non-canonical apocalyptic symbolism. So, our safest course is to look throughout Scripture for the meanings of Revelation's many symbols.

Third, apocalyptic literature focuses on the end of time. Though general prophecy often predicts the future, too, it usually is more concerned with current issues facing the prophet and his contemporaries. It doesn't give the cosmic sweep of history so apparent in biblical apocalyptic literature. In contrast, biblical apocalyptic literature characteristically presents an outline of history from the prophet's day to the Second Advent. Consider, for example, the focus of Daniel's prophecies. In each one, the outline of history culminates in an eschatological climax. That focus on the end time is true of the prophecies of Revelation too—in every one, the cosmic sweep of history climaxes in the second coming of Jesus Christ. The obvious intent of the Divine Author is to convince us that the accurate prediction of historical events underlines the certainty of the Second Coming, when earthly evil powers will be subjugated by the dramatic intervention of our Lord Jesus Christ.

For the believer, Revelation's focus on the end time is enormously enlightening and encouraging. John assures us: "He who testifies to these things says, 'Surely I am coming quickly.' " And the believer responds as enthusiastically as did John, "Amen. Even so, come, Lord Jesus!" (Rev. 22:20, NKJV).

LITERARY STRUCTURE OF REVELATION

The book of Revelation is constructed in a way unfamiliar to most of us today. Generally, our documents follow the simple literary structure of A-B-C-D-E, in which the content is presented progressively from beginning to end and the last section contains the conclusion— the main point of the document. However, many ancient documents, including the book of Revelation, had the distinctive literary structure called inverse parallelism, or chiasm. In this structure, the first section of the document parallels the last section, the second section parallels the next-to-the-last section, and so on, and the climactic message stands at the center of the document.

The following statement is an example of synonymous parallelism, the second line repeating in different wording the thought of the first line:

John walked
> to the country;
he hiked
> to the hills.

When that statement is expressed as a chiasm (or inverted parallelism), it becomes:

John walked
> *to the country;*
> *to the hills*
he hiked.

There are two lines at the center of this chiasm. Sometimes there's just one line at the center of the chiasm, a single line that expresses the author's main thought—what he or she considered most important.

I've broken the book of Revelation into its individual parts (see the "Breakdown of the Book of Revelation," page 31) and then placed those parts in the chiastic form that I think John used as the structure of Revelation (see "Tentative Chiastic Structure of Revelation," page 32). This chiasm may be explained as follows.

A and A': The history of the Christian church (the church militant) culminates ultimately in God's saved people experiencing eternity with Christ (the church triumphant).

B and B': Christ's mediatorial and judgment ministries end shortly before His second advent, at which time He translates His redeemed people to heaven and conducts the millennial judgment of the lost. The parallel between Revelation 4:1–8:1 and 19:1–20:15 is dramatic. In Revelation 4 and 5 we can see the mediatorial and judgment ministries of Christ.

Judgment motifs emerge in the prophecy of the seals. For example, balances in the hand of the rider of the black horse suggest judgment (Rev. 6:5). The name of the rider of the fourth horse, "Death and Hades," indicates the carrying out of judgment (Rev. 6:8). The cry of the righteous dead that is part of the fifth seal is a cry for judgment and vindication (Rev. 6:9, 10). The events of the sixth seal (Rev. 6:12–17) depict execution of judgment upon the wicked at Jesus' second coming.

Parallel to these events are the events of Revelation 19:1–20:15. Revelation 19:1–9 tells us that the pre-Advent judgment has ended. The cry of the righteous dead in Revelation 6:10 was, "How long, O Lord, holy and true, until You judge and avenge our blood on those who dwell on the earth?" (NKJV). The answer to their cry is the announcement of the end of the judgment: "His judgments are true and just; he has judged the great harlot who corrupted the earth with her fornication, and he has avenged on her the blood of his servants" (Rev. 19:2). The white robes given to the righteous dead (Rev. 6:11), symbolizing their final vindication in the pre-Advent judgment, are spoken of again in Revelation 19:7, 8. The marriage of the Lamb, the pre-Advent judgment, results in God's faithful people being "clothed with fine linen, bright and pure"—the righteousness of Jesus Christ. Thus they are qualified to take part in the marriage supper of the Lamb (Rev. 19:9, 10).

The coming of Christ, depicted in Revelation 6:12–17, is paralleled by the symbolic representation of His appearing the second time riding a white horse and leading the armies of heaven (Rev. 19:11–21).

The triumphant picture of Christ's sealed saints, who have suffered so intensely, enjoying the joys of heaven (Rev. 7:1–17) is paralleled by the scene of faithful believers in heaven conducting the millennial judgment (Rev. 20:4–6), the result of which is the ultimate condemnation of the wicked (Rev. 20:11–14) and their final destruction along with Satan (Rev. 20:7–10).

C(a) and C(a)': The third section of Revelation (Rev. 8:2–11:19) is the prophecy of the trumpets, which is the subject of this book. *The trumpets represent Satan's destructive work, and the plagues are God's counteracting work* (Rev. 15:1, 5–8; 16:1–21). The parallel between the seven trumpets and the seven last plagues has often been pointed out. The parallel may be outlined as shown on the chart titled "Parallels Between the Trumpets and the Plagues" (see page 33).

C(b) and C(b)': Revelation 12 and 13 portray Christ's great controversy with Satan, beginning with Satan's rebellion in heaven and climaxing in his use of antitypical Babylon to attempt to destroy God's church and people. The focus of the controversy is on the last days, when Babylon passes a death decree against Christ's faithful followers. But Revelation 17 and 18 teach that God deals with end-time Babylon, calling His people to come out of her and punishing those who are aligned with her.

Historically, Revelation 12 and 13 cover the same eras as does the prophecy of the trumpets, but those chapters focus on different events and culminate in the end-time conflict between Christ and Satan. Revelation 17 and 18 add to the scenario of the seven last plagues by describing God's punishment of antitypical Babylon.

D: Revelation 14:1–20 and 15:2–4 present the central message and climax of the book. The people who will be translated to Mount Zion, the heavenly Jerusalem (Heb. 12:22), are those who have received God's seal because, by His grace, they are spiritually spotless (Rev. 14:1–5). The spiritual qualifications of God's redeemed people result from their acceptance of, and commitment to, the three angels' messages. These are God's final messages to the world, and those who respond to them "keep the commandments of God and the faith of Jesus" (Rev. 14:12). They are the ones referred to in verses 14–16 as being harvested from the earth. By contrast, those who don't respond positively to the three angel's messages are subject to the destruction described in verses 17–20. Revelation 15:2–4, then, describes the triumph of God's people in heaven.

In the light of the chiastic structure of the Revelation, the book is thoroughly systematic and coherent. The central focus is on our loving Lord's earnest appeal to the peoples of earth to repent of sin and apostasy and to accept the only means of victory and salvation. No wonder Jesus says, "Blessed is he who reads and those who hear the words of this prophecy, and keep those things which are written in it; for the time is near" (Rev. 1:3, NKJV)!

BREAKDOWN OF THE BOOK OF REVELATION

Rev. 1–3: Christ our High Priest cares for His church through the ages.

Rev. 4:1–8:1: Christ our Mediator and pre-Advent Judge sends messages to those who live on the earth.

Rev. 8:2–11:19: Christ allows Satan to work but imparts encouraging end-time messages.

Rev. 12:1–13:18: Christ's great controversy with Satan and antitypical Babylon throughout history culminates in the end-time conflict.

Rev. 14:1–20; 15:2–4: Christ translates His believing people to heaven in view of their acceptance of the three angels' messages.

Rev. 15:1, 5–8; 16:1–21: Christ counteracts Satan's destructive work by punishing the wicked.

Rev. 17:1–18:24: Christ punishes antitypical Babylon.

Rev. 19:1–20:15: Christ ends the pre-Advent judgment and comes to earth again; He conducts the millennial judgment.

Rev. 21:1–22:21: Christ lives with His people for eternity.

Tentative Chiastic Structure of Revelation[11]

A Rev. 1–3: Christ our High Priest cares for His church through the ages.

B Rev. 4:1–8:1: Christ our Mediator and pre-Advent Judge sends messages to those who live on the earth.

C(a) Rev. 8:2–11:19: Christ allows Satan to work but imparts encouraging end-time messages.

C(b) Rev. 12:1–13:18: Christ's great controversy with Satan and antitypical Babylon throughout history culminates in the end-time conflict.

D Rev. 14:1–20; 15:2–4: Christ translates His believing people to heaven in view of their acceptance of the three angels' messages.

C(a)' Rev. 15:1, 5–8; 16:1–21: Christ counteracts Satan's destructive work by punishing the wicked.

C(b)' Rev. 17:1–18:24: Christ punishes antitypical Babylon.

B' Rev. 19:1–20:15: Christ ends the pre-Advent judgment and comes to earth again; He conducts the millennial judgment.

A' Rev. 21:1–22:21: Christ lives with His people for eternity.

PARALLELS BETWEEN THE TRUMPETS AND THE PLAGUES

Trumpets	Plagues
1. Rev. 8:7: Hail and fire on the earth.	1. Rev. 16:2: Poured out on the earth.
2. Rev. 8:8, 9: A mountain into the sea.	2. Rev. 16:3: The sea becomes blood.
3. Rev. 8:10, 11: A star falls on rivers and fountains of water.	3. Rev. 16:4–7: Rivers and fountains of water become blood.
4. Rev. 8:12, 13: Darkening of the sun, moon, and stars.	4. Rev. 16:8, 9: The sun scorches people with fire.
5. Rev. 9:1–12: Locusts from the bottomless pit torture mankind.	5. Rev. 16:10, 11: Torture for those who give allegiance to the beast.
6. Rev. 9:13–21: Four angels released at the river Euphrates.	6. Rev. 16:12–16: The great river Euphrates dried up.
7. Rev. 11:15–19: The kingdoms of the world become Christ's kingdom.	7. Rev. 16:17–21: A voice from heaven says, "It is done."

1. Ellen G. White, *Testimonies for the Church* (Boise, ID: Pacific Press® Publishing Association, 1948), 8:302.
2. Ellen G. White, *Testimonies to Ministers and Gospel Workers* (Boise, ID: Pacific Press®, 1923), 114.
3. Ellen G. White, Christ's Object Lessons (Hagerstown, MD: Review and Herald® Publishing Association, 1900), 133.
4. In chapter 12 of my book, *You Ask, God Answers,* "Will the Rapture Be Secret or Public?" I have pointed out the error of this position; see Erwin R. Gane, *You Ask, God Answers* (Ukiah, CA: Orion Publishing, 1998), 218–233.
5. Kenneth A. Strand, *Interpreting the Book of Revelation* (Ann Arbor, MI: Ann Arbor Publishers, 1976), 14–16.
6. Erwin R. Gane, *Heaven's Open Door* (Boise, ID: Pacific Press®, 1989).
7. Ranko Stefanovic regards Revelation 4 and 5 as "the coronation of the ascended and glorified Christ on the heavenly throne at the right hand of the Father after the incarnation and his death and resurrection." *Revelation of Jesus Christ* (Berrien Springs, MI: Andrews University Press, 2002), 209. Possibly Revelation 4 and 5 depict the beginning of Christ's period of intercession in the heavenly sanctuary (AD 31 on), which sets the stage for the pre-Advent judgment (1844 on).
8. All of this is spelled out in much greater detail in my book, *Heaven's Open Door.*
9. Compare Stefanovic, *Revelation of Jesus Christ,* 275–355; Jon Paulien, *Decoding Revelation's Trumpets* (Berrien Springs, MI: Andrews University Press, 1987), 307–420; C. Mervyn Maxwell, *God Cares* (Boise, ID: Pacific Press®, 1985), 2:223–265.
10. Paulien, *Decoding Revelation's Trumpets,* 46.
11. Compare the tentative outline of the book of Revelation in Strand, *Interpreting the Book of Revelation,* 51, 52; Stefanovic, *Revelation of Jesus Christ,* 35–45; Maxwell, *God Cares,* 2:54–62.

Chapter 2
The Close of Probation

Revelation 8:1 records the opening of the seventh seal; thus it belongs to the prophecy of the seals. Verse 2 marks the introduction of a new prophecy, the vision of the seven trumpets. The prophecy of the trumpets begins with these words: "Then I saw the seven angels who stand before God, and seven trumpets were given to them."

Who are "the seven angels who stand before God"? Luke 1:19 records the words of the angel to Zechariah, the father of John the Baptist. "I am Gabriel, who stands in the presence of God." But here, in Revelation 8:2, we have seven angels standing in the presence of God. They are spoken of again in Revelation 15:1: "Then I saw another portent in heaven, great and wonderful, seven angels with seven plagues, which are the last, for with them the wrath of God is ended." Because of the parallel between the trumpets and the plagues, we argue that chapters 8 and 15 refer to the same seven angels.

The seven angels with the seven last plagues are described in more detail in Revelation 15:6–8; 16:1:

After this I looked, and the temple of the tent of witness in heaven was opened, and out of the temple came the seven angels with the seven plagues, robed in pure bright linen, and their breasts girded with golden girdles. And one of the four living creatures gave the seven angels seven golden bowls full of the wrath of God who lives for ever and ever, and the temple was filled with smoke from the glory of God and from his power, and no one could enter the temple until the seven plagues of the seven angels were ended. Then I heard a loud voice from the temple telling the seven angels, "Go and pour out on the earth the seven bowls of the wrath of God."

The four living creatures who give the seven angels "seven bowls full of the wrath of God" first appear in Revelation 4:6–8. They are cherubim, commanders of the heavenly hosts (Ezek. 1; 10). They minister before the throne of God (Rev. 4:6), receiving their commands directly from God and passing them on to the angelic hosts (Rev. 6:1, 3, 5, 7). During the mediatorial and pre-Advent judgment ministries of Christ, depicted in Revelation 4 and 5, the living creatures send messages to the earth (Rev. 6:1–8). But Revelation 15:8 tells us that now "the temple was filled with smoke from the glory of God and from his power, and no one could enter the temple until the seven plagues of the seven angels were ended."

Now Christ's mediation and pre-Advent judgment have ended; now the living creatures have left the heavenly temple; now probation has closed; now every person on earth has decided whether or not to serve God.

The same seven angels appear in Revelation 17:1: "Then one of the seven angels who had the seven bowls came and said to me, 'Come, I will show you the judgment of the great harlot who is seated upon many waters.' " Chapter 17 goes on to reveal the destructive activities of antitypical Babylon in both historical times and the end time, and chapter 18 describes the ultimate judgments meted out upon her. Hence, we may justifiably conclude that chapters 17 and 18 are an extension of the plagues itemized in chapter 16.

The prophet speaks of these seven angels again in Revelation 21:9, 10:

> Then came one of the seven angels who had the seven bowls full of the seven last plagues, and spoke to me, saying, "Come, I will show you the Bride, the wife of the Lamb." And in the Spirit he carried me away to a great, high mountain, and showed me the holy city Jerusalem coming down out of heaven from God.

Evidently, the seven angels who are given the trumpets (Rev. 8:2) and the seven last plagues (Rev. 15:1) signal the angelic hosts commissioned to execute God's judicial decisions: condemnation of the wicked and acquittal and deliverance of God's faithful people. The number seven seems to represent the perfection of God's work of executive justice.

THE BLOWING OF THE TRUMPETS

These, then, are the angels who introduce the seven trumpets: "I saw the seven angels which stood before God; and to them were given seven trumpets" (Rev. 8:2, KJV).

In Scripture, trumpets are blown for a number of reasons. Often, the blowing of trumpets was a call to worship. For example, when God descended upon Mount Sinai to give His law, a trumpet blast announced that the people were to approach the mountain in a spirit of reverent devotion and worship. God commanded that no one was to touch the mountain when He descended upon it (Exod. 19:12, 13), but He said, "When the trumpet sounds a long blast, they shall come up to the mountain" (verse 13). Clearly the trumpet blast was supernatural; it came from the throne of God.

On the morning of the third day there were thunders and lightnings, and a thick cloud upon the mountain, and a very loud trumpet blast, so that all the people who were in the camp trembled. Then Moses brought the people out of the camp to meet God; and they took their stand at the foot of the mountain. And Mount Sinai was wrapped in smoke, because the LORD descended upon it in fire; and the smoke of it went up like the smoke of a kiln, and the whole mountain quaked greatly. And as the sound of the trumpet grew louder and louder, Moses spoke, and God answered him in thunder (Exod. 19:16–19).

Numbers 10:1–10 lists three purposes for the blowing of trumpets in Israel: (1) as a call to worship; (2) as an announcement that the Israelites should move camp; and (3) as a call to go to war against their enemies.

The LORD said to Moses, "Make two silver trumpets; of hammered work you shall make them; and you shall use them for summoning the congregation, and for breaking camp. And when both are blown, all the congregation shall gather themselves to you at the entrance of the tent of meeting. But if they blow only one, then the leaders, the heads of the tribes of Israel, shall gather themselves to you. When you blow an alarm, the camps that are on the east side shall set out. And when you blow an alarm the second time, the camps that are on the south side shall set out. An alarm is to be blown whenever they are to set out. But when the assembly is to be gathered together, you shall blow, but you shall not sound an alarm. And the sons of Aaron, the priests, shall blow the trumpets. The trumpets shall be to you for a perpetual statute throughout your generations. And when you go to war in your land against the adversary who oppresses you, then you shall sound an alarm with the trumpets, that you may be remembered before the LORD your God, and you shall be saved from your enemies. On the day of your gladness also, and at your appointed feasts, and at the beginnings of your months, you shall blow the trumpets over your burnt offerings and over the sacrifices of your peace offerings; they shall serve you for remembrance before your God: I am the LORD your God."

The feast of trumpets, which was celebrated on the first day of the seventh month, was a special time for the blowing of the trumpets. The Lord instructed that this day was to be observed as "a day of solemn rest, a memorial proclaimed with blasts of trumpets, a holy convocation. You shall do no laborious work; and you shall present an offering by fire to the LORD" (Lev. 23:24, 25; cf. Num. 29:1–6). In the time of Ezra after the Babylonian captivity, the returnees celebrated the feast of trumpets by reading the Law of Moses (Neh. 8:1–3). The effect on the people was dramatic; they wept and repented of their sins (Neh. 8:9–17).[1]

Significantly, the feast of trumpets came a few days before the Day of Atonement, which was observed on the tenth day of the seventh month (Lev. 23:27). The Day of Atonement was a day of judgment on which the sanctuary was to be cleansed of the sins that had been transferred to it during the year (Lev. 4). On this day God's people were to examine themselves to be sure that their sins were forgiven and that they no longer considered sin a normal part of life (Lev. 16:29–34; 23:26–32; Num. 29:7–11). The feast of trumpets served as a time of preparation for this important day—as in Ezra's day, providing people an opportunity to prepare for judgment.

One of the most significant occasions when trumpets were blown was at the conquest of Jericho (Josh. 6:4–21). At the command of God, the first six days of the week the Israelites marched around the city one time while seven priests blew trumpets. On the seventh day, however, they marched around the city seven times, and then the priests blew great blasts of sound from their trumpets, the walls protecting the city collapsed, and the Israelites attacked and destroyed it.

The blowing of trumpets played a significant role in Gideon's overthrow of the Midianite army (Judg. 7:15–23); Job refers to the battle horse that "cannot stand still at the sound of the trumpet" (Job 39:24, 25); the psalmist writes that God's sovereign rule over the earth is announced with the sound of a trumpet (Ps. 47:1–7); Hosea speaks of a trumpet blast calling attention to the unfaithfulness of God's people and to the judgments that will be meted out upon them in consequence (Hosea 5:8–10), and Amos sounds the same alarm (Amos 2:2; 3:6–8).

In the book of Joel, God calls for the "day of the LORD" to be heralded with a trumpet blast: "Blow the trumpet in Zion; sound the alarm on my holy mountain! Let all the inhabitants of the land tremble, for the day of the LORD is coming, it is near, a day of darkness and gloom, a day of clouds and thick darkness!" (Joel 2:1, 2). The context suggests that the day of the Lord spoken of there, in which God's unfaithful people were punished for their apostasy, was a type of the ultimate day of the Lord, when the sun and the moon are darkened, and the stars withdraw their shining. The LORD utters his voice before his army, for his host is exceedingly great; he that executes his word is powerful. For the day of the LORD is great and very terrible; who can endure it? (Joel 2:10, 11).

The parallel with Revelation 6:12–17 and other passages in Revelation is impressive.

In view of the coming calamity, Joel urges: "Blow the trumpet in Zion; sanctify a fast; call a solemn assembly; gather the people. Sanctify the congregation; assemble the elders; gather the children, even nursing infants. Let the bridegroom leave his room, and the bride her chamber" (Joel 2:15, 16). The trumpet not only announces the coming day of the Lord, but it also calls God's people to repentance.

Zephaniah repeats Joel's call to repentance in view of the approaching "day of the LORD" (Zeph. 1:14–18). This is "a day of trumpet blast and battle cry against the fortified cities and against the lofty battlements" (verse 16). Isaiah identifies the trumpet blast as announcing both the destruction of the unfaithful and the vindication of the faithful (Isa. 18:3–7; 27:12, 13). Jeremiah urges the blowing of trumpets to warn about the coming of the Babylonians, who, with God's acquiescence, would take captive His apostate people (Jer. 4:5–8, 19, 21; 6:1, 17). Then another trumpet blast warns of the demise of ancient Babylon, Jeremiah explaining that God will punish that nation by bringing the Medes against them (Jer. 51:27–33). The nation that God used to punish His people was itself punished for its wickedness. And Ezekiel speaks of the day of the Lord as a day of doom and terrible destruction that was to be proclaimed by the blowing of the trumpet (Ezek. 7:10–27). He writes eloquently of the judgments poured out upon the unfaithful. Finally, in most instances in the New Testament, trumpet blasts are associated with the second coming of Jesus (Matt. 24:31; 1 Cor. 15:52; 1 Thess. 4:16).

We may summarize the roles of trumpets in the Bible:

- Trumpets were blown as a call to worship.
- Trumpets announced the coming judgment, the Day of Atonement.
- Trumpet blasts were a call for God's people to war against their enemies.
- The sounding of trumpets symbolized God's call for unbelieving nations to punish His apostate people.
- Trumpet blasts initiated God's judgments against the unholy nations that He had permitted to punish His people.
- And trumpets announced the coming of the local day of the Lord as a type of the end-time Day of the Lord, when the unfaithful among His professed people and the unfaithful among the nations will suffer punishment, and the faithful will experience ultimate vindication and deliverance.

The relationship between the Bible's general discussion of trumpets and the role trumpets play in Revelation will become clearer as we study them. In anticipation of our later conclusions, we can say that the purpose of Revelation's trumpets is as follows: (1) to call God's people, who are facing historical and end-time challenges, to repentance and genuine worship; (2) to warn of Satan's attacks against God's professed people; (3) to warn of the coming antitypical Day of Atonement, the pre-Advent, investigative judgment that ends with the close of probation; and (4) to announce the approaching end-time Day of the Lord on which the unfaithful will be destroyed and the faithful delivered.

THE ALTAR AND THE INCENSE

Returning to where we left off in Revelation, we read next:

> And another angel came and stood at the altar with a golden
> censer; and he was given much incense to mingle with the
> prayers of all the saints upon the golden altar before the
> throne; and the smoke of the incense rose with the prayers of
> the saints from the hand of the angel before God (Rev. 8:3, 4).

The Greek word translated "altar" in Revelation 8:3 is *thusiastērion*. This Greek word is used in the Septuagint (a translation of the Hebrew Old Testament into Greek—abbreviated LXX) and the New Testament for both the altar of burnt offering in the court of the ancient Israelite sanctuary (Exod. 29:38, LXX; 1 Cor. 9:13) and the altar of incense in the Holy Place of the sanctuary (Exod. 30:1, LXX; Luke 1:11). Revelation 8:3 is clearly a reference to the altar of incense in heaven, which is the great original and of which the altar of incense in the earthly sanctuary was a copy (Heb. 8:5).

The altar of incense in the ancient Israelite sanctuary is described in Exodus 30:1–10. It was made of acacia wood overlaid with gold. Moses was instructed: "You shall overlay it with pure gold, its top and its sides round about and its horns; and you shall make for it a molding of gold round about" (Exod. 30:3). "And Aaron shall burn fragrant incense on it; every morning when he dresses the lamps he shall burn it, and when Aaron sets up the lamps in the evening, he shall burn it, a perpetual incense before the LORD throughout your generations" (Exod. 30:7, 8).

The golden altar of incense stood in the Holy Place in front of the veil between the Holy Place and the Most Holy Place (Exod. 40:26), and every morning and evening the smoke of the incense burnt on the altar ascended over the veil into the presence of God. The offering of incense represented the prayers of the people ascending to God. The psalmist wrote: "Let my prayer be counted as incense before thee" (Ps. 141:2). Revelation 5:8 identifies incense as representing "the prayers of the saints." As every morning and evening the priest burnt incense on the altar in the Holy Place of the sanctuary, the people stood outside in the court with the sure knowledge that God heard their prayers. This was the scenario when Zechariah, the father of John the Baptist, was serving in the temple:

> Now while he was serving as priest before God when his division was on duty, according to the custom of the priesthood, it fell to him by lot to enter the temple of the Lord and burn incense. And the whole multitude of the people were praying outside at the hour of incense (Luke 1:8–10).

When sin offerings were performed on behalf of the high priest or the entire community of Israelites, some of the blood of the sacrificial animal was sprinkled on the horns of the altar of incense (Lev. 4:7, 18). This symbolized the transference of the forgiven sin to the sanctuary. Then, on the Day of Atonement, the high priest took "a censer full of coals of fire from the altar before the LORD, and two handfuls of sweet incense beaten small," and he brought it "within the veil and put the incense on the fire before the Lord, that the cloud of the incense may cover the mercy seat which is upon the testimony [the tables of stone on which were written the Ten Commandments], lest he die" (Lev. 16:12, 13). Then the high priest sprinkled the blood of the sin offering on the mercy seat and before the mercy seat, after which he went into the Holy Place and sprinkled some of the blood on the horns of the altar of incense (Lev. 16:16; Exod. 30:10). Then he went into the court and sprinkled some of the blood of the sin offering on the horns of the altar of burnt offering (Lev. 16:18, 19).

The sprinkling of blood in the Most Holy Place, the Holy Place, and on the altar of burnt offering in the court symbolized the cleansing of the sanctuary (Lev. 16:20). These actions and the others that the priest performed on the Day of Atonement, as described in Leviticus 16, provided atonement (cleansing from sin, purgation, reconciliation) for both the sanctuary and the people. The Lord told Moses,

> On this day shall atonement be made for you, to cleanse you; from all your sins you shall be clean before the Lord. . . . He shall make atonement for the sanctuary, and he shall make atonement for the tent of meeting and for the altar, and he shall make atonement for the priests and for all the people of the assembly (Lev. 16:30, 33).

The services carried out in the wilderness tabernacle were later regularly performed in the temple Solomon built (1 Kings 7:48–51; 2 Chron. 4:19–22).

The offering of incense morning and evening represented the prayers of the people ascending to God so that their hearts could be made ready for the other services of the sanctuary, and especially for the events of the Day of Atonement, the great annual judgment day when sin was to be finally eliminated from both the sanctuary and the people.

WHO IS THE ANGEL?

At this point, one might logically ask, "Who is the angel whom John saw standing before the altar in heaven offering incense?"

The short answer is that it is Christ, our heavenly High Priest, who intercedes for His believing people, as Hebrews 8 makes clear: "We have such a high priest, one who is seated at the right hand of the throne of the Majesty in heaven, a minister in the sanctuary and the true tent which is set up not by man but by the Lord" (Heb. 8:1, 2). Hebrews 9 explains that

> when Christ appeared as a high priest of the good things that have come, then through the greater and more perfect tent (not made with hands, that is, not of this creation) he entered once for all into the Holy Place [the heavenly sanctuary], taking not the blood of goats and calves but his own blood, thus securing an eternal redemption (Heb. 9:11, 12).

The "angel" offering incense at the heavenly, golden altar of incense is Christ, the only true Mediator between us and God. Scripture says, "There is one God, and there is one mediator between God and men, the man Christ Jesus" (1 Tim. 2:5; cf. 1 John 2:1; Heb. 8:6; 9:15, 24; 12:24). The Holy Spirit cooperates with Christ's work of mediation (Rom. 8:26, 27), and the twenty-four elders and four living creatures of Revelation 4 and 5 function as assistants to Christ our High Priest (Rev. 5:8), just as the regular Israelite priests assisted the earthly high priest (Luke 1:9–11). Nevertheless, we have only one Mediator, and He is qualified to plead our cause because He has lived on earth as a man and suffered for the sins of the whole world on Calvary's cross (1 John 2:2).

Why would Christ be referred to in Revelation 8:3 as an angel?

The Deity is often spoken of as an "angel," or "the angel of the Lord" in Scripture. For instance, when Jacob blessed Joseph and his sons, he said, "The God before whom my fathers Abraham and Isaac walked, the God who has led me all my life long to this day, the angel who has redeemed me from all evil, bless the lads" (Gen. 48:15, 16).

Scripture says "the angel of the Lord appeared" to Moses from the burning bush (Exod. 3:2); and just two verses down, it says "God called to him out of the bush" (verse 4). The Angel of the Lord, the Messenger, was God Himself (cf. Acts 7:30–34). It was Christ who accompanied the Israelites in their wilderness wanderings, dwelling in the pillar of cloud by day and the pillar of fire by night (1 Cor. 10:1, 2), but He is spoken of in the Old Testament as "the angel of God" (Exod. 14:19; cf. 23:20–24). So, the "angel of the Lord" who spoke to the people (Judg. 2:1–4) was the Lord Himself, as was the "angel of the Lord" who appeared to Gideon (Judg. 6:11–24).

Christ is the "angel" whom Revelation 8:3, 4 pictures offering incense. This in no way implies that He is a created being, as are heaven's angels. "In him the whole fulness of deity dwells bodily" (Col. 2:9). He is the I AM who appeared to Moses (John 8:58, 59; Exod. 3:13–15). Christ is equal with the Father in authority and power (John 5:18). To know Him is to know the Father (John 14:8–11).

Revelation 8:3, 4 presents the magnificent picture of Christ, our heavenly High Priest, mingling the merits of His intercession with our prayers. His incense is said to "mingle *with* the prayers of all the saints" (verse 3; italics added). John says, "The smoke of the incense rose *with* the prayers of the saints from the hand of the angel before God" (verse 4; italics added; compare Revelation 5:8, which identifies incense with "the prayers of the saints"). We need have no fear that our prayers aren't heard—and answered. Jesus, our loving Lord, accepts our prayers and presents them before the Father's throne as acceptable because He mingles with them the merits of His divine intercession.

Ellen G. White spelled out the meaning of Revelation 8:3, 4 in these words:

As in that typical service the priest looked by faith to the mercy seat which he could not see, so the people of God are now to direct their prayers to Christ, their great High Priest, who, unseen by human vision, is pleading in their behalf in the sanctuary above.

The incense, ascending with the prayers of Israel, represents the merits and intercession of Christ, His perfect righteousness, which through faith is imputed to His people, and which can alone make the worship of sinful beings acceptable to God. Before the veil of the most holy place was an altar of perpetual intercession, before the holy, an altar of continual atonement. By blood and by incense God was to be approached—symbols pointing to the great Mediator, through whom sinners may approach Jehovah, and through whom alone mercy and salvation can be granted to the repentant, believing soul.[2]

THE CENSER

Revelation continues: "Then the angel took the censer and filled it with fire from the altar and threw it on the earth; and there were peals of thunder, voices, flashes of lightning, and an earthquake" (Rev. 8:5).

Priests burned incense in the censers as part of the morning and evening services (Num. 4:14, KJV; 1 Kings 7:50). On the Day of Atonement, the high priest used a censer to burn incense in the Most Holy Place (Lev. 16:12, 13). The "angel" (Christ) now ceases to offer incense. Instead, He fills the censer with fire from the altar and then casts it upon the earth, an act that symbolically betokens punishment for the unfaithful (Ezek. 9:8–10; 10:2, 6, 7; 11:5–12 ; Ps. 18:6–15; Gen. 19:24, 25; Luke 12:49).

The end of Christ's intercession for humankind, represented here by His ceasing to offer incense, is the close of probation.[3] That is when Christ's loving appeals to humanity cease, when every living human being has decided either before or against God.

This same event is referred to in other passages in the book of Revelation. For instance, when the fourth seal was broken (Rev. 6:7, 8), John saw "a pale horse, and its rider's name was Death, and Hades followed him; and they were given power over a fourth of the earth, to kill with sword and with famine and with pestilence and by wild beasts of the earth." Here is a picture of God withdrawing His protection from those who have rejected the first three messages (Rev. 6:1–6). They were given the righteousness-and-salvation-by-faith message (the white horse and its rider, Rev. 6:1, 2), but they rejected it. They were given warnings (Rev. 6:3, 4) and more warnings (Rev. 6:5, 6), but they scorned them. Then came judgment, when God pronounced them guilty, followed by destruction and death. Such judgment has occurred many times throughout history; the ultimate, final judgment will take place shortly before the second coming of Jesus.

The end-time close of probation is referred to in Revelation 7:1–3. God restrains the angels commissioned to punish the wicked till, as He says, "we have sealed the servants of our God upon their foreheads" (Rev. 7:3). Only when the end-time sealing work is complete and probation closes are the winds of strife let loose.

The same end-time close of probation is depicted in Revelation 15:5–8. The "temple of the tent of witness in heaven" will be opened, and the seven last plagues will be poured out. And no one will be permitted to enter the heavenly temple until the plagues have been administered (cf. Lev. 16:17). The opening of the heavenly temple at the beginning of the outpouring of the plagues symbolizes the close of probation.

The same end-time close of probation is announced in Revelation 22: "Let the evildoer still do evil, and the filthy still be filthy, and the righteous still do right, and the holy still be holy. Behold, I am coming soon, bringing my recompense, to repay every one for what he has done" (Rev. 22:11, 12). H. B. Swete comments:

> It is not only true that the troubles of the last days will tend to fix the character of each individual according to the habits which he has already formed, but there will come a time when change will be impossible—when no further opportunity will be given for repentance on the one hand or for apostasy on the other. . . . The moment has been reached when the Master of the house has arisen and shut the door, and those that are without will knock in vain (Matt. 25:10; Luke 13:25); men can then no longer recede from the position which they have chosen to take up.[4]

Ellen G. White clearly identifies Christ's casting down the censer (Rev. 8:5) as initiating the end-time close of probation:

> I saw angels hurrying to and fro in heaven. An angel with a writer's inkhorn by his side returned from the earth and reported to Jesus that his work was done, and the saints were numbered and sealed. Then I saw Jesus, who had been ministering before the ark containing the ten commandments, throw down the censer. He raised His hands, and with a loud voice said, *"It is done."* And all the angelic host laid off their crowns as Jesus made the solemn declaration, "He that is unjust, let him be unjust still: and he which is filthy, let him be filthy still: and he that is righteous, let him be righteous

still: and he that is holy, let him be holy still."

Every case had been decided for life or death. While Jesus had been ministering in the sanctuary, the judgment had been going on for the righteous dead, and then for the righteous living. Christ had received His kingdom, having made the atonement for His people and blotted out their sins. The subjects of the kingdom were made up. The marriage of the Lamb was consummated. And the kingdom, and the greatness of the kingdom under the whole heaven, was given to Jesus and the heirs of salvation, and Jesus was to reign as King of kings and Lord of lords.[5]

Speaking of the close of probation in her book *The Great Controversy,* Ellen White adds:

When the work of the investigative judgment closes, the destiny of all will have been decided for life or death. Probation is ended a short time before the appearing of the Lord in the clouds of heaven. Christ in the Revelation, looking forward to that time, declares: "He that is unjust, let him be unjust still: and he which is filthy, let him be filthy still: and he that is righteous let him be righteous still: and he that is holy, let him be holy still. And, behold, I come quickly; and My reward is with Me, to give every man according as his work shall be." Revelation 22:11, 12.[6]

ANOTHER PROBATION

Apart from this end-time close of probation, Bible prophecy speaks of a historical close of probation for Israel as a nation. In the sixth century BC, Gabriel told Daniel, "Seventy weeks are determined for your people and for your holy city, to finish the transgression, to make an end of sins, to make reconciliation for iniquity, to bring in everlasting righteousness, to seal up vision and prophecy, and to anoint the Most Holy" (Dan. 9:24, NKJV).

Translated literally, the Hebrew says "seventy sevens" rather than "seventy weeks." Although the word *years* isn't in the text, it is generally agreed by scholars that these seventy sevens represent 490 years.[7] They must represent years rather than days because this prophetic period reaches to the time of the Messiah. It was the Messiah's sacrifice that put an end to guilt in the lives of those who have given themselves to Him in faith and obedience. It was His work on the cross that made reconciliation for iniquity and brought in everlasting righteousness. Moreover, the next verse, Daniel 9:25, informs us that these seventy sevens began with "the going forth of the command to restore and build Jerusalem" and reached "until Messiah the Prince." Seventy times seven days, or 490 days, would certainly not span the specified time, but 490 years does.

Daniel 9:24 says, "Seventy weeks [of years] are determined [or decreed] for your people and for your holy city" (NKJV). In other words, this 490-year span is said to be a period of probation for the Israelite nation, a period that began with "the going forth of the command to restore and build Jerusalem" (verse 25). Ezra 6:14 mentions three decrees that call for the rebuilding of Jerusalem—three decrees that direct people to carry out God's command: "So the elders of the Jews built. . . . And they built and finished it, according to the commandment of the God of Israel, and according to the command of Cyrus, Darius, and Artaxerxes king of Persia" (NKJV).

Cyrus decreed the return of the Jews after the captivity in about 537 BC. The decree of Darius I was passed about 519 or 518 BC. The decree of Artaxerxes I Longimanus was certainly put into operation in the autumn of 457 BC.[8] Since three human decrees applied God's command (Ezra 6:14), we are justified in dating "the command to restore and build Jerusalem" (Dan. 9:25) from the third decree, that of Artaxerxes I Longimanus in 457 BC.

Four hundred and ninety years from 457 BC bring us to AD 34. Hence, AD 34 was the year that Daniel specified as the end of the probationary period for Israel. Why do we regard this year as the close of probation for Israel as God's chosen nation? Because of the events that occurred during that 490-year period.

According to Daniel's prophecy, the Messiah, the Anointed One, would arise sixty-nine weeks of years, or 483 years, after 457 BC (Dan. 9:25). Four hundred and eighty-three years after 457 BC bring us to AD 27. (There was no year zero; 1 BC was immediately followed by AD 1.)

In AD 27, Jesus became the Anointed One, because He was anointed by the Holy Spirit at His baptism (Acts 10:38; Matt. 3:16, 17). Luke 3:1–3, 21 reveals that Jesus was baptized in the fifteenth year of Tiberius Caesar, which was AD 27.

The emperor Augustus died on August 19, AD 14. If we apply the antedating, or the non-accession-year method of numbering regnal years, Tiberius's first year was August–October, AD 14. In AD 14, the Jewish New Year's Day occurred in October. Thus, Tiberius's second year was October AD 14 to October AD 15, and so on.

Also, Luke followed the Tishri-to-Tishri civil year of the Jews. Therefore Tiberius's fifteenth year was autumn to autumn AD 27/28. Hence, the historical event of the anointing of Jesus the Messiah at His baptism took place in the year that Daniel had prophesied.

What else occurred during that 490-year period of probation for ancient Israel? After the seven-plus-sixty-two weeks of years, or 483 years, the Messiah was to be "cut off" (Dan. 9:26). The next verse tells us that the Messiah would "bring an end to sacrifice and offering" in the middle of the final week (Dan. 9:27). The final week of years was the seven-year period from AD 27 to 34. In the middle of that week, or three and a half years after the autumn of AD 27, the Messiah would bring the Israelite system of sacrifices and offerings to an end by offering Himself as the ultimate Divine Sacrifice for the sins of the world. In other words, the Messiah would be cut off in the spring of AD 31.

And so it was. Since Jesus' ministry began with His baptism, and He was baptized in the autumn of AD 27, He attended four Passovers during His ministry—the Passovers of AD 28, 29, 30, and 31. The Gospel of John reveals that Jesus did, indeed, attend four Passovers (John 2:13; 5:1; 6:4; 13:1).

The point is that throughout His three and a half years of ministry, Jesus was opposed and rejected by the Israelite leaders and ultimately condemned to an unjust death on the cross. The Jews closed their probation as God's chosen nation by rejecting Jesus Christ as the Messiah. Now, "they are not all Israel who are of Israel" (Rom. 9:6, NKJV). Individual Jews, of course, may be saved as Gentiles are saved, by accepting Jesus Christ as Savior and Lord (Rom. 11:1–5). "They [the Jews] also, if they do not continue in unbelief, will be grafted in, for God is able to graft them in again" (Rom. 11:23). So now, those who believe in Jesus Christ, whether Jew or Gentile, are the true Israel of God (Gal. 3:7, 26–29).

The significance of all this for the prophecy of the trumpets is quite dramatic. We can view the trumpets as prophetic of the major retributive political upheavals God permitted throughout the Christian era after the close of probation for Israel as the chosen nation in AD 34. John informs us that after Christ's intercession ceased, "there were noises, thunderings, lightnings, and an earthquake" (Rev. 8:5,

NKJV). Certainly there were major political and social upheavals for the Jewish nation after they rejected Jesus as the Messiah. Daniel said as much. He wrote that after the Messiah was cut off, "the people of the prince who is to come shall destroy the city and the sanctuary. The end of it shall be with a flood. And till the end of the war desolations are determined" (Dan. 9:26, NKJV). Surely Daniel was foreseeing the destruction of Jerusalem by the Romans in AD 70. Hence, we may view the seven trumpets as prophetic of events from the rejection of the Israelite nation as the chosen people in AD 34 until the second coming of Jesus.

THE TRUMPETS AND THE CLOSE OF PROBATION

Daniel also predicted the end-time close of probation at the conclusion of the pre-Advent judgment.

> At that time Michael shall stand up, the great prince who stands watch over the sons of your people; and there shall be a time of trouble, such as never was since there was a nation, even to that time. And at that time your people shall be delivered, every one who is found written in the book (Dan. 12:1, NKJV).

In the book of Daniel, Michael is the Messiah. He is "the great prince" who watches over the people of God. He is the Son of man, who entered the heavenly court at the beginning of the pre-Advent judgment (Dan. 7:13, 14). Jesus is our Advocate in the judgment, at the conclusion of which He stands up and leaves the heavenly court. This is the end-time close of probation, which is followed by an unprecedented time of trouble.

As we have seen, Revelation 8:5 also refers to the end-time close of probation. Therefore, the trumpets may be viewed eschatologically as events occurring after the end-time close of probation, which comes at the conclusion of the pre-Advent judgment.[9] A comparison of Revelation 7:1 with 8:7 supports this interpretation. Revelation 7:1 says no harm is to come to "earth," "sea," or "tree" prior to the conclusion of the sealing work. But the first trumpet pictures fire burning "earth," "trees," and "green grass" (Rev. 8:7). Hence, the casting of the censer into the earth (Rev. 8:5) marks the end of the sealing work (Rev. 7:1–4). Looked at this way, the trumpets are chronologically parallel with the plagues (Rev. 15; 16).

Nevertheless, there seems to be a marked distinction between the trumpets and the plagues. The trumpets are devil-inspired scourges that God allows because of the unfaithfulness of humanity. For example, the locusts of the fifth trumpet represent satanic forces that God permits to wreak partial destruction, but which He keeps from harming His sealed people (Rev. 9:3, 4).

By contrast, the plagues are curses God metes out upon portions of the ungodly as punishments meant to counteract and restrain the destructive work of Satan pictured in the trumpets. They are said to emanate from "the seven bowls of the wrath of God" (Rev. 16:1), and the third plague is said directly to be God's response to humanity's unjust destructiveness: "Men have shed the blood of saints and prophets, and thou hast given them blood to drink" (Rev. 16:6). Under the sixth trumpet, the four angels "who are bound at the great river Euphra'tes" (Rev. 9:14) are released, and international conflict results. By contrast, the sixth plague results in the drying up of the river Euphrates "to prepare the way for the kings from the east" (Rev. 16:12). Satan's work of destruction and bloodshed (trumpets) is countered by God's work of restraint (plagues).

ANOTHER PERSPECTIVE

Every form of evil is to spring into intense activity. Evil angels unite their powers with evil men, and as they have been in constant conflict and attained an experience in the best modes of deception and battle, and have been strengthening for centuries, they will not yield the last great final contest without a desperate struggle. All the world will be on one side or the other of the question. The battle of Armageddon will be fought, and that day must find none of us sleeping. Wide awake we must be, as wise virgins having oil in our vessels with our lamps. . . . The power of the Holy Ghost must be upon us, and the Captain of the Lord's host will stand at the head of the angels of heaven to direct the battle. *Solemn events before us are yet to transpire. Trumpet after trumpet is to be sounded, vial after vial poured out one after another upon the inhabitants of the earth. Scenes of stupendous interest are right upon us.*[10]

When He [Christ] leaves the sanctuary, darkness covers the inhabitants of the earth. In that fearful time the righteous must live in the sight of a holy God without an intercessor. The restraint which has been upon the wicked is removed, and Satan has entire control of the finally impenitent. God's long-suffering has ended. The world has rejected His mercy, despised His love, and trampled upon His law. The wicked have passed the boundary of their probation; the Spirit of God, persistently resisted, has been at last withdrawn. Unsheltered by divine grace, they have no protection from the wicked one. Satan will then plunge the inhabitants of the earth into one great final trouble. As the angels of God cease to hold in check the fierce winds of human passion, all the elements of strife will be let loose. The whole world will be involved in ruin more terrible than that which came upon Jerusalem of old.

A single angel destroyed all the first-born of the Egyptians and filled the land with mourning. When David offended against God by numbering the people, one angel caused that terrible destruction by which his sin was punished. The same destructive power exercised by holy angels when God commands, will be exercised by evil angels when He permits. There are forces now ready, and only waiting the divine permission, to spread desolation everywhere.[11]

The wrath of Satan increases as his time grows short, and his work of deceit and destruction will reach its culmination in the time of trouble.[12]

The Saviour's prophecy concerning the visitation of judgments upon Jerusalem is to have another fulfillment, of which that terrible desolation was but a faint shadow. In the fate of the chosen city we may behold the doom of a world that has rejected God's mercy and trampled upon His law. Dark are the records of human misery that earth has witnessed during its long centuries of crime. The heart sickens and the mind grows faint in contemplation. Terrible have been the results of rejecting the authority of heaven. But a scene yet darker is presented in the revelations of the future. The records of the past—the long procession of tumults, conflicts, and revolutions, the "battle of the warrior . . . with confused noise, and garments rolled in blood" (Isaiah 9:5)—what are these, in contrast with the terrors of that day when the restraining Spirit of God shall be wholly withdrawn from the wicked, no longer to hold in check the outburst of human passion and satanic wrath! The world will then behold, as never before, the results of Satan's rule.[13]

When Christ ceases His intercession in the sanctuary, the unmingled wrath threatened against those who worship the beast and his image and receive his mark (Rev. 14:9, 10), will be poured out. The plagues upon Egypt when God was about to deliver Israel were similar in character to those more terrible and extensive judgments which are to fall upon the world just before the final deliverance of God's people. . . . These plagues are not universal, or the inhabitants of the earth would be wholly cut off. Yet they will be the most awful scourges that have ever been known to mortals. All the judgments upon men, prior to the close of probation, have been mingled with mercy. The pleading blood of Christ has shielded the sinner from receiving the full measure of his guilt; but in the final judgment, wrath is poured out unmixed with mercy.[14]

Conclusion

The historical application of the trumpets portrays international conflicts inspired by Satan and allowed by God after the close of probation for the ancient Israelite nation in AD 34, events that have occurred throughout the Christian era. However, these events serve as prophetic types of the destructive operations of Satan and evil people after the eschatological close of probation.

The prophecy pictures seven angels receiving the trumpets before

Christ's intercession for His believing people (Rev. 8:2); however, it doesn't portray them as blowing the trumpets until the end of Christ's mediatorial work, when He casts the censer onto the earth (Rev. 8:5, 6). Hence, the interpretation that the trumpets have a special application after the close of probation is supported by the order of events in the passage.

1. On the significance of trumpets in Leviticus 23 and Numbers 10, see Roy Gane, *Leviticus, Numbers: The NIV Application Commentary* (Grand Rapids, MI: Zondervan, 2004), 401, 402, 571.

2. Ellen G. White, *Patriarchs and Prophets* (Oakland, CA: Pacific Press®, 1890), 353. Cf. White, *Christ's Object Lessons,* 156, 157.

3. Christ's casting the censer into the earth is not generally interpreted as the close of probation. My view is unique. Alternative interpretations emphasize the pouring out of judgments upon the earth but do not identify a close of probation. See Stefanovic, *Revelation of Jesus Christ,* 285, 286; Maxwell, *God Cares,* 2:229, 230; Paulien, *Decoding Revelation's Trumpets,* 321–323; William Barclay, *The Revelation of John* (Philadelphia: Westminster Press, 1959), 2:51, 52; George Eldon Ladd, *A Commentary on the Revelation of John* (Grand Rapids, MI: Eerdmans, 1972), 125, 126; Richard C. H. Lenski, *The Interpretation of St. John's Revelation* (Minneapolis, MN: Augsburg, 1943), 271; Robert Mounce, *The Book of Revelation,* The New International Commentary on the New Testament (Grand Rapids, MI: Eerdmans, 1977), 182, 183; R. H. Charles, *A Critical and Exegetical Commentary on the Revelation of St. John* (Edinburgh: T. & T. Clark, 1920), 1:231, 232; Henry Barclay Swete, *The Apocalypse of St. John* (Grand Rapids, MI: Eerdmans, 1968), 109.

4. Swete, *Apocalypse of St. John,* 305.

5. Ellen G. White, *Early Writings* (Battle Creek, MI: Review and Herald®, 1882), 279, 280.

6. Ellen G. White, *The Great Controversy* (Mountain View, CA: Pacific Press®, 1911), 490, 491. Cf. 613, 614, 627–629.

7. John F. Walvoord, *Daniel, the Key to Prophetic Revelation* (Chicago: Moody Press, 1971), 217–220. Leon Wood, *A Commentary on Daniel* (Grand Rapids, MI: Zondervan, 1973), 247, 248. James A. Montgomery, *A Critical and Exegetical Commentary on the Book of Daniel* (Edinburgh: T. & T. Clark, 1927), 372.

8. Siegfried H. Horn and Lynn H. Wood, *The Chronology of Ezra 7* (Washington, DC: Review and Herald®, l953), 124–127.

9. David E. Aune comments, "The use of the metaphor of the sounding of a trumpet for introducing a series of eschatological divine punishments has an inherent logic, if only because of the use of the trumpet in ancient warfare to deploy successive units of troops and cavalry in attacking the enemy forces at a variety of points." Later in the same volume he adds: "The parallels between Exod 7:8–13:16 (the ten Exodus plagues) and Rev 8:1–11:19 and 15:1–16:21 indicate that Exodus provided the model for the author's vision of the eschatological punishments inflicted by God on the unbelieving inhabitants of the world." *Revelation 6–16,* Word Biblical Commentary, vol. 52B (Nashville: Thomas Nelson, 1998), 497, 546.

10. *Seventh-day Adventist Bible Commentary* (Washington, DC: Review and Herald®, 1957), 7:982; italics added.

11. White, *The Great Controversy,* 614.

12. Ibid., 623.

13. Ibid., 36, 37.

14. Ibid., 627–629.

CHAPTER 3

THE FIRST TRUMPET

We will now start looking closely, chapter by chapter, at each of the trumpets individually. Revelation 8:7 says,

> The first angel blew his trumpet, and there followed hail and fire, mixed with blood, which fell on the earth; and a third of the earth was burnt up, and a third of the trees were burnt up, and all the green grass was burnt up.

Hail, fire, and blood are symbols used throughout Scripture, primarily in three ways: (1) they refer to God's punishment of His enemies who are also the enemies of His people; (2) they refer to God's judgments upon His own people when they are unfaithful, and often these judgments are meted out by unbelieving nations whom God has permitted to punish His apostate people; (3) they refer to end-time judgments that will be poured out in various ways before and during the second coming of Christ. We will consider the Bible evidence for each of these points in turn.

HAIL, FIRE, AND BLOOD

Hail, fire, and blood are symbols of God's punishment of His enemies who are also the enemies of His people. The seventh plague that fell upon Egypt was hail mingled with fire. "There was hail, and fire flashing continually in the midst of the hail, very heavy hail, such as had never been in all the land of Egypt since it became a nation" (Exod. 9:24). During the war that Israel fought against the Amorites, more of the enemy died because of the large hailstones that struck them than were killed by Israel's army (Josh. 10:11).

Of fire, the psalmist wrote: "On the wicked he will rain coals of fire and brimstone; a scorching wind shall be the portion of their cup. For the Lord is righteous, he loves righteous deeds; the upright shall behold his face" (Ps. 11:6, 7). Of course, that was the experience of Sodom and Gomorrah. "The Lord rained on Sodom and Gomorrah brimstone and fire from the Lord out of heaven" (Gen. 19:24). Amos prophesied that fire would destroy Damascus (Amos 1:4), Gaza (verse 7), Tyre (verse 10), Edom (verse 12), Ammon (verse 14), and Moab (Amos 2:2). Isaiah's prophecy against Assyria employed fire as a symbol of destruction.

> Therefore the Lord, the Lord of hosts, will send wasting sickness among his stout warriors, and under his glory a burning will be kindled, like the burning of fire. The light of Israel will become a fire, and his Holy One a flame (Isa. 10:16, 17).

As for blood, in the first plague brought upon Egypt in the time of Moses, the water of the rivers and ponds was turned to blood (Exod. 7:14–24). The psalmist uses blood as a symbol of the destruction that will be the experience of Israel's enemies: "The righteous will rejoice when he sees the vengeance; he will bathe his feet in the blood of the wicked" (Ps. 58:10). Isaiah employs blood as a symbol of the judgments to be poured out on Edom:

> My sword has drunk its fill in the heavens; behold, it descends for judgment upon Edom, upon the people I have doomed. The Lord has a sword; it is sated with blood, it is gorged with fat, with the blood of lambs and goats, with the fat of the kidneys of rams. For the Lord has a sacrifice in Bozrah, a great slaughter in the land of Edom (Isa. 34:5, 6; cf. Ezek. 21:32; 28:23; 32:6; 35:1–7).

Thus, it seems very clear that hail, fire, and blood are symbols of God's judgments upon His unfaithful people. Often, these judgments were meted out by unbelieving nations whom the Lord allowed to attack His apostate people. Through Haggai, He explained to Israel: "I smote you and all the products of your toil with blight and mildew and hail; yet you did not return to me, says the Lord" (Hag. 2:17). Predicting the overthrow of the apostates in Samaria, Isaiah wrote: "Behold, the Lord has one who is mighty and strong; like a storm of hail, a destroying tempest, like a storm of mighty, overflowing waters, he will cast down to the earth with violence" (Isa. 28:2). Speaking of the attack on Israel God permitted the Assyrians to make, Isaiah wrote: "Hail will sweep away the refuge of lies" (Isa. 28:17): And prophesying against the false prophets in Israel, Ezekiel warned: "There will be a deluge of rain, great hailstones will fall, and a stormy wind break out" (Ezek. 13:11; cf. verses 13, 16).

Grieving at the unfaithfulness of his people, Hosea conveyed the message the Lord gave him: "Israel has forgotten his maker, and built palaces; and Judah has multiplied fortified cities; but I will send a fire upon his cities, and it shall devour his strongholds" (Hosea 8:14). Joel bemoaned the fact that because of the apostasy of the people, fire had "devoured the pastures of the wilderness" and flames had "burned all the trees of the field" (Joel 1:19). Because Israel had rejected His law, the Lord decreed through Amos: "I will send fire upon Judah, and it shall devour the strongholds of Jerusalem" (Amos 2:5; cf. Isa. 5:24). Jeremiah foresaw the imminent invasion of Israel by Babylon and passed along the Lord's warning to repent "lest my wrath go forth like fire, and burn with none to quench it, because of the evil of your doings" (Jer. 4:4; cf. 11:16). The Lord's rebuke was stern: "I will make you serve your enemies in a land which you do not know, for in my anger a fire is kindled which shall burn for ever" (Jer. 15:14). Micah also used fire as a symbol of God's destruction of His people (Mic. 1:4, 7).

John the Baptist added to the warnings of the Old Testament prophets. The Jews' history of apostasy followed by destruction would recur unless they repented. John proclaimed: "Even now the axe is laid to the root of the trees; every tree therefore that does not bear good fruit is cut down and thrown into the fire." "The chaff he will burn with unquenchable fire" (Matt. 3:10, 12). Jesus underlined the warnings of John the Baptist: "Every tree that does not bear good fruit is cut down and thrown into the fire" (Matt. 7:19). God's people of that day were not bearing good fruit, and divine retribution was coming.

Returning to the theme of blood, we find that the psalmist laments the destruction that Jerusalem was suffering. The heathen had "poured out their [Israel's] blood like water round about Jerusalem, and there was none to bury them" (Ps. 79:3). The blood of God's people was to be shed because their hands were "full of blood" (Isa. 1:15).

Ezekiel's predictions of tragedy upon Israel in view of her spiritual harlotry are terrible to consider (see Ezek. 16:35–43). The Lord spoke through the prophet: "I will judge you as women who break wedlock and shed blood are judged, and bring upon you the blood of wrath and jealousy" (Ezek. 16:38). God would forsake Israel to the ravages of her enemies.

The Lord made it abundantly clear that when His people turned away from the path of righteousness, He would allow calamity to come upon them. He warned,

> If I send a pestilence into that land, and pour out my wrath upon it with blood, to cut off from it man and beast; even if Noah, Daniel, and Job were in it, as I live, says the Lord God, they would deliver neither son nor daughter; they would deliver but their own lives by their righteousness (Ezek. 14:19, 20; cf. 22:1–6, 9–16, 27–31; 36:18).

Jesus reiterated the warnings of the prophets in a manner that could not be misunderstood.

> "Woe to you, scribes and Pharisees, hypocrites! For you build the tombs of the prophets and adorn the monuments of the righteous, saying, 'If we had lived in the days of our fathers, we would not have taken part with them in shedding the blood of the prophets.' Thus you witness against yourselves, that you are sons of those who murdered the prophets. Fill up, then, the measure of your fathers. You serpents, you brood of vipers, how are you to escape being sentenced to hell? Therefore I send you prophets and wise men and scribes, some of whom you will kill and crucify, and some you will scourge in your synagogues and persecute from town to town, that upon you may come all the righteous blood shed

on earth, from the blood of innocent Abel to the blood of Zechari'ah the son of Barachi'ah, whom you murdered between the sanctuary and the altar. *Truly, I say to you, all this will come upon this generation*" (Matt. 23:29–36; italics added; cf. Luke 11:45–52).

Jesus added, "Behold, your house is forsaken and desolate" (verse 38), and the mob at Jesus' trial confirmed that verdict when they cried out, "His blood be on us and on our children!" (Matt. 27:25).

Clearly, hail, fire, and blood sometimes refer to end-time judgments that will be poured out in various ways before and during the second coming of Christ.

It seems clear that the psalmist is referring to God's end-time intervention in the affairs of humankind when he writes:

Then the earth reeled and rocked;
    the foundations also of the mountains trembled
    and quaked, because he was angry.
Smoke went up from his nostrils,
    and devouring fire from his mouth;
    glowing coals flamed forth from him.
He bowed the heavens, and came down;
    thick darkness was under his feet.
He rode on a cherub, and flew;
    he came swiftly upon the wings of the wind.
He made darkness his covering around him,
    his canopy thick clouds dark with water.
Out of the brightness before him
    there broke through his clouds
    hailstones and coals of fire.

The LORD also thundered in the heavens,
    and the Most High uttered his voice,
    hailstones and coals of fire.
And he sent out his arrows, and scattered them;
    he flashed forth lightnings, and routed them.
Then the channels of the sea were seen,
    and the foundations of the world were laid bare,
at thy rebuke, O LORD,
    at the blast of the breath of thy nostrils (Ps. 18:7–15).

The Lord rains hailstones upon Gog: "With pestilence and bloodshed I will enter into judgment with him; and I will rain upon him and his hordes and the many peoples that are with him, torrential rains and hailstones, fire and brimstone" (Ezek. 38:22; cf. Rev. 20:7–9). When the temple of God is opened at the return of Jesus, "heavy hail" will be one of the destructive forces unleashed upon the world (Rev. 11:19; 16:21).

In describing the horrors of the local day of the Lord when Israel was under attack, Joel seems to be forecasting the ultimate Day of the Lord. Speaking of the destructive power of the Lord's army, Joel writes, "Fire devours before them, and behind them a flame burns. The land is like the garden of Eden before them, but after them a desolate wilderness, and nothing escapes them" (Joel 2:3). "The earth quakes before them, the heavens tremble. The sun and the moon are darkened, and the stars withdraw their shining. The Lord utters his voice before his army, for his host is exceedingly great; he that executes his word is powerful. For the day of the Lord is great and very terrible; who can endure it?" (Joel 2:10, 11).

Obadiah describes the same end-time Day of the Lord (Obad. 1:15, 16). As part of this event, he tells us, "The house of Jacob shall be a fire, and the house of Joseph a flame, and the house of Esau stubble; they shall burn them and consume them, and there shall be no survivor to the house of Esau; for the Lord has spoken" (Obad. 1:18).

Zephaniah speaks of the same event: "The great day of the Lord is near, near and hastening fast." "In the fire of his jealous wrath, all the earth shall be consumed; for a full, yea, sudden end he will make of all the inhabitants of the earth" (Zeph. 1:14, 18).

In chapter 29 of his prophecy, Isaiah also seems to be using the local day of the Lord as a type of the end-time Day of the Lord (Isa. 29:5–8): "You will be visited by the Lord of hosts with thunder and with earthquake and great noise, with whirlwind and tempest, and the flame of a devouring fire" (Isa. 29:6).

In predicting the end of the world, Jesus reiterated the warnings of the ancient prophets:

> The harvest is the close of the age, and the reapers are angels. Just as the weeds are gathered and burned with fire, so will it be at the close of the age. The Son of man will send his angels, and they will gather out of his kingdom all causes of sin and all evildoers, and throw them into the furnace of fire; there men will weep and gnash their teeth. Then the righteous will shine like the sun in the kingdom of their Father (Matt. 13:39–43; cf. 25:41; Luke 12:49; 17:29, 30; 1 Cor. 3:13, 15; 2 Thess. 1:7, 8; Rev. 18:8; 20:9).

Of the end of the world, Isaiah wrote, "Behold, the Lord is coming forth out of his place to punish the inhabitants of the earth for their iniquity, and the earth will disclose the blood shed upon her, and will no more cover her slain" (Isa. 26:21; cf. 34:1–4). Forecasting the suffering of the Messiah, Isaiah spoke of His garments sprinkled with the lifeblood of those for whom He was to die (Isa. 63:3). Then he notes the retribution those who reject the Messiah will suffer: "I trod down the peoples in my anger, I made them drunk in my wrath, and I poured out their lifeblood on the earth" (Isa. 63:6; cf. 9:2–5).

Jeremiah also foresaw the Day of the Lord on which "the sword shall devour and be sated, and drink its fill of their blood" (Jer. 46:10; cf. Ps. 68:21–23).

The book of Revelation speaks of antitypical Babylon. "In her was found the blood of prophets and saints, and of all who have been slain on earth" (Rev. 18:24; cf. 17:6). The blood of the dead saints cries out from the ground: "How long before thou wilt judge and avenge our blood on those who dwell upon the earth?" (Rev. 6:10). At that point they are given white clothing, symbolizing their ultimate vindication in the pre-Advent judgment (verse 11). Then follows the retribution for their persecutors: "He has judged the great harlot who corrupted the earth with her fornication, and he has avenged on her the blood of his servants" (Rev. 19:2).

THE EARTH

Before we determine just how the Bible's discussions of hail, fire, and blood relate to the prophecy of the trumpets, we must consider the meaning of the other symbols used in Revelation 8:7. John wrote, "The first angel blew his trumpet, and there followed hail and fire, mixed with blood, *which fell on the earth*" (Rev. 8:7; italics added). Although the "earth" is very often a symbol of all the world's peoples, on occasion the word refers in a special, restrictive sense to Israel, which is the subject of God's supreme regard. Israel (spoken of as the earth) is blessed or cursed depending on its obedience or disobedience to Jehovah. The various Babylonian captivities resulted from Israel's (the earth's) neglect of the everlasting covenant relationship.

For example, Isaiah 26:9 uses *earth* in the sense of the entire world: "My soul yearns for thee in the night, my spirit within me earnestly seeks thee. For when thy judgments are in the earth, the inhabitants of the world learn righteousness" (Isa. 26:9; cf. verse 21). On the other hand, Isaiah 28 uses *earth* to signify God's unfaithful people, upon whom judgments will fall: "Behold, the Lord has one who is mighty and strong; like a storm of hail, a destroying tempest, like a storm of mighty, overflowing waters, he will cast down to the earth with violence. The proud crown of the drunkards of Ephraim will be trodden under foot" (Isa. 28:2). The Assyrians would attack Israel, "for I [Isaiah] have heard from the Lord GOD of hosts of decisive destruction on all the earth" (verse 22, NASB).

Jeremiah also addressed Israel as the "earth." He wrote, "Hear, O earth; behold I am bringing evil upon this people, the fruit of their devices, because they have not given heed to my words; as for my law, they have rejected it" (Jer. 6:19). "O earth, earth, earth, hear the word of the LORD" (Jer. 22:29, KJV).

Jesus instructed His disciples: "Whatever you bind upon the earth shall have been bound in heaven, and whatever you loose upon the earth shall have been loosed in heaven" (Matt. 18:18).[1] The binding and loosing upon the earth is in fact binding and loosing within the church (cf. the context, verses 15–17). Paul asked, "What have I to do with judging outsiders? Is it not those inside the church whom you are to judge? God judges those outside" (1 Cor. 5:12, 13).

In Revelation 13, the lamblike beast "rose out of the earth" (verse 11), in contrast with the leopardlike beast (verses 1–10), which rose out of the sea (verse 1). The sea, or waters, represents "peoples and multitudes and nations and tongues" (Rev. 17:15; cf. Dan. 7:3, 17).

The sea represents the peoples of earth from among whom the nations rise. In symbolic prophecy, when the earth is contrasted with the sea, it seems to represent the professed people of God, both those who are faithful and those who are apostate. The power represented by the lamblike beast (Rev. 13:11–18) rose out of the earth in two senses: (1) it rose out of a previously uninhabited region;[2] and (2) it rose out of churches committed to specific religious and ecclesiastical principles.

A similar contrast is to be observed between the first and second trumpets. When the first is sounded, destruction falls upon "the earth" (Rev. 8:7). When the second is sounded, "a great mountain, burning with fire, was thrown into the sea" (verse 8). Considering the manner in which the symbols "earth" and "sea" are used in Scripture, we receive the impression that the contrast is between judgments upon the church and more extensive judgments upon the world in general.

The same contrast is apparent in the description of the first and second plagues (Rev. 16:2, 3). The first is poured out on "the earth," and the second is poured out upon "the sea."

THE TREES

The impression is now mounting that after the close of both the historical and eschatological periods of probation, God's professed people are attacked. What follows reinforces that impression. "The first angel blew his trumpet, and there followed hail and fire, mixed with blood, which fell on the earth; and a third of the earth was burnt up, *and a third of the trees were burnt up*" (Rev. 8:7, italics added).

In Scripture, trees are often employed as symbolizing God's professed people. In so far as the people are faithful to God, they are represented as flourishing, healthy trees. But when they are unfaithful, they are symbolized by trees that are no longer productive and will be cut down or destroyed by fire.

Psalm 1:3 depicts the righteous person as resembling "a tree planted by streams of water, that yields its fruit in its season, and its leaf does not wither. In all that he does, he prospers." Speaking of himself, the psalmist says, "I am like a green olive tree in the house of God. I trust in the steadfast love of God for ever and ever" (Ps. 52:8). Again he proclaims,

> The righteous flourish like the palm tree, and grow like a cedar in Lebanon. They are planted in the house of the LORD; they flourish in the courts of our God. They still bring forth fruit in old age, they are ever full of sap and green, to show that the LORD is upright; he is my rock, and there is no unrighteousness in him (Ps. 92:12–15; cf. Jer. 17:7, 8; Hosea 14:4–7).

Trees sometimes represent the leaders of God's professed people. Referring to Zedekiah and the manner in which he broke his covenant with the Babylonian monarch, God announced through Ezekiel that he would take a sprig from the top of a lofty cedar and plant it upon a high mountain. It would then become a flourishing tree under which animals would rest and in whose branches the birds would nest. "And all the trees of the field shall know that I the LORD bring low the high tree, and make high the low tree, dry up the green tree, and make the dry tree flourish. I the LORD have spoken, and I will do it" (Ezek. 17:24). In other words, God would bless the faithful leaders of His people and reduce the unfaithful to nothingness.

The Lord spoke through Jeremiah, "To the house of the king of Judah [Zedekiah] say, 'Hear the word of the LORD, O house of David' "

(Jer. 21:11). "I will kindle a fire in her forest, and it shall devour all that is round about her" (verse 14).

The Lord also spoke through Jeremiah to other leaders of the people:

Thus says the LORD concerning the house of the king of Judah: "You are as Gilead to me, as the summit of Lebanon, yet surely I will make you a desert, an uninhabited city. I will prepare destroyers against you, each with his weapons; and they shall cut down your choicest cedars, and cast them into the fire" (Jer. 22:6, 7).

Isaiah had a prophecy for the king of Assyria (see Isa. 10:12). He said, "The remnant of the trees of his forest will be so few that a child can write them down" (verse 19). And John the Baptist warned the Israelite leaders of his day: "Even now the axe is laid to the root of the trees; every tree therefore that does not bear good fruit is cut down and thrown into the fire" (Matt. 3:10).

Again and again in Scripture, the burning of trees is a symbol of judgments upon God's unfaithful people. The psalmist wrote, "I have seen a wicked man overbearing, and towering like a cedar of Lebanon. Again I passed by, and lo, he was no more; though I sought him, he could not be found" (Ps. 37:35, 36). Jeremiah wrote that because the people of Judah had broken their covenant with God, "the Lord once called you, 'A green olive tree, fair with goodly fruit'; but with the roar of a great tempest he will set fire to it, and its branches will be consumed" (Jer. 11:16; cf. Joel 1:5–7, 19, 20; Ezek. 15:6–8; Zech. 11:1–6).

Early in His ministry, Jesus used trees to symbolize the danger of spiritual fruitlessness: "Every sound tree bears good fruit, but the bad tree bears evil fruit. . . . Every tree that does not bear good fruit is cut down and thrown into the fire. Thus you will know them by their fruits" (Matt. 7:17–20; cf. 12:33; Luke 6:43–45).

Jesus represented the Jews of His day as an unfruitful tree that would eventually be destroyed. During the final week of His earthly ministry, Jesus cursed the fruitless fig tree; His action symbolized what would happen to the Israelite nation (Mark 11:12–14, 20). The tree looked promising; outwardly it was attractive. But it was unproductive. Like that tree, the religious leaders put on a great display of piety but they were spiritually barren. How significant that on the day on which Jesus cursed the fig tree, He also drove the traders and money-changers out of the temple court. His actions dramatized His disapproval of the fruitless nation (Mark 11:15–19).

Jesus' parable of the wicked tenants (Mark 12:1–12) harked back to Isaiah 5:1–7. The man who planted the vineyard represented the Lord Himself. The wicked tenants symbolized the unresponsive Israelite nation that rejected the prophets sent to them and eventually rejected the Messiah Himself. Jesus revealed the outcome: "What will the owner of the vineyard do? He will come and destroy the tenants, and give the vineyard to others" (Mark 12:9).

Jesus was illustrating the perfidy of the Israelite leaders, who were listening to His teaching. "They tried to arrest him, but feared the multitude, for they perceived that he had told the parable against them; so they left him and went away" (verse 12).

The statement Jesus made to His female followers who were accompanying Him as He was being led to Calvary reiterated the impending doom of the unfaithful nation:

"Daughters of Jerusalem, do not weep for me, but weep for yourselves and for your children. For behold, the days are coming when they will say, 'Blessed are the barren, and the

wombs that never bore, and the breasts that never gave suck!'
Then they will begin to say to the mountains, 'Fall on us';
and to the hills, 'Cover us.' For if they do this when the wood
is green, what will happen when it is dry?" (Luke 23:28–31).

The grass

"The first angel blew his trumpet, and there followed hail and fire
mixed with blood, which fell on the earth; and a third of the earth
was burnt up, and a third of the trees were burnt up, *and all the green
grass was burnt up*" (Rev. 8:7; italics added). In Scripture, grass is
sometimes used as a symbol of all the inhabitants of the earth. The
psalmist said of God, "Thou dost sweep men away; they are like a
dream, like grass which is renewed in the morning: in the morning it
flourishes and is renewed; in the evening it fades and withers. For we
are consumed by thy anger; by thy wrath we are overwhelmed" (Ps.
90:5–7). "As for man, his days are like grass; he flourishes like a
flower of the field; for the wind passes over it, and it is gone, and its
place knows it no more" (Ps. 103:15, 16; cf. Isa. 40:6–8; 51:12;
1 Pet. 1:24, 25).

Grass can also symbolize the faithful people of God. Job was reassured, "You shall know also that your descendants shall be many, and
your offspring as the grass of the earth" (Job 5:25). Uttering a prayer
for the righteous king, the psalmist pleaded for his subjects: "May
men blossom forth from the cities like the grass of the field!" (Ps.
72:16).

On yet other occasions, grass represents the unfaithful people of
God, and the destruction of grass designates their destruction. Addressing Sennacherib, whom He had permitted to punish His unfaithful people, the Lord proclaimed, "Have you not heard that I determined
it long ago? I planned from days of old what now I bring to pass, that

you should turn fortified cities into heaps of ruins, while their inhabitants, shorn of strength, are dismayed and confounded, and have become like plants of the field, and like tender grass, like grass on the housetops; blighted before it is grown?" (2 Kings 19:25, 26).

King David had every reason to know of the evil designs of enemies and of God's willingness to care for His people. He wrote, "Fret not yourself because of the wicked; be not envious of wrongdoers! For they will soon fade like the grass, and wither like the green herb" (Ps. 37:1, 2). Again, the psalmist wrote, "Though the wicked sprout like grass and all evildoers flourish, they are doomed to destruction for ever, but thou, O LORD, art on high for ever" (Ps. 92:7, 8; cf. 129:5–7).

Why does Revelation 8:7 announce, however, that *a third* of the earth and of the trees would be burnt up, and *all* the green grass would be burnt up? Why a third of some and all of the grass?

This scenario seems to suggest that the destruction would not be universal. The punishment that God would bring upon His unfaithful people would be partial.

God instructed Ezekiel to cut the hair of his head and beard and divide the hair into three parts (Ezek. 5:1–4). He was to burn a third of the hair in a fire; another third he was to "take and strike with the sword round about the city"; and the final third he was to "scatter to the wind." The thirds denoted the three ways in which God would permit His unfaithful people to be punished. Here's how the Lord applied the acted prophecy:

> Thus says the Lord God: This is Jerusalem; I have set her in the center of the nations, with countries round about her. And she has wickedly rebelled against my ordinances, more than the nations, and against my statutes more than the

countries round about her, by rejecting my ordinances and not walking in my statutes. Therefore thus says the Lord God: Because you are more turbulent than the nations that are round about you, have not walked in my statutes or kept my ordinances, but have acted according to the ordinances of the nations that are round about you; therefore thus says the Lord God: Behold, I, even I, am against you; and I will execute judgments in the midst of you in the sight of the nations. And because of all your abominations I will do with you what I have never yet done, and the like of which I will never do again. Therefore fathers shall eat their sons in the midst of you, and sons shall eat their fathers; and I will execute judgments on you, and any of you who survive I will scatter to all the winds. . . . A third part of you shall die of pestilence and be consumed with famine in the midst of you; a third part shall fall by the sword round about you; and a third part I will scatter to all the winds and will unsheathe the sword after them (Ezek. 5:5–10, 12; cf. Zech. 13:8, 9).

Revelation 8:7 tells us that *a third* of the earth and of the trees were to be burnt up, but *all* the green grass. Evidently, all the grass would be burnt up in the third where the trees were to be burnt.[3]

THE FIRST TRUMPET

In the light of the symbolic meanings that we have discovered in Scripture, how should we now interpret the first trumpet (Rev. 8:7)?

We have discovered that often hail, fire, and blood are symbols of God's judgments upon His unfaithful people—judgments that are meted out by unbelieving nations whom the Lord permits to attack His apostate people. We have discovered that *earth* often represents

Israel, God's professed people. We have noted that *trees* are sometimes symbols of the leaders of God's professed people, and *grass* often symbolizes the unfaithful people of God who will be destroyed. We also observed that a third of the earth and the trees being burnt up implies that a portion of the population of Israel and of her leaders will be destroyed as retribution for their sins. All the green grass being burnt up means that all the green grass will be destroyed in the territory in which the third of the trees are destroyed. In other words, the unfaithful in that area would be wiped out.

Now, let's put the first trumpet in its historical setting. As we have seen, Revelation 8:5, describing Christ's casting the censer into the earth, refers to the close of probation. Daniel predicted a close of probation for the Jews at the end of the seventy weeks of years—that is, at the conclusion of the 490 years, which began in 457 BC and ended in AD 34 (Dan. 9:24–27). The Jews rejected Christ, so the "probationary time" for their position as a chosen nation, God's special people, ended in AD 34. Daniel predicted that after that event, "the people of the prince who is to come shall destroy the city and the sanctuary. The end of it shall be with a flood. And till the end of the war desolations are determined" (Dan. 9:26, NASB).

Quoting Daniel, Jesus also predicted the destruction of Jerusalem and the temple (Matt. 24:15–21). As we have seen, during His ministry Jesus often warned of this coming destruction (Matt. 22:7; 23:37–39; Mark 12:1–9; Luke 19:42–44: 23:28–31).

The first trumpet sounded after the close of probation for Israel as a nation. Significantly, the predicted destruction of Jerusalem and the temple occurred in AD 70. At that time, "hail and fire, mixed with blood" were poured out on the earth—in the sense that the professed church of God, centered in Jerusalem, was the brunt of the Roman attack upon the Jews. The faithful Christians escaped, but many Jews were killed. A third of the earth was burnt up in the sense that, although the slaughter was devastating, it didn't comprise a total massacre of the professed people of God. A large number of the Israelite religious leaders ("trees") was destroyed, and retribution was meted out upon the unfaithful people ("grass") within the city.[4]

Ellen White's comments are crucial here:

> When Christ should hang upon the cross of Calvary, Israel's day as a nation favored and blessed of God would be ended. The loss of even one soul is a calamity infinitely outweighing the gains and treasures of a world; but as Christ looked upon Jerusalem, the doom of a whole city, a whole nation, was before Him—that city, that nation, which had once been the chosen of God, His peculiar treasure.[5]

> The cursing of the fig tree was an acted parable. That barren tree, flaunting its pretentious foliage in the very face of Christ, was a symbol of the Jewish nation. The Saviour desired to make plain to His disciples the cause and the certainty of Israel's doom. For this purpose He invested the tree with moral qualities, and made it the expositor of divine truth. The Jews stood forth distinct from all other nations, professing allegiance to God. They had been specially favored by Him, and they laid claim to righteousness above every other people. But they were corrupted by the love of the world and the greed of gain. They boasted of their knowledge, but they were ignorant of the requirements of God, and were full of hypocrisy. Like the barren tree, they spread their pretentious branches aloft, luxuriant in appearance, and beautiful to the eye, but they yielded "nothing but leaves."

The Jewish religion, with its magnificent temple, its sacred altars, its mitered priests and impressive ceremonies, was indeed fair in outward appearance, but humility, love, and benevolence were lacking.[6]

Not one Christian perished in the destruction of Jerusalem. Christ had given His disciples warning, and all who believed His words watched for the promised sign. "When ye shall see Jerusalem compassed with armies," said Jesus, "then know that the desolation thereof is nigh. Then let them which are in Judea flee to the mountains; and let them which are in the midst of it depart out." Luke 21:20, 21. After the Romans under Cestius had surrounded the city, they unexpectedly abandoned the siege when everything seemed favorable for an immediate attack. The besieged, despairing of successful resistance, were on the point of surrender, when the Roman general withdrew his forces without the least apparent reason. But God's merciful providence was directing events for the good of His own people. The promised sign had been given to the waiting Christians, and now an opportunity was offered for all who would, to obey the Saviour's warning. Events were so overruled that neither Jews nor Romans should hinder the flight of the Christians. Upon the retreat of Cestius, the Jews, sallying from Jerusalem, pursued after the retiring army; and while both forces were thus fully engaged, the Christians had an opportunity to leave the city. At this time the country also had been cleared of enemies who might have endeavored to intercept them. At the time of the siege, the Jews were assembled at Jerusalem to keep the Feast of Tabernacles, and thus the Christians throughout the land were able to make their escape unmolested. Without delay they fled to a place of safety—the city of Pella, in the land Perea, beyond Jordan.[7]

In the siege and the slaughter that followed, more than a million of the people perished; the survivors were carried away as captives, sold as slaves, dragged to Rome to grace the conqueror's triumph, thrown to wild beasts in the amphitheaters, or scattered as homeless wanderers throughout the earth. . . .

The horrible cruelties enacted in the destruction of Jerusalem are a demonstration of Satan's vindictive power over those who yield to his control.[8]

CONCLUSION OF FIRST TRUMPET

We have observed that Revelation 8:5 refers to the universal end-time close of probation as well as to previous occasions on which probation was closed for limited numbers of earth's inhabitants. This trumpet then indicates that there will be a massive, devil-inspired attack on all the members of the professed Christian church (the "earth")—both upon sealed believers (Rev. 12:17; 13:7, 8, 15–17) and upon unsealed adherents of antitypical Babylon (Rev. 18:4) who profess to belong to God's true church. Many unfruitful professed Christians—leaders ("trees") and erstwhile believers ("grass") who have not made the necessary spiritual preparation but have given allegiance to the image of the beast—will be wiped out. But just as the faithful servants of God were able to escape the destruction of Jerusalem, so those in the universal church who are God's sealed saints will escape the end-time close of probation unharmed (Rev. 7:1–4; 9:4).

At the same time that this attack on His professed people is in progress, God will pour out the first of the seven plagues upon many of those who have the metaphorical "mark of the beast" and who are worshiping its "image" (Rev. 16:2). The plague of "foul and evil sores" will not only punish the adherents of antitypical Babylon, but will also counteract and somewhat restrain the destructive work of Satan. Here, too, Ellen White brings some important insights that help us understand what all this means.

> Christ saw in Jerusalem a symbol of the world hardened in unbelief and rebellion, and hastening on to meet the retributive judgments of God. The woes of a fallen race, pressing upon His soul, forced from His lips that exceeding bitter cry. He saw the record of sin traced in human misery, tears, and blood; His heart was moved with infinite pity for the afflicted and suffering ones of earth; He yearned to relieve them all. But even His hand might not turn back the tide of human woe; few would seek their only Source of help. He was willing to pour out His soul unto death, to bring salvation within their reach; but few would come to Him that they might have life. . . .
>
> Jesus, looking down to the last generation, saw the world involved in a deception similar to that which caused the destruction of Jerusalem. The great sin of the Jews was their rejection of Christ; the great sin of the Christian world would be their rejection of the law of God, the foundation of His government in heaven and earth. The precepts of Jehovah would be despised and set at nought. Millions in bondage to sin, slaves of Satan, doomed to suffer the second death, would refuse to listen to the words of truth in their day of visitation. Terrible blindness! strange infatuation![9]

Noah was shut in, and the rejecters of God's mercy were shut out. The seal of Heaven was on that door; God had shut it, and God alone could open it. So when Christ shall cease his intercession for guilty men, before his coming in the clouds of heaven, the door of mercy will be shut. Then divine grace will no longer restrain the wicked, and Satan will have full control of those who have rejected mercy. They will endeavor to destroy God's people; but as Noah was shut into the ark, so the righteous will be shielded by divine power.[10]

When He [Christ] leaves the sanctuary, darkness covers the inhabitants of the earth. In that fearful time the righteous must live in the sight of a holy God without an intercessor. The restraint which has been upon the wicked is removed, and Satan has entire control of the finally impenitent. God's long-suffering has ended. The world has rejected His mercy, despised His love, and trampled upon His law. The wicked have passed the boundary of their probation; the Spirit of God, persistently resisted, has been at last withdrawn. Unsheltered by divine grace, they have no protection from the wicked one. Satan will then plunge the inhabitants of the earth into one great, final trouble. As the angels of God cease to hold in check the fierce winds of human passion, all the elements of strife will be let loose. The whole world will be involved in ruin more terrible than that which came upon Jerusalem of old. . . .

Those who honor the law of God have been accused of bringing judgments upon the world, and they will be regarded as the cause of the fearful convulsions of nature and the strife and bloodshed among men that are filling the earth with woe.

The power attending the last warning has enraged the wicked; their anger is kindled against all who have received the message, and Satan will excite to still greater intensity the spirit of hatred and persecution. . . .

When God's presence was finally withdrawn from the Jewish nation, priests and people knew it not. . . . So when the irrevocable decision of the sanctuary has been pronounced and the destiny of the world has been forever fixed, the inhabitants of the earth will know it not. The forms of religion will be continued by a people from whom the Spirit of God has been finally withdrawn; and the satanic zeal with which the prince of evil will inspire them for the accomplishment of his malignant designs, will bear the semblance of zeal for God.

As the Sabbath has become the special point of controversy throughout Christendom, and religious and secular authorities have combined to enforce the observance of the Sunday, the persistent refusal of a small minority to yield to the popular demand will make them objects of universal execration.[11]

---

1. My translation. The two verbs are future perfect passive periphrastics: *estai dedemena* and *estai lelumena*. The decision made by the church simply underlines the decision already made in heaven. Randolph O. Yeager translates the verse: "Whatever you may bind upon the earth shall be that which has already been bound in heaven; and whatever you may loose upon the earth shall be that which has already been loosed in heaven." Randolph O. Yeager, *The Renaissance New Testament* (Bowling Green, KY: Renaissance Press, 1976), 2:632.

2. White, *The Great Controversy*, 440, 441.

3. See Jon Paulien, *Decoding Revelation's Trumpets*, 379.

4. Jon Paulien, Ranko Stefanovic, and Mervyn Maxwell agree substantially with my historical applications of the first four trumpets, but for the most part they do not see end-time applications after the close of probation.

J. Massyngberde Ford does not identify specific historical events as fulfillments of the first four trumpets. She summarizes her comments on Revelation 8: "Thus Rev 8 shows Yahweh beginning to bring his weapons and troops into action, to war against his people in order that they may repent, Rev 9:20. As in Isa 42:13, Yahweh is portrayed as a furious man of war." *Revelation,* The Anchor Bible, vol. 38 (Garden City, NY: Doubleday, 1975), 139.

Without identifying any historical fulfillment, Leon Morris summarizes his discussion of the first trumpet as follows: "John does not tell us who it was who cast the fire and hail upon the earth. We should understand some heavenly being, but precisely which does not matter. What matters is that God sends His plagues on evil men. This is true throughout the ages and it will be so till the End." *The Revelation of St. John* (Grand Rapids, MI: Eerdmans, 1969), 123. Just so, in his discussion of the second, third, and fourth trumpets, Morris specifies no historical fulfillments. He simply refers to the "punishment of ungodly men" (124) by the judgments of God.

5. White, *The Great Controversy,* 21.

6. White, *The Desire of Ages,* 582, 583.

7. White, *The Great Controversy,* 30, 31.

8. Ibid., 35, 36.

9. Ibid., 22, 23.

10. White, *Patriarchs and Prophets,* 98.

11. White, *The Great Controversy,* 614, 615.

CHAPTER 4

THE SECOND TRUMPET

The second angel blew his trumpet, and something like a great mountain, burning with fire, was thrown into the sea; and a third of the sea became blood, a third of the living creatures in the sea died, and a third of the ships were destroyed (Rev. 8:8, 9).

In Scripture, a mountain often symbolizes a nation or power. The closest imagery to that employed regarding the second trumpet of Revelation is to be found in the writings of Jeremiah:

"I will requite Babylon and all the inhabitants of Chalde'a before your very eyes for all the evil that they have done in Zion, says the LORD. Behold, I am against you, O destroying mountain, says the LORD, which destroys the whole earth; I will stretch out my hand against you, and roll you down from the crags, and make you a burnt mountain. No stone shall be taken from you for a corner and no stone for a foundation, but you shall be a perpetual waste, says the LORD. . . . The sea has come up on Babylon; she is covered with its tumultuous waves" (Jer. 51:24–26, 42).[1]

During the rule of Nebuchadnezzar, Babylon had invaded Palestine three times (in 605, 597, and 586 BC) and had taken many Israelites captive. Although Babylon was the instrument that God permitted to punish His apostate people, eventually Babylon was to be punished for rejecting God's counsels. Jeremiah wrote,

> "The sea has come upon Babylon; she is covered with its tumultuous waves. . . . Go out of the midst of her, my people! Let every man save his life from the fierce anger of the LORD! . . . For the LORD is laying Babylon waste, and stilling her mighty voice. Their waves roar like many waters, the noise of their voice is raised. . . . Thus says the Lord of hosts: the broad wall of Babylon shall be leveled to the ground and her high gates shall be burned with fire. The peoples labor for naught, and the nations weary themselves only for fire" (Jer. 51:42, 45, 55, 58).

Jeremiah instructed Seraiah, who went to Babylon with Zedekiah, the king of Judah, "When you finish reading this book, bind a stone to it, and cast it into the midst of the Euphra'tes, and say, 'Thus shall Babylon sink, to rise no more, because of the evil that I am bringing upon her' " (Jer. 51:63, 64). Babylon, a burnt mountain, was to be thrown into the water.

Isaiah also used the imagery of the destruction of mountains to warn of God's punishment of unfaithful nations: "The Lord of hosts has a day against all that is proud and lofty, against all that is lifted up and high; . . . against all the high mountains, and against all the lofty hills" (Isa. 2:12, 14). Isaiah longed for the day when the Lord would manifest His presence to the nations. "O that thou wouldst rend the heavens and come down," he prayed, "that the mountains might quake at thy presence—as when fire kindles brushwood and the fire causes water to boil—to make thy name known to thy adversaries, and that the nations might tremble at thy presence!" (Isa. 64:1, 2; cf. Ps. 83:13–15).

Speaking of Babylon's coming doom, Isaiah wrote, "Hark, a tumult on the mountains as of a great multitude! Hark, an uproar of kingdoms, of nations gathering together! The LORD of hosts is mustering a host for battle" (Isa. 13:4).

Eventually, God's mountain, His kingdom, will supersede all earthly mountains; it will be exalted above the nations and rule the world in righteousness.

> It shall come to pass in the latter days that the mountain of the house of the LORD shall be established as the highest of the mountains, and shall be raised above the hills; and all the nations shall flow to it, and many peoples shall come, and say: "Come, let us go up to the mountain of the LORD, to the house of the God of Jacob; that he may teach us his ways and that we may walk in his paths" (Isa. 2:2, 3).

In view of this divine intervention in the affairs of humankind, God's people should have no fear when the mountains (the nations) are subject to heaven's judgments (Ps. 46:2; Isa. 54:10). As Daniel predicted, God's kingdom will be like "a great mountain" that will fill the whole earth (Dan. 2:35, 44, 45).

Revelation 8:8 pictures a strange sight: "The second angel blew his trumpet, and something like a great mountain, *burning with fire, was thrown into the sea*" (italics added). As we have observed, fire is often a symbol of God's punishment of those who are opposed to Him and His faithful people.

The sea refers to peoples, nations, the teeming masses of humanity. The four beasts that Daniel saw coming up out of the sea (Dan. 7:2, 3) represented nations that would arise "out of the earth" (verse 17). In Revelation 17, the harlot Babylon is depicted as "seated upon many waters" (verse 1). And John was told, "The waters that you saw, where the harlot is seated, are peoples and multitudes and nations and tongues" (verse 15).

The text continues, now with this image: "And a third of the sea *became blood*" (Rev. 8:9; italics added). In our study of the first trumpet we found that in Scripture, blood is often a symbol of God's judgments upon His enemies, who are the enemies of His faithful people. The first plague upon Egypt in Moses' time consisted of the turning of the water in the rivers and ponds to blood. The limitation to a "third" of the sea implies that the particular judgment referred to was not universal in extent. Only a portion of the forces arrayed against God and His people would be destroyed.

The second trumpet concludes with more symbols: "A third of the living creatures in the sea died, and a third of the ships were destroyed" (Rev. 8:9). The creatures in the sea are the people who comprise the great sea of humanity in the area in which this judgment is meted out, and the ships symbolize their material possessions and the sources of their wealth (Zeph. 1:2, 3; Hab. 1:14; Ps. 48:4–8; 107:23–27; Ezek. 27:9, 25, 29; Rev. 18:17–19).

THE ROMAN EMPIRE

How are we to interpret the symbolism used in this prophecy? What is God telling us through the second trumpet?[2]

When Revelation 8:8, 9 is placed in its historical context, it is clear that the events described in those verses were to occur after the close of probation for the Jewish nation (AD 34; Rev. 8:5). Furthermore, we can expect that these events would transpire sometime after the Roman attack on the Jews in AD 70—that is, after the events outlined in the first trumpet. Babylon didn't exist as a nation at that time; the apostles used the name of that ancient enemy of God's people to refer to Rome. Writing of Rome, the apostle Peter said, "She who is at Babylon, who is likewise chosen, sends you greetings" (1 Pet. 5:13), and in Revelation, John speaks of the harlot "Babylon" (see Rev. 17:1–6) as "the great city which has dominion over the kings of the earth" (verse 18). Moreover, "during the early Christian centuries the cryptic designation Babylon for the city and empire of Rome appears commonly in both Jewish and Christian literature."[3] The suggestion, therefore, is that the second trumpet is speaking of the decline and fall of the Roman Empire. A prominent message in the book of Daniel is that all the nations that succeeded Neo-Babylonia would meet the same fate as Babylon because of their rejection of the divine purpose for their existence (Dan. 2; 7; 8; 11).

The Roman Empire figures largely in Daniel's prophecies. Daniel 2 presents Rome as "a fourth kingdom, strong as iron, because iron breaks to pieces and shatters all things; and like iron which crushes, it shall break and crush all these" (Dan. 2:40). But the prophecy makes it clear that this great, destructive power would be superseded by a divided Europe, which was symbolized by the mixture of iron and clay that comprised the feet and toes of the image (verse 41).

Daniel 7 provides more detail. In the vision described in that chapter, four wild beasts represent four successive empires. Rome is represented by the fourth beast, which is basically indescribable other than that it has ten horns (Dan. 7:7). The "fourth kingdom on earth" (verse 23) after Babylon was Rome. The ten horns on the symbolic beast's head denote the powers that would dismember the Roman Empire (verse 24).

Daniel 8 brings to view a "little horn" power that represents both the Roman Empire and the papacy, which arose out of it. Daniel foresaw that Rome would persecute the people of God; attack Christ, "the Prince of the host"; and destroy "the place of his sanctuary" (Dan. 8:9–11). The Roman Empire did all this, but the prophecy envisioned its ultimate downfall, and the Roman Empire did indeed fall.

The eleventh chapter of Daniel depicts Rome as the king of the north who would subjugate the nations of the eastern Mediterranean (Dan. 11:14–20). But this prophecy also says Rome would lose its power, and it indicates that the papacy would take its place (verse 21ff.). Similarly, Revelation 12 likens the Roman Empire to "a great red dragon" waiting to destroy Christ as soon as He was born (Rev. 12:1–5). But Revelation indicates that Rome failed in this attempt and eventually was replaced by the medieval papacy (cf. Rev. 13:2).

Revelation 17 describes John's vision of a scarlet beast with seven heads and ten horns. He was told: "The seven heads are seven mountains on which the woman is seated; they are also seven kings, five of whom have fallen, one is, the other has not yet come" (verse 10). The five fallen nations are usually considered to be those opponents of Israel that preceded the Roman Empire: Egypt, Assyria, Babylon, Media-Persia, and Greece. The Roman Empire of John's day was the sixth "head"—the one that "is." And the seventh foretold the emergence of a power that in John's day had "not yet come" (Rev. 17:10). The point is, John predicts that the days of the Roman Empire were numbered, which was the case: the fifth and sixth centuries AD witnessed the gradual decline and fall of that great empire. Edwin R. Thiele describes it graphically:

> After the fall of Jerusalem and the end of the Jewish state, the next scene of judgment is one on a much broader and vaster

scale, one in which a large share of the creatures in the international scene were to be involved. The second trumpet calls for some terrible, fiery, destructive force to fall into the troubled seas of the ancient world and to turn their turbid waters into blood. After the fall of Jerusalem came the fall of Rome. As the Jews had outlived their days of national usefulness, so also had Rome. Avarice and greed, lewdness and intemperance, extravagance and voluptuousness, cruelty and rapaciousness—every vice known to demons and men—had so weakened the moral fiber of the inhabitants of the Roman world that they were ripe for dissolution. The empire of the Caesars was doomed. The ax of divine retribution must fall. Like flames of fire from heaven came Genseric the Vandal, Alaric the Goth, and Attila the Hun, leaving in their wake scenes of ruin, desolation, carnage, and blood. Irresistible and destructive as a flaming mountain, the hordes of barbarians fell upon the peoples of Rome, till all the empire was involved in a grand and irretrievable catastrophe. Rome was gone and justice again had had its way.[4]

The papacy (historical application)

As we have seen, the trumpets depict events that occur after the end-time close of probation (Rev. 8:5).[5] The first trumpet informs us that, after the close of probation, earthly apostate powers will conduct a concerted attack on professed Christians. But these apostate powers are themselves to suffer under the judgments of God. The second trumpet warns us that the secular authority undergirding the end-time false religious union will be torn away. Earth's superpowers that—like the ancient Roman Empire—support false, unbiblical religion will be divested of their prowess and, as it were, "like a great mountain, burning with fire . . . thrown into the sea" (Rev. 8:8). To understand in a general way these events of the future, we must consult the prophecies of both Daniel and Revelation.

Daniel 7 reveals that the little horn power is the papacy, whose "dominion shall be taken away" by the pre-Advent judgment, and it tells us that the papacy will be destroyed at the end of time (Dan. 7:26). Daniel 8 provides further details. The little horn power in this chapter is both pagan and papal Rome. Gabriel explained to Daniel that the prophecy pertains to events at the end of time. He said, "Behold, I will make known to you what shall be at the latter end of the indignation; for it pertains to the appointed time of the end" (Dan. 8:19).

Gabriel spelled out the end-time activities of the little horn power in graphic detail:

> His power shall be great, and he shall cause fearful destruc-
> tion, and shall succeed in what he does, and destroy mighty
> men and the people of the saints. By his cunning he shall
> make deceit prosper under his hand, and in his own mind he
> shall magnify himself. Without warning he shall destroy
> many; and he shall even rise up against the Prince of princes;
> but, by no human hand, he shall be broken. The vision of the
> evenings and the mornings which has been told is true; but
> seal up the vision, for it pertains to many days hence (Dan.
> 8:24–26).

The papacy, a religious power, could never have accomplished these horrors without support from secular nations. The undergirding power of western European nations supported the political domi-nance of the papacy in the Middle Ages, and prophecy indicates that

European power, with the added support of the United States, will again bolster the claims and activities of the papacy.

Daniel 11 brings the events of the future into clearer focus. In this chapter, the king of the north refers to those powers that throughout history have threatened Palestine from the north. Initially, Persia, Greece, Syria, and the Roman Empire fulfilled this prophesied role. Egypt and those powers that supported it were represented as the king of the south.

Daniel 11:20 refers to the Emperor Augustus: "There shall arise in his place one who imposes taxes on the glorious kingdom; but within a few days he shall be destroyed, but not in anger or in battle" (NKJV). Augustus, the raiser of taxes, was reigning when Christ was born (cf. Luke 2:1–7). Augustus had an illustrious and relatively peaceful reign and died of natural causes on August 19, AD 14.

The next verse introduces the papacy. "His place will be taken by a contemptible man, on whom royal majesty was not conferred; he will come in unawares and seize the kingdom through trickery" (Dan. 11:21, NJPS). The verse doesn't refer to the Roman emperor Tiberius; royal majesty was conferred upon him. But papal Rome succeeded the Roman Empire, and, as the prophecy specified, it came to power by craft, force, treachery, and deceit (cf. Dan. 7:24, 25; 8:23–25). Also in fulfillment of the prophecy, throughout the medieval period, papal Rome usurped Christ's mediatorial role, replacing Him and His ministry in heaven with the pope and his sacerdotal (priestly) system. The popes also used deception and false religion to control the nations of Western Europe. Because of the alliances between the papacy and those nations, Europe became known as the *Respublica Christiana,* the "Christian republic."

Daniel 11:24–30 outlines the crusades the Christian west undertook against the Islamic east and south. The king of the north—the papacy in league with the nations of Western Europe—attacked the king of the south, the Islamic world, which at that time controlled Palestine. As Philip Schaff commented, the Crusades "were a succession of tournaments between two continents and two religions, struggling for supremacy,—Europe and Asia, Christianity and Mohammedanism."[6]

TIME OF THE END (FUTURE APPLICATION)

Prophecies are quite specific; however, we must always regard our interpretation of prophecies concerning the future as tentative. But history does repeat itself. The final verses of Daniel 11 suggest that in the future there will be a massive clash between the professedly Christian west and the world of Islam. Daniel 11:40 informs us, "At the time of the end the king of the South shall attack him; and the king of the North shall come against him like a whirlwind, with chariots, horsemen, and with many ships; and he shall enter the countries, overwhelm them, and pass through" (NKJV).

The king of the south was last mentioned in verses 25 and 29, which describe the papal crusades against the Islamic powers in the Middle East. Subsequent verses (verses 31–39) focus on the activities of the papacy leading up to 1798, the year the "time of the end" began (verse 35), and beyond (verses 36–39—still referring to the time of the end). Verse 40 begins a description of events "in" that prophetic period: The king of the south (the Islamic powers) will attack the king of the north (the Western world), and all-out war will result. The king of the north (the Western powers, including the United States, in league with the papacy) will invade the territories of the Islamic world with a huge military force and take over some of the countries. Verse 41 says, "He shall also enter the Glorious Land, and many countries shall be overthrown; but these shall escape from his hand: Edom, Moab, and the prominent people of Ammon" (NKJV). The Western powers will invade Palestine, but some of the Islamic countries that are allied with the West will escape being attacked.

Verse 42 continues: "He shall stretch out his hand against the countries, and the land of Egypt shall not escape" (Dan. 11:42, NKJV). As the Western powers continue their attack on the Islamic world, Egypt will join the Islamic alliance and, as a consequence, will be attacked.

"He shall have power over the treasures of gold and silver, and over all the precious things of Egypt; also the Libyans and Ethiopians shall follow at his heels" (Dan. 11:43, NKJV). In league with the papacy, the Western powers, including the United States, will subjugate the Islamic powers and will then appropriate the wealth of the Islamic world (oil).

"But news from the east and the north shall trouble him; therefore he shall go out with great fury to destroy and annihilate many" (Dan. 11:44, NKJV). The book of Revelation indicates that the "kings from the east" (Rev. 16:12; cf. 17:12–18) are Christ and His angels, who will come to destroy unfaithful earthly nations. The preaching of Christ's coming will alarm the king of the north, and he will turn his attention to destroying those who preach this message. Having conquered the Islamic world, the king of the north—the papacy in league with the United States and other Western powers—will at that point be in the position of being able to enforce worldwide "the image to the beast" (Rev. 13:14) and the mark of the beast (verse 16). The only serious resistance to the "image" and the "mark" consists of God's faithful people around the world. They reject the image and the mark of the beast and, with unprecedented spiritual power, announce the imminent coming of Christ.

And he shall plant the tents of his palace between the seas and the glorious holy mountain; yet he shall come to his end, and no one will help him. At that time Michael shall stand up, the great prince who stands watch over the sons of your people; and there shall be a time of trouble, such as never was since there was a nation, even to that time. And at that time your people shall be delivered, every one who is found written in the book (Dan. 11:45–12:1, NKJV).

The glorious holy mountain is Jerusalem. The suggestion seems to be that the king of the north—the papacy, the United States, and other Western powers—will establish a center of papal rule in Palestine. At this crucial point, "Michael [Christ] shall stand up" (Dan. 12:1) at the conclusion of the pre-Advent, investigative judgment (cf. Dan. 7:9–14). This is the end-time close of probation. Then the power of the nations represented as the king of the north will be broken: "He shall come to his end, and no one will help him."

CONCLUSION OF THE SECOND TRUMPET

The events described above comprise the fulfillment of the second trumpet. National apostasy results in national ruin—nations that have turned away from the truths of God's Word, espousing in its place unbiblical tradition, and then have sought to enforce the edicts of fallen religious organizations, will suffer decline and dissolution.

The "beast" of Revelation 17 is another symbol of the power depicted in Revelation 13:11–18. This "beast" power, which supports the harlot Babylon (Rev. 17:1–6), is likened to a "mountain" (Rev. 17:9–11). It is the secular power that supports the great satanic religious system of the end time, bolstering the claims of the papacy. "It exercises all the authority of the first beast in its presence, and makes the earth and its inhabitants worship the first beast, whose mortal wound was healed" (Rev. 13:12). The prophecy indicates that the United States of America, in league with the papacy and those churches that are in union with it, will provide state support for a church-state union similar to that which existed in the Middle Ages. This last-day church-state union will be the "image of the beast" (Rev. 13:14–17).

Revelation indicates that the United States and supporting nations will enforce the religious decrees of antitypical Babylon; they are the powers that will carry out the attack on professed believers referred to under the first trumpet. But the end-time application of the prophecy of the second trumpet indicates that the United States and supporting nations—"the great mountain, burning with fire"—will be destroyed.

> When the Protestant churches shall unite with the secular power to sustain a false religion, for opposing which their ancestors endured the fiercest persecution; when the state shall use its power to enforce the decrees and sustain the institutions of the church—then will Protestant America have formed an image to the papacy, *and there will be a national apostasy which will end only in national ruin.* . . .
>
> History will be repeated. False religion will be exalted. The first day of the week, a common working day, possessing no sanctity whatever, will be set up as was the image at Babylon. All nations and tongues and peoples will be commanded to worship this spurious Sabbath. This is Satan's plan to make of no account the day instituted by God, and given to the world as a memorial of creation. . . .
>
> The papacy has exercised her power to compel men to obey her, and she will continue to do so. We need the same

spirit that was manifested by God's servants in the conflict with paganism. . . .

A time is coming when the law of God is, in a special sense, to be made void in our land. The rulers of our nation will, by legislative enactments, enforce the Sunday law, and thus God's people be brought into great peril. When our nation, in its legislative councils, shall enact laws to bind the consciences of men in regard to their religious privileges, enforcing Sunday observance, and bringing oppressive power to bear against those who keep the seventh-day Sabbath, the law of God will, to all intents and purposes, be made void in our land; *and national apostasy will be followed by national ruin.*[7]

In Revelation, the second plague reveals the ultimate fulfillment of the second trumpet. John wrote, "The second angel poured his bowl into the sea, and it became like the blood of a dead man, and every living thing died that was in the sea" (Rev. 16:3). The second angel pores out the plague he bears as a restraint and as a retributive judgment upon those who, guided by Satan, align themselves with false religion.

---

1. After quoting this passage from Jeremiah, G. B. Caird comments: "If John is indeed alluding to this passage, then he is preparing the way for the most subtle of hints, not only for those later visions in which he treats Rome as the current embodiment of Babylon, but also for his theological exposition of the self-destroying power of evil. God uses the 'blazing mountain' of Babylon, the 'destroyer of the whole earth', to pollute the sea on which Babylon itself depends for the maintenance of its commercial empire (cf. xviii.9-19)." *The Revelation of St. John the Divine* (New York: Harper and Row, 1966), 114.

2. Donald Grey Barnhouse comments on the second trumpet: "We have previously noted that the earth is frequently a symbol of Palestine and that the sea by contrast represents the Gentile nations. This judgment, then, if taken symbolically, is a judgment that falls more especially upon the Gentile nations. . . . There is in view here a great power filled with eruptive forces which shall be cast into the midst of the nations." *Revelation, an Expository Commentary* (Grand Rapids, MI: Zondervan, 1971), 163. He offers a number of historical suggestions but fails to identify the fall of the Roman Empire.

3. See the evidence presented in the comment on Revelation 14:8 in *Seventh-day Adventist Bible Commentary* (Washington, DC: Review and Herald®, 1957), 7:830.

4. Edwin R. Thiele, *Outline Studies in Revelation* (Angwin, CA: Pacific Union College, 1980) 166.

5. After suggesting that the second trumpet may be referring to the eruption of Vesuvius, which desolated the Bay of Naples in AD 79, J. Massyngberde Ford adds: "However, the author may be referring not to a specific incident, but rather to an eschatological event." *Revelation,* 138.
Robert H. Mounce summarizes his discussion of the second trumpet: "It represents an eschatological judgment which goes beyond any explanation in terms of natural phenomena. It affects but one-third of the sea, its life and commerce. The purpose is to warn and lead to repentance." *The Book of Revelation,* 187.

6. Philip Schaff, *History of the Christian Church* (Grand Rapids, MI: Eerdmans, 1907), 5:214.

7. F. D. Nichol, ed., *Seventh-day Adventist Bible Commentary* (Washington, DC: Review and Herald®, 1957), 7:976, 977; italics added.

CHAPTER 5

THE THIRD TRUMPET

After the second trumpet, of course, comes the third.

The third angel blew his trumpet, and a great star fell from heaven, blazing like a torch, and it fell on a third of the rivers and on the fountains of water. The name of the star is Wormwood. A third of the waters became wormwood, and many men died of the water, because it was made bitter (Rev. 8:10, 11).

What is going on here?

In Scripture, stars sometimes symbolize Satan and his demons, who were cast out of heaven. Speaking of Lucifer, Isaiah writes:

How you are fallen from heaven, O Day Star [Lucifer], son of Dawn! How are you cut down to the ground, you who laid the nations low! You said in your heart, "I will ascend to heaven; above the stars of God I will set my throne on high; I will sit on the mount of assembly in the far north; I will ascend above the heights of the clouds, I will make myself like the Most High." But you are brought down to Sheol, to the depths of the Pit (Isa. 14:12–15).

Revelation 12 gives us somewhat more detail regarding Satan's expulsion from heaven. John saw a great red dragon whose "tail swept down a third of the stars of heaven, and cast them to the earth" (Rev. 12:4). A few verses later John writes,

> Now war arose in heaven, Michael and his angels fighting against the dragon; and the dragon and his angels fought, but they were defeated and there was no longer any place for them in heaven. And the great dragon was thrown down, that ancient serpent, who is called the Devil and Satan, the deceiver of the whole world—he was thrown down to the earth, and his angels were thrown down with him (Rev. 12:7–9).

From this passage we conclude that when Satan was cast out of heaven, a third of heaven's angels had allied themselves with him and were also cast out. Since heaven has myriads of angels, we can only assume that a huge number of angels were cast out and that now they are roaming around our world, bent on destroying humanity's fellowship with God.

John continues his story by letting us know that Jesus' death on the cross conclusively confirmed the casting out of Satan.

> I heard a loud voice in heaven, saying, "Now the salvation and the power and the kingdom of our God and the authority of his Christ have come, for the accuser of our brethren has been thrown down, who accuses them day and night before God. And they have conquered him *by the blood of the Lamb* and by the word of their testimony, for they loved not their lives even unto death. Rejoice then, O heaven and you that dwell therein! But woe to you, O earth and sea, for the devil

has come down to you in great wrath, because he knows that his time is short!" (Rev. 12:10–12; italics added).

When Jesus' disciples returned with joy from their evangelistic tour, they reported: " 'Lord, even the demons are subject to us in your name!' And he said to them, 'I saw Satan fall like lightning from heaven. Behold, I have given you authority to tread upon serpents and scorpions, and over all the power of the enemy; and nothing shall hurt you' " (Luke 10:17, 18). Through His disciples, Jesus manifests His power to subjugate the influence of fallen demons.

In Scripture, stars sometimes represent heathen deities, who at times His apostate people have worshiped. The prophet Amos recorded God's words: " 'You shall take up Sakkuth your king, and Kaiwan your star-god, your images, which you made for yourselves; therefore I will take you into exile beyond Damascus,' says the LORD, whose name is the God of hosts" (Amos 5:26, 27). In Stephen's great sermon, which is recorded in Acts 7, he spoke of the apostasy of ancient Israel in the wilderness: "God turned and gave them over to worship the host of heaven, as it is written in the book of the prophets: . . . 'And you took up the tent of Moloch, and the star of the god Rephan, the figures which you made to worship; and I will remove you beyond Babylon' " (Acts 7:42, 43). And Jude described unfaithful, immoral, rebellious people as "wandering stars for whom the nether gloom of darkness has been reserved for ever" (Jude 13). Hence, throughout Scripture, star symbolism may refer to Satan, his demons, false deities who have no existence, and the unfaithful people who have identified themselves with them.

However, stars sometimes have a positive application in Scripture. They may denote heaven's angels (Job 38:7) or God's faithful people who are subject to persecution by the devil, his demons, and those who serve them (Dan. 8:10). They also are used to represent the ministers of Christ's church on earth (Rev. 1:20), and Jesus Himself is called "the bright morning star" (Rev. 22:16; cf. 2:28; 2 Pet. 1:19). But since the star depicted in the third trumpet falls from heaven and then does an evil thing, embittering the rivers and fountains of water, we can assume that it represents Satan and not Christ or His faithful people.

The text says the great star that fell from heaven was "blazing like a torch" (Rev. 8:10). The Greek word translated "torch" is *lampas*, the word used in the Septuagint to refer to the lamps on the lamp stand[1] in the Holy Place of the sanctuary (Exod. 25:37; 37:23; Lev. 24:1–4). The light of the sanctuary lamps symbolized Christ, the Light of the world (John 8:12; 1:4, 9), whose people are to reflect His glory (Matt. 5:14; Acts 13:47).

But in Revelation 8:10, 11, the star that falls from heaven "blazing like a torch" embitters the "rivers" and "fountains of water" so that men die when they partake of the water. Hence, this star must not refer to Christ or His people. The light of the lamp spoken of in this passage is a counterfeit to the light of Christ reflected through His Word and His people.

WATER IMAGERY

What happens next?

"And it fell on a third of the rivers and on the fountains of water" (Rev. 8:10). In Scripture, rivers and fountains of water sometimes represent God's love and truth extended to humanity. Psalm 36:7–9 provides an example:

> How precious is thy steadfast love, O God! The children of
> men take refuge in the shadow of thy wings. They feast on

the abundance of thy house, and thou givest them drink from the river of thy delights. For with thee is the fountain of life; in thy light do we see light.

The psalmist also wrote, "There is a river whose streams make glad the city of God, the holy habitation of the Most High. God is in the midst of her, she shall not be moved; God will help her right early" (Ps. 46:4, 5), and "Thou visitest the earth and waterest it, thou greatly enrichest it; the river of God is full of water; thou providest their grain, for so thou hast prepared it" (Ps. 65:9; cf. 105:41; Isa. 66:12; Jer. 17:7, 8; Ezek. 47:1–12; Rev. 22:1, 2).

The spiritual fountain of life and truth emanates from God. "As a hart earnestly desires the fountains of water, so my soul earnestly longs for thee, O God" (Ps. 42:1, LXX). "Tremble, O earth, at the presence of the LORD, at the presence of the God of Jacob, who turns the rock into a pool of water, the flint into a spring of water" (Ps. 114:7, 8). "The mouth of the righteous is a fountain of life, but the mouth of the wicked conceals violence" (Prov. 10:11). "The fear of the LORD is a fountain of life, that one may avoid the snares of death" (Prov. 14:27; cf. Isa. 12:3).

The Lord grieves because His people have rejected Him, the Fountain of life. "My people have committed two evils: they have forsaken me, the fountain of living waters, and hewed out cisterns for themselves, broken cisterns, that can hold no water" (Jer. 2:13; cf. 17:13).

Rivers and fountains of water that don't convey life may designate sources of evil for individuals and nations. Because of the nations' rebellion against God, He is said to dry up and pollute their rivers and fountains of water, in the sense that He allows other nations to destroy them. "He turns rivers into a desert, springs of water into thirsty ground, a fruitful land into a salty waste, because of the wickedness of its inhabitants" (Ps. 107:33, 34; cf. Ps. 78:44; Isa. 8:7; 11:15; 19:5–8; 27:12, 13; Ezek. 29:3, 9; Zech. 10:11; Nah. 1:4; Jer. 51:36, 37).

In most of its uses in the New Testament, the word for "spring" or "fountain" (*pege*) refers to the love, truth, and salvation that God gives freely to the believer in Christ. For example, John 4:14: "Whoever drinks of the water that I shall give him will never thirst; the water that I shall give him will become in him a spring of water welling up to eternal life" (cf. Rev. 7:17; 21:6).

But the word may also refer to those who are not directed and controlled by God. Peter speaks of rebellious, deliberate sinners as "waterless springs and mists driven by a storm; for them the nether gloom of darkness has been reserved" (2 Pet. 2:17).

WORMWOOD

The third trumpet doesn't leave us wondering, though. It directly tells us that "the name of the star is Wormwood" (Rev. 8:11). The Greek word translated "Wormwood" is *apsinthos*, which is the name of a bitter herb now called *Artemisia absinthium*. The word *apsinthos* is not used in the Septuagint or anywhere else in the New Testament. The Hebrew equivalent used in the Old Testament is *laᵃnâ*. The *Interpreter's Dictionary of the Bible* comments:

> A plant with a bitter taste, probably referring to several species of the genus Artemisia, of which *Artemisia herba-alba* Asso is most common. The Hebrew word is often used with "Gall" (Deut. 29:18 KJV–H 29:17; Jer. 9:15 KJV; 23:15 KJV; Lam. 3:19; Amos 6:12 KJV), and is always used metaphorically of bitterness and sorrow. The LXX never translates

as "wormwood," but uses various words meaning "bitterness."

Youth is warned against the "loose woman," whose honeyed words lead to bitter experiences (Prov. 5:4). The prophets describe the judgment of God in terms of being fed with wormwood (Jer. 9:15; 23:15), condemn those who "turn justice to wormwood" (Amos 5:7; cf. 6:12), and compare the destruction of Jerusalem in 586 B.C. to the bitterness of wormwood and gall (Lam. 3:15, 19).

Rev. 8:10-11 describes the blazing star called "Wormwood" as falling from heaven and turning the waters bitter with wormwood until "many men died of the water" (wormwood is not poisonous). *Artemisia absinthium* . . . is the sage known to the Greeks and thus could be the wormwood of John of Patmos. Cf. Heb. 12:15, where the LXX of Deut. 29:18–G 29:17, "root of bitterness," is quoted.[2]

The fact mentioned in the above quote that "wormwood is not poisonous" is substantially irrelevant to the meaning of Revelation 8:11. "The waters became wormwood" so that "many men died of the water." This was the opposite of Israel's experience at Marah (Exod. 15:22–26). The symbolism in Revelation suggests that the water was so polluted as to be not drinkable; death was the inevitable result of drinking it. The Hebrew word is consistently used in contexts that speak of humankind's spiritual defection from the everlasting covenant relationship with God. When the truth of God is turned into wormwood and gall, the people suffer spiritual extinction.

Church history (historical application)

During the post-apostolic period of the church's history, Satan the great star and his followers polluted the spiritual and theological rivers and fountains of water. Especially in the period represented by the church of Pergamum (AD 313–538; Rev. 2:12–17), truth was mingled with error—and spiritual apostasy resulted. It was during this period that the papacy rose to ecclesiastical predominance. The church mingled Bible teaching with pagan philosophy and religion, leading to spiritual death for many professed Christians.

Four major ecclesiastical developments during this period poisoned the sources of divine truth and salvation: (1) the development of the monarchical episcopate; (2) the rise to primacy of the Roman episcopate; (3) the development of theological dogmas that intermingled Greek and oriental ideas with Christian motifs; and (4) the growth of a church-state union that became characteristic of the Middle Ages. Here is what the four developments portended:

1. The development of the monarchical episcopate made bishops virtual monarchs in the regions they served. They became ecclesiastical rulers rather than spiritual leaders, and their parishioners were obliged to conform to the ideas and practices the bishops stipulated.

2. In the period following the conversion of Constantine and his formulation of the Edict of Milan (AD 313), which recognized Christianity as a legal religion, the Christian church witnessed the Roman Church's gradual rise to ecclesiastical supremacy.[3] Later, Justinian decreed the recognition of the bishop of Rome as head of all the churches (AD 533), although that action did not take effect until AD 538, when the Gothic siege of Rome was broken. Hence, this date marks the commencement of the Middle Ages and the beginning of the period of papal ecclesiastical supremacy.

3. In the quarter century after AD 313, pagan and Greek concepts became intermingled with New Testament Christianity. It was this period that saw the doctrine of the immortality of the soul become more widely accepted[4]—along with sacerdotal concepts of the priesthood and sacramental religious practices, both of which denigrated the New Testament teaching of the heavenly priesthood of Christ and the apostolic teaching of righteousness and salvation by faith.

> While the good-will of the emperors aimed to advance the Christian religion, the indiscreet piety of the bishops obscured its true nature and oppressed its energies, by the multiplication of rites and ceremonies. . . . For the Christian bishops introduced, with but slight alteration, into the Christian worship, those rites and institutions by which, formerly, the Greeks and Romans and others had manifested their piety and reverence toward their imaginary deities; supposing that the people would more readily embrace Christianity, if they perceived the rites handed down to them from their fathers, still existing unchanged among the Christians, and saw, that Christ and the martyrs were worshipped in the same manner as formerly their gods were. There was, accordingly, little difference in these times between the public worship of the Christians and that of the Greeks and Romans. In both there were splendid robes, mitres, tiaras, wax-tapers, crosiers, processions, lustrations, images, golden and silver vases, and innumerable other things.
>
> No sooner had Constantine renounced the religion of his ancestors, than magnificent temples were everywhere erected, adorned with pictures and images, and both in external and internal form very similar to the fanes and temples of the gods.[5]

It was in this period as well that the professed Christian church's recognition of Sunday as a sacred day of worship became more widely accepted.[6]

4. In this period, emperors and prelates worked together to establish political, theological, and ecclesiastical unity—theological unity being fostered in the interests of political unity. The result was the gradual development of the church-state union that was characteristic of the Middle Ages.

> Since Constantine's policy was to unite the Christian Church to the secular state by the closest possible ties, it was natural that even before he formally professed Christianity himself, he should be concerned with the internal affairs of the Church. . . .
>
> A similar appeal from the contending parties led Constantine to summon the Council of Nicaea (325) to settle the Arian dispute about the Person of Christ. The emperor himself presided, though unbaptized, a circumstance which foreshadows the Byzantine theory of the emperors as supreme rulers of Church and State alike.[7]

> Justinian's religious policy was upheld by the imperial conviction that the unity of the empire unconditionally presupposed unity of faith; and with him it was a matter of course that this faith could be only the orthodox. Those of a different belief had to recognize that the process which had been begun by imperial legislation from Constantius down was now to be vigorously continued. . . .
>
> The like despotism was also shown in the emperor's ecclesiastical policy. He regulated everything, both in religion and in law.[8]

The work of Daniel's little horn power matches this pollution of God's truth at the beginning of the Middle Ages (Dan. 7:8, 19–25;

8:9–14). Jesus spoke of the great medieval apostasy that would begin with the erection of the "desolating sacrilege" (Matt. 24:15–22). And Paul predicted apostasy leading to the development of the "man of sin" (2 Thess. 2:1–11; cf. Acts 20:29). Because people chose not to believe in Christ, they were permitted to be deceived by Satan and his human agent, the "man of lawlessness" (2 Thess. 2:3, 11). The inevitable result was rejection by God (verse 12).

In its historical application, the third trumpet refers to Satan's strenuous and successful attempts to pollute the sources of truth Christ had so lovingly provided, with the consequence that multitudes were encouraged to espouse a hybrid religion consisting of New Testament motifs interwoven with pagan beliefs and practices.

> Little by little, at first in stealth and silence, and then more openly as it increased in strength and gained control of the minds of men, "the mystery of iniquity" carried forward its deceptive and blasphemous work. Almost imperceptibly the customs of heathenism found their way into the Christian church. The spirit of compromise and conformity was restrained for a time by the fierce persecutions which the church endured under paganism. But as persecution ceased, and Christianity entered the courts and palaces of kings, she laid aside the humble simplicity of Christ and His apostles for the pomp and pride of pagan priests and rulers; and in place of the requirements of God, she substituted human theories and traditions. The nominal conversion of Constantine, in the early part of the fourth century, caused great rejoicing; and the world, cloaked with a form of righteousness, walked into the church. Now the work of corruption rapidly progressed. Paganism, while appearing to be vanquished, became

the conqueror. Her spirit controlled the church. Her doctrines, ceremonies, and superstitions were incorporated into the faith and worship of the professed followers of Christ.

This compromise between paganism and Christianity resulted in the development of "the man of sin" foretold in prophecy as opposing and exalting himself above God. That gigantic system of false religion is a masterpiece of Satan's power—a monument of his efforts to seat himself upon the throne to rule the earth according to his will. . . .

To secure worldly gains and honors, the church was led to seek the favor and support of the great men of earth; and having thus rejected Christ, she was induced to yield allegiance to the representative of Satan—the bishop of Rome.[9]

Even so, in the period represented by Pergamum there were faithful believers who resisted the paganizing trend in the church. Jesus Himself spoke to them: "I know where you dwell, where Satan's throne is; you hold fast my name and you did not deny my faith even in the days of Antipas my witness, my faithful one, who was killed among you, where Satan dwells" (Rev. 2:13). We don't know who Antipas was. Perhaps he was an individual martyred for his faith either in Pergamum or Rome, or perhaps the name is symbolic of the many who suffered for their rejection of Roman Christianity.[10] The significant point is that there were those who upheld Christ's name and who, when confronted by widespread apostasy and persecution, refused to deny the true faith.

SATAN'S GAMBIT (END-TIME APPLICATION)

In its end-time application, the third trumpet predicts that after the close of probation, Satan will make an especially successful attack on God's truth. Satan is the "great star" that fell from heaven. "Blazing like a torch," he will use all his highly practiced means of confirming unbelievers in their apostasy and will attempt to turn true believers from their commitment to Christ.

Our Lord predicted this. He warned,

> If anyone says to you, "Lo, here is the Christ!" or "There he is!" do not believe it. For false Christs and false prophets will arise and show great signs and wonders, so as to lead astray, if possible, even the elect. Lo, I have told you beforehand. So, if they say to you, "Lo, he is in the wilderness," do not go out; if they say, "Lo, he is in the inner rooms," do not believe it. For as the lightning comes from the east and shines as far as the west, so will be the coming of the Son of man (Matt. 24:23–27; cf. Mark 13:21–23).

Christ's statement indicates that some being or beings will pose as Him. He warns us to reject such claims and says we shouldn't even investigate those making them. Why? Because His second coming will be like the lightning flashing from east to west, so bright that the whole world will see it. "Behold, he is coming with clouds, and every eye will see him, everyone who pierced him; and all tribes of the earth will wail on account of him" (Rev. 1:7).

Moreover, when Jesus comes the second time, He won't touch the earth. Paul informs us that "the dead in Christ will rise first; then we who are alive, and who are left, shall be caught up together with them in the clouds to meet the Lord in the air; and so we shall always be with the Lord" (1 Thess. 4:16, 17). And where is it that we will be with Him? Jesus answered that clearly. He said, "In my Father's house are many rooms; if it were not so, would I have told you that

I go to prepare a place for you? And when I go and prepare a place for you, *I will come again and will take you to myself, that where I am you may be also*" (John 14:2, 3; italics added). Jesus plans to take His believing people to heaven at His second coming. He won't appear someplace on earth only to disappear and then show up somewhere else. He will appear in the sky, His translated people will meet Him there, and He will take them to be with Him in heaven. There the redeemed will be "before the throne of God, and serve him day and night within his temple; and he who sits upon the throne will shelter them with his presence" (Rev. 7:15). God's throne is in His temple, which is in heaven (Rev. 11:19).

But back to Satan: by masquerading as the Christ, Satan will appear to have His authority. He'll use it to confirm the beliefs of those who have turned away from the clear teachings of Scripture, and also in strenuous attempts to deceive Christ's elect people. Why will he do this after probation has closed? First, because he probably doesn't know when probation closes; and second, because even if he deduces that it has closed, he wants to retain the allegiance of the many who have espoused his false teachings. He also wants to prove that God's people, who have been sealed (Rev. 7:1–3) can be induced to forsake their faith and accept his lying pretensions.

The apostle Paul underlined Jesus' prediction that Satan would impersonate Him. He wrote of "false apostles, deceitful workmen" who disguise themselves "as apostles of Christ." "And no wonder," he says, "for even Satan disguises himself as an angel of light. So it is not strange if his servants also disguise themselves as servants of righteousness. Their end will correspond to their deeds" (2 Cor. 11:13–15). Satan and his servants pose as sources of light and truth, but they are transmitters of death and destruction.

Fearful sights of a supernatural character will soon be revealed in the heavens, in token of the power of miracle-working demons. The spirits of devils will go forth to the kings of the earth and to the whole world, to fasten them in deception, and urge them to unite with Satan in his last struggle against the government of heaven. By these agencies, rulers and subjects will be alike deceived. Persons will arise pretending to be Christ Himself, and claiming the title and worship which belong to the world's Redeemer. They will perform wonderful miracles of healing and will profess to have revelations from heaven contradicting the testimony of the Scriptures.

As the crowning act in the great drama of deception, Satan himself will personate Christ. The church has long professed to look to the Saviour's advent as the consummation of her hopes. Now the great deceiver will make it appear that Christ has come. In different parts of the earth, Satan will manifest himself among men as a majestic being of dazzling brightness, resembling the description of the Son of God given by John in the Revelation. Revelation 1:13–15. The glory that surrounds him is unsurpassed by anything that mortal eyes have yet beheld. The shout of triumph rings out upon the air: "Christ has come! Christ has come!" The people prostrate themselves in adoration before him, while he lifts up his hands and pronounces a blessing upon them, as Christ blessed His disciples when He was upon the earth. His voice is soft and subdued, yet full of melody. In gentle, compassionate tones he presents some of the same gracious, heavenly truths which the Saviour uttered; he heals the diseases of the people, and then, in his assumed character of Christ, he claims to have changed the Sabbath to Sunday, and commands all to hallow the day which he has blessed. He declares that those who persist in keeping holy the seventh day are blaspheming his name by refusing to listen to his angels sent to them with light and truth. This is the strong, almost overmastering delusion. Like the Samaritans who were deceived by Simon Magus, the multitudes, from the least to the greatest, give heed to these sorceries, saying: This is "the great power of God." Acts 8:10.

But the people of God will not be misled. The teachings of this false christ are not in accordance with the Scriptures. His blessing is pronounced upon the worshipers of the beast and his image, the very class upon whom the Bible declares that God's unmingled wrath shall be poured out. . . .

Only those who have been diligent students of the Scriptures and who have received the love of the truth will be shielded from the powerful delusion that takes the world captive.[11]

In order to counteract the deceptive designs of Satan and his many followers, the Lord pours out the third plague:

The third angel poured his bowl into the rivers and fountains of water, and they become blood. And I heard the angel of water say, "Just art thou in these thy judgments, thou who art and wast, O Holy One. For men have shed the blood of saints and prophets, and thou hast given them blood to drink. It is their due!" And I heard the altar cry, "Yea, Lord God the Almighty, true and just are thy judgments!" (Rev. 16:4–7).

1. "Candlestick" in the King James Version. However, candles weren't used in the Middle East until four hundred years after Christ's time. And note that Zechariah 4:12, for instance, speaks of olive trees providing a continuous supply of oil for the sanctuary lamps.

2. *The Interpreter's Dictionary of the Bible* (New York: Abingdon Press, 1962), 4:878, 879.

3. LeRoy Edwin Froom, *The Prophetic Faith of Our Fathers* (Washington, DC: Review and Herald®, 1950), 1:492–517, 931–936.

4. LeRoy Edwin Froom, *The Conditionalist Faith of Our Fathers* (Washington, DC: Review and Herald®, 1966), 1:757–1079.

5. J. L. Mosheim, *Institutes of Ecclesiastical History, Ancient and Modern* (London: Longmans, 1845), 1:366, 367.

6. Kenneth A. Strand, ed., *The Sabbath in Scripture and History* (Washington, DC: Review and Herald®, 1982), 132–145, 190–214, 323–332.

7. F. L. Cross, ed., *The Oxford Dictionary of the Christian Church* (London: Oxford University Press, 1958), 334.

8. S. M. Jackson, ed., *The New Schaff-Herzog Encyclopedia of Religious Knowledge* (Grand Rapids, MI: Baker, 1963), 6:285, 286.

9. White, *The Great Controversy,* 49, 50.

10. *Antipas* is a compound of the Greek words *anti,* meaning "instead of," "in place of," and *pas,* an abbreviation of *pater,* meaning "father." Hence, some interpreters regard Antipas as symbolic of those who were replacing the Roman "holy father" by the Lord Jesus Christ as head of the church. For this they were persecuted.

11. White, *The Great Controversy,* 624, 625.

Chapter 6

The Fourth Trumpet

We now come to the fourth trumpet and the truths and warnings it gives.

> The fourth angel blew his trumpet, and a third of the sun was struck, and a third of the moon, and a third of the stars, so that a third of their light was darkened; a third of the day was kept from shining, and likewise a third of the night (Rev. 8:12).

In the Old Testament, the sun sometimes symbolizes God Himself and the spiritual light that emanates from Him. "The Lord God is a sun and shield; he bestows favor and honor. No good thing does the Lord withhold from those who walk uprightly. O Lord of hosts, blessed is the man who trusts in thee!" (Ps. 84:11, 12). "Blessed be the name of the Lord from this time forth and for evermore! From the rising of the sun to its setting the name of the Lord is to be praised! The Lord is high above all nations, and his glory above the heavens!" (Ps. 113:2–4). Psalm 148:1–6 associates heaven's angels with the sun, moon, and stars that praise the Lord. And through

Malachi, the Lord promised, "For you who fear my name the sun of righteousness shall rise, with healing in its wings" (Mal. 4:2).

The Old Testament also relates the sun's shining to the light that emanates from the leaders of the people: the patriarchs (Gen. 37:9); kings (Pss. 72:5, 6; 89:35–37; Isa. 24:21–23); and prophets (Mic. 3:5, 6). In other contexts, the sun symbolizes God's faithful people themselves. "So perish all thine enemies, O LORD! But thy friends be like the sun as he rises in his might" (Judg. 5:31). When they become unfaithful, their light is obliterated.

In the New Testament, the sun often symbolizes Christ and His righteousness. On the Mount of Transfiguration, "his face shone like the sun, and his garments became white as light" (Matt. 17:2). Christ's light shone upon Saul (Paul) when he was on the way to Damascus to persecute the Christians. In his defense before King Agrippa, Paul reported, "I journeyed to Damascus with the authority and commission of the chief priests. At midday, O king, I saw on the way a light from heaven, brighter than the sun, shining round me and those who journeyed with me" (Acts 26:12, 13). Then Jesus identified Himself to Paul, saying, "I am Jesus whom you are persecuting" (verse 15).

When John received a vision of Christ on the island of Patmos, "his [Jesus'] face was like the sun shining in full strength" (Rev. 1:16). Later John saw a "mighty angel" representing Christ "wrapped in a cloud, with a rainbow over his head, and his face was like the sun, and his legs like pillars of fire" (Rev. 10:1). In the heavenly city there is "no need of the sun or moon to shine upon it, for the glory of God is its light, and its lamp is the Lamb. By its light shall the nations walk" (Rev. 21:23, 24; cf. 22:5). And Christ's church is depicted in Revelation as a pure woman, "clothed with the sun, with the moon under her feet" (Rev. 12:1). We conclude, therefore, that the sun denotes the righteousness of Christ that clothes His people. The New Testament also likens God's faithful people to the sun because they are reflectors of Christ's character. That's why "the righteous will shine like the sun in the kingdom of their Father" (Matt. 13:43; cf. 1 Cor. 15:41; Rev. 12:1).

At other times, the sun represents false deities that are worshiped by those who turn away from the Lord. Ancient Israelites were warned:

> Beware lest you lift up your eyes to heaven, and when you see the sun and the moon and the stars, all the host of heaven, you be drawn away and worship them and serve them, things which the Lord your God has allotted to all the peoples under the whole heaven (Deut. 4:19; cf. 17:2–5; 2 Kings 23:5, 11; Jer. 8:1, 2; Ezek. 8:16).

THE DARKENING

The darkening of the sun, moon, and stars (alluded to in the fourth trumpet) is an Old Testament symbol of God's judgments upon people and nations in view of their wickedness. The darkening of the sun, part of the local "day of the Lord," was a symbol of that which will occur on the end-time "Day of the Lord." This darkening represents God's final withdrawal of His favor. Any divine enlightenment from God, heavenly angels, national or spiritual leaders, or from God's people generally will be finally withdrawn, and satanic darkness and apostasy will reign supreme. Such a state is followed immediately by death and destruction.

Isaiah associated the darkening of the sun, moon, and stars with the local day of the Lord, a type of the end-time Day of the Lord.

Behold, the day of the LORD comes, cruel, with wrath and fierce anger, to make the earth a desolation and to destroy its sinners from it. For the stars of the heavens and their constellations will not give their light; the sun will be dark at its rising and the moon will not shed its light. I will punish the world for its evil, and the wicked for their iniquity (Isa. 13:9–11).

Similarly, Joel describes the local day of the Lord that presages the ultimate Day of the Lord:

The earth quakes before them, the heavens tremble. The sun and the moon are darkened, and the stars withdraw their shining. The LORD utters his voice before his army, for his host is exceedingly great; he that executes his word is powerful. For the day of the LORD is great and very terrible; who can endure it? (Joel 2:10, 11; cf. 3:15; Amos 8:9, 10; Ezek. 32:7, 8; Mic. 3:5, 6).

Joel tells us that some time after the end-time outpouring of the Holy Spirit upon God's people, "the sun shall be turned to darkness, and the moon to blood, before the great and terrible day of the LORD comes" (Joel 2:31). Jesus underlined Joel's prediction as He foresaw an ultimate, quintessential time of trouble for the world (Matt. 24:21), followed by the darkening of the sun, moon, and stars before His second coming.

"Immediately after the tribulation of those days the sun will be darkened, and the moon will not give its light, and the stars will fall from heaven, and the powers of the heavens will be shaken; then will appear the sign of the Son of man in heaven, and then all tribes of the earth will mourn, and they will see the Son of man coming on the clouds of heaven with power and great glory" (Matt. 24:29, 30; cf. Mark 13:24; Luke 21:25; Acts 2:20; Rev. 6:12–17).

The point is that the darkening of the sun, moon, and stars at various stages of history and at the end of history denotes the withdrawal of God's favor in view of the fact that His truth has been denigrated, His people scorned, and His love repudiated.

APOSTASY AND PERSECUTION (HISTORICAL APPLICATION)

The fourth trumpet seems clearly to refer to the tragic results of the third. After the rise of the papacy during the period represented by Pergamum in the prophecy of the seven churches (AD 313–538; Rev. 2:12–17), spiritual and theological darkness resulted in the Middle Ages, the period represented in the churches by Thyatira (Rev. 2:18–29).[1] The church-state union of the medieval period obviated divine enlightenment. Christ and His righteousness, as revealed in Scripture and reflected through His faithful people, were denigrated. Consequently, western Europe experienced centuries of spiritual and theological darkness. The "sun of righteousness" (Mal. 4:2) ceased to shine for part of the world: "a third of the day was kept from shining, and likewise a third of the night" (Rev. 8:12).

"The woman Jezebel," spoken of in the message to Thyatira, is a fitting symbol of the medieval church. Jesus counseled that church: "I have this against you, that you tolerate the woman Jezebel, who calls herself a prophetess and is teaching and beguiling my servants to practice immorality and to eat food sacrificed to idols" (Rev. 2:20). Spiritual immorality, involving the worship of idols and the substitution of earthly priestly mediation for the heavenly mediation of Jesus Christ, cast a pall of spiritual darkness over western Europe.

Jesus continued:

> "I gave her time to repent, but she refuses to repent of her immorality. Behold, I will throw her on a sickbed, and those who commit adultery with her I will throw into great tribulation, unless they repent of her doings; and I will strike her children dead. And all the churches shall know that I am he who searches mind and heart, and I will give to each of you as your works deserve" (Rev. 2:21–23).

The mention of "churches" (verse 23) establishes that Jezebel is a symbol of apostasy within the established church—apostasy that infected numerous Christian churches.

But the apostasy wasn't universal. Jesus encouraged those who resisted the demands of the apostate established church. "But to the rest of you in Thyatira," He said, "who do not hold this teaching, who have not learned what some call the deep things of Satan, to you I say, I do not lay upon you any other burden; only hold fast what you have, until I come" (Rev. 2:24, 25).

The faithful did precisely that. The Waldenses and other evangelical groups; John Wycliffe (ca. 1329–1384) and the Lollards; then John Hus (ca. 1369–1415) and Jerome of Prague (ca. 1365–1416)—who were burnt at the stake by the Council of Constance—stood firmly for biblical Christianity and opposed the unbiblical traditions of the Roman Catholic Church. They were faithful forerunners of the sixteenth-century Reformation, which cast a ray of divine light into the deep darkness of the Middle Ages.

"The woman Jezebel" (Rev. 2:20) is an appropriate parallel symbol to the little horn power of Daniel 7 and 8. The dark work of the established medieval church is accurately spelled out in Daniel 7:25: "He shall speak words against the Most High, and shall wear out the saints of the Most High, and shall think to change the times and the law; and they shall be given into his hand for a time, two times, and half a time." The exaggerated claims of the medieval popes can only be described as "words against the Most High." The widespread slaughter of those who rejected the claims of the papacy wore "out the saints of the Most High." And the papal tampering with the Ten Commandments and promotion of the change of the Sabbath from the seventh day of the week to the first day of the week fulfilled the prediction that the little horn power would "think to change the times and the law."

The "time, two times, and half a time" referred to in Daniel 7:25 is identified in Scripture as a period of 1,260 years (Dan. 12:7; Rev. 11:2, 3; 12:6, 14).[2] From the application in AD 538 of the decree Justinian made in 533 that recognized the bishop of Rome as head of all the churches, until 1798, when Napoleon's general took the pope prisoner, was a period of 1,260 years. For the greater part of that period of papal ecclesiastical supremacy, spiritual and theological darkness reigned in western Europe. The fourth trumpet was strikingly fulfilled. "A third of the sun was struck, and a third of the moon, and a third of the stars, so that a third of their light was darkened; a third of the day was kept from shining, and likewise a third of the night" (Rev. 8:12).

The accession of the Roman Church to power marked the beginning of the Dark Ages. As her power increased, the darkness deepened. Faith was transferred from Christ, the true foundation, to the pope of Rome. Instead of trusting in the Son of God for forgiveness of sins and for eternal salvation, the people looked to the pope, and to the priests and prelates to whom he delegated authority. They were taught that the pope was their earthly mediator and that none could approach God except through him; and, further, that he stood in the place of God to them and was therefore to be implicitly obeyed. A deviation from his requirements was sufficient cause for the severest punishment to be visited upon the bodies and souls of the offenders. Thus the minds of the people were turned away from God to fallible, erring, and cruel men, nay, more, to the prince of darkness himself, who exercised his power through them. Sin was disguised in a garb of sanctity. When the Scriptures are suppressed, and man comes to regard himself as supreme, we need look only for fraud, deception, and debasing iniquity. With the elevation of human laws and traditions was manifest the corruption that ever results from setting aside the law of God.

Those were days of peril for the church of Christ. The faithful standard-bearers were few indeed. Though the truth was not left without witnesses, yet at times it seemed that error and superstition would wholly prevail, and true religion would be banished from the earth. The gospel was lost sight of, but the forms of religion were multiplied, and the people were burdened with rigorous exactions.

They were taught not only to look to the pope as their mediator, but to trust to works of their own to atone for sin. Long pilgrimages, acts of penance, the worship of relics, the erection of churches, shrines, and altars, the payment of large sums to the church—these and many similar acts were enjoined to appease the wrath of God or to secure His favor; as if God were like men, to be angered at trifles, or pacified by gifts or acts of penance![3]

DELUSIONS (END-TIME APPLICATION)

History will be repeated. Satan's impersonation of Christ (under the third trumpet; Rev. 8:10, 11) after the close of probation will result in the widespread union of apostate people under his banner. The doctrines and practices that for centuries Satan has tried to inculcate will be accepted by multitudes, and the greatest spiritual darkness of human history will result. Because of their rejection of Satan's doctrines, God's faithful people will be judged guilty of a capital offense.

Satan's impersonation of Christ

is the strong, almost overmastering delusion. Like Samaritans who were deceived by Simon Magus, the multitudes, from the least to the greatest, give heed to these sorceries, saying: This is "the great power of God." Acts 8:10. . . .

Only those who have been diligent students of the Scriptures and who have received the love of the truth will be shielded from the powerful delusion that takes the world captive. By the Bible testimony these will detect the deceiver in his disguise. To all the testing time will come. By the sifting of temptation the genuine Christian will be revealed. Are the people of God so firmly established upon His word that they would not yield to the evidence of their senses? Would they, in such a crisis, cling to the Bible and the Bible only? Satan will, if possible, prevent them from obtaining a preparation to stand in that day. He will so arrange affairs as to hedge up their way, entangle them with earthly treasures, cause them to carry a heavy, wearisome burden, that their hearts may be overcharged with the cares of this life and the day of trial may come upon them as a thief.

As the decree issued by the various rulers of Christendom against the commandment keepers shall withdraw the protection of government and abandon them to those who desire their destruction, the people of God will flee from the cities and villages and associate together in companies, dwelling in the most desolate and solitary places. Many will find refuge in the strongholds of the mountains. Like the Christians of the Piedmont valleys, they will make the high places of the earth their sanctuaries and will thank God for "the munitions of rocks." Isaiah 33:16. But many of all nations and of all classes, high and low, rich and poor, black and white, will be cast into the most unjust and cruel bondage. The beloved of God pass weary days, bound in chains, shut in by prison bars, sentenced to be slain, some apparently left to die of starvation in dark and loathsome dungeons. No human ear is open to hear their moans; no human hand is ready to lend them help.

Will the Lord forget His people in this trying hour? Did He forget faithful Noah when judgments were visited upon the antediluvian world?[4]

As a means of counteracting and restraining the multitudes who will commit themselves to the almost universal satanic darkness, the Lord will pour out the fourth plague. Speaking in the past tense of events that will occur in the future, John wrote:

The fourth angel poured his bowl on the sun, and it was allowed to scorch men with fire; men were scorched by the fierce heat, and they cursed the name of God who had power over these plagues, and they did not repent and give him glory (Rev. 16:8, 9).

The fourth trumpet involves the light of the sun being darkened, the light of God's truth being replaced by error. The fourth plague will involve the literal light of the sun scorching those who have dared to obliterate God's truth.

---

1. Jacques B. Doukhan comments on the third and fourth trumpets: "With the third shofar, truth is corrupted, and with the fourth, it is blotted out. The third and fourth shofar depict the Dark Ages, the period of the church's greatest usurpation of divine attributes (sixth to tenth centuries). Rome replaces the 'city of God.' Tradition and power sweep aside spirituality. Truth becomes a vestige, and the people die of spiritual hunger and thirst, as they did in the third seal (Rev. 6:6). Because of its thirst for power, the church loses its sense of mission and of truth. Having sought to hoist itself up to God's level, it now finds itself, not unlike the ancient city of Babel, condemned to confusion." *Secrets of Revelation: The Apocalypse Through Hebrew Eyes* (Hagerstown, MD: Review and Herald®, 2002), 84.
2. Applying the year-day principle. For a detailed interpretation of Daniel chapter 7, see Maxwell, *God Cares,* 1:115–149.
3. White, *The Great Controversy,* 55, 56.
4. White, *The Great Controversy,* 624–626.

Chapter 7
The Fifth Trumpet

We now come to the fifth trumpet:

> Then I looked, and I heard an eagle crying with a loud voice, as it flew in midheaven, "Woe, woe, woe to those who dwell on the earth, at the blasts of the other trumpets which the three angels are about to blow!"

> And the fifth angel blew his trumpet, and I saw a star fallen from heaven to earth, and he was given the key of the shaft of the bottomless pit; he opened the shaft of the bottomless pit, and from the shaft rose smoke like the smoke of a great furnace, and the sun and the air were darkened with the smoke from the shaft. Then from the smoke came locusts on the earth, and they were given power like the power of scorpions of the earth; they were told not to harm the grass of the earth or any green growth or any tree, but only those of mankind who have not the seal of God upon their foreheads; they were allowed to torture them for five months, but not to kill them, and their torture was like the torture of a

scorpion, when it stings a man. And in those days men will seek death and will not find it; they will long to die, and death will fly from them. In appearance the locusts were like horses arrayed for battle; on their heads were what looked like crowns of gold; their faces were like human faces, their hair like women's hair, and their teeth like lions' teeth; they had scales like iron breastplates, and the noise of their wings was like the noise of many chariots with horses rushing into battle. They have tails like scorpions, and stings, and their power of hurting men for five months lies in their tails. They have as king over them the angel of the bottomless pit; his name in Hebrew is Abad'don, and in Greek he is called Apol'lyon. The first woe has passed; behold, two woes are still to come (Rev. 8:13–9:12).

THE EAGLE

Chapter 8 concludes with the announcement that the last three trumpets will bring woe—in other words, great suffering—to the inhabitants of the earth (Rev. 8:13). The "eagle crying with a loud voice" is a symbol of judgments to come. The Lord warned ancient Israel that, if they should be unfaithful, He would "bring a nation against you from afar, from the end of the earth, as swift as the eagle flies, a nation whose language you do not understand" (Deut. 28:49; cf. Ezek. 32:4; 39:17). Hosea repeated the warning: "Set the trumpet to your lips, for a vulture ["eagle," NKJV] is over the house of the LORD, because they have broken my covenant, and transgressed my law" (Hosea 8:1).

Jesus repeated the symbolism, using an eagle to denote the destruction to occur at His second advent. "As the lightning comes from the east and shines as far as the west, so will be the coming of the Son of man. Wherever the body is, there the eagles will be gathered together" (Matt. 24:27, 28; cf. Luke 17:37).

John employed similar symbolism in Revelation 19:17, 18:

> I saw an angel standing in the sun, and with a loud voice he called to all the birds that fly in midheaven, "Come, gather for the great supper of God, to eat the flesh of kings, the flesh of captains, the flesh of mighty men, the flesh of horses and their riders, and the flesh of all men, both free and slave, both small and great."

The second coming of Jesus will be a time of great destruction for those who have rejected His loving sacrifice and have despised His truth.

As an introduction to the last three trumpets, the eagle's announcement that woe would come to those who dwell on the earth indicates that demonic forces were about to be released that would bring unprecedented torment and destruction to those who hadn't sought shelter in the arms of our heavenly Shepherd.

FALLEN STAR

"And the fifth angel blew his trumpet, and I saw a star fallen from heaven to earth" (Rev. 9:1). As I indicated in my discussion of Revelation 8:10, Scripture uses stars to represent (1) Satan and his angels (Isa. 14:12, 13; Rev. 12:4, 9); (2) heathen deities, whom God's apostate people sometimes worshiped (Amos 5:26; Acts 7:43); (3) lost souls (Jude 13); (4) Christ, the Bright Morning Star (Rev. 2:28; 22:16; 2 Pet. 1:19); (5) heavenly angels (Job 38:7); (6) God's people on earth (Dan. 8:10); and (7) the ministry of the church (Rev. 1:16, 20).

There can be no serious doubt that the fallen star of Revelation 9:1 represents Satan. The Greek literally says: "And I saw a star having fallen [*peptokota*] from heaven to the earth." The use of the perfect participle indicates that the falling took place in the past but we're still living with the results of that fall. The work of this fallen angel is evil. He releases smoke from the bottomless pit that causes darkness, from which come locusts that have the torturing power of scorpions (Rev. 9:2, 3).

Satan is called by name in Revelation 9:11: "They have as king over them the angel of the bottomless pit; his name in Hebrew is Abad'don, and in Greek he is called Apol'lyon." These names are certainly appropriate for Satan. The Hebrew word *abaddon* means "destruction, ruin."[1] In the Hebrew Old Testament, *abaddon* refers to the destruction associated with death and the grave. Job declared, "Sheol is naked before God, and Abaddon has no covering" (Job 26:6). Adultery "would be a fire which consumes unto Abaddon, and it would burn to the root all my increase" (Job 31:12; compare Ps. 88:10–12; Prov. 15:11; 27:20). Satan is the personification of destruction.

The Greek word *Apollyon* means "the Destroyer,"[2] and the verbal form of this word is *apollumi,* which means "to destroy." Satan is the ultimate destroyer. Scripture says, "The LORD said to Satan, 'Have you considered my servant Job, that there is none like him on the earth, a blameless and upright man, who fears God and turns away from evil? He still holds fast his integrity, although you moved me against him, to destroy him without cause' " (Job 2:3). In the story of Job, Satan was the destroyer. God allowed Satan to attack Job; He sometimes allows Satan and fallen earthly powers to work their will (Isa. 14:12–20; Ezek. 28:12–19; 37:11).

Satan, depicted in Revelation as a great red dragon, sought to destroy Jesus as soon as He was born (Rev. 12:4, 9; cf. Matt. 2:13). Satan was the would-be destroyer of the possessed boy whom Jesus healed (Mark 9:22). He is "the thief" who "comes only to steal and kill and destroy" (John 10:10). He causes the ruin of those who accept his deceptions (2 Thess. 2:9, 10). He is our "adversary the devil" who "prowls around like a roaring lion, seeking some one to devour" (1 Pet. 5:8). He is the one about whom Revelation 12:12 warns us: "Woe to you, O earth and sea, for the devil has come down to you in great wrath, because he knows that his time is short!"

G. B. Caird comments pertinently concerning this fallen star:

> At the blowing of the fifth trumpet John sees an angel whom he describes as a fallen star. There is all the difference in the world between this fallen angel, to whom was given the key to the shaft of the abyss, and the angel of xx.1, whom John sees descending from heaven with the key of the abyss in his hand. The difference is not just that the one releases the destroyers and the other locks them up. The one is an evil agent acting by divine permission—he was given (*edothē*) the key . . . , the other a good agent voluntarily carrying out the beneficent purpose of God. It is not God's gracious purpose that men or angels should disobey him, but he allows them to do so, knowing that he can use even their disobedience to further his own good designs. It is not God's gracious purpose that the denizens of the abyss be let loose to ravage the earth, but he allows evil to be evil's own destruction.[3]

THE PIT

"And he was given the key of the shaft of the bottomless pit" (Rev. 9:1).

The Greek word translated "shaft" is *phrear*. It means "a well," "a pit," or "a shaft."[4] This word is used in the Septuagint to refer to "slime-pits" (Gen. 14:10), a "well" (Gen. 16:14), the "pit of destruction"

139

(Ps. 55 [54]:23; cf. Ps. 69 [68]:15; Jer. 48 [41]:7). In most instances of its use in the Septuagint, *phrear* refers to literal wells of water. In Psalms, the word is used to symbolize the pit of destruction into which the wicked are cast. In Revelation 9:1, 2, the word is used to depict a well or shaft leading to the bottomless pit.

What is the bottomless pit? The Greek word is *abussos*. The word means "abyss, depth, underworld," "the abode of the dead," "the dungeon where the devil is kept Rv 20:3."[5] In the Septuagint, *abussos* consistently refers to large accumulations of water—the sea, rivers, wells, or springs. This is the word used in Genesis 1:2 (LXX) to describe the state of the earth on the first day of Creation week: "The earth was unsightly and unfurnished, and darkness was over the deep [*abussos*], and the Spirit of God moved over the water." (See also LXX, Deut. 8:7; 33:13; Pss. 33 [32]:7; 78 [77]:15; 106 [105]:9; Jon. 2:6, 7.)

Occasionally, the waters of the deep symbolize destroying nations. In prophesying the destruction of ancient Tyre, Ezekiel said:

> Thus saith the LORD God; when I shall make the city desolate, as the cities that shall not be inhabited, when I have brought the deep [*abusson*] up upon thee, and great waters shall cover thee; and I shall bring thee down to them that go down to the pit; to the people of old time, and shall cause thee to dwell in the depths of the earth, as in everlasting desolation, with them that go down to the pit, that thou mayest not be inhabited, nor stand upon the land of life; I will make thee a destruction, and thou shalt be no more for ever, saith the LORD God (Ezek. 26:19–21, LXX).

In the New Testament, *abussos* denotes the realm of Satan and his demons. When Jesus was about to cast the evil spirits out of the possessed man in the country of the Gerasenes, "they begged him not to command them to depart into the abyss [*abusson*]" (Luke 8:31). In Revelation 11:7, the "beast that ascends from the bottomless pit [*abussou*]" is Satan, who uses an earthly power to attack the people of God and His truth. In Revelation 17:8, the beast that "is to ascend from the bottomless pit and go to perdition" is an apostate earthly power used by Satan in his end-time destructive work. At the second coming of Jesus, Satan himself will be cast into "the bottomless pit [*abusson*] . . . so that he should deceive the nations no more till the thousand years were finished" (Rev. 20:3, NKJV).

We conclude that the "star fallen from heaven" (Rev. 9:1), who is given "the key of the shaft of the bottomless pit," and who releases darkening smoke and locusts like scorpions upon the earth (Rev. 9:2, 3) is none other than Satan, who, from his realm of darkness, ascends with his demons to pervert God's truth and to torture those who are not sheltered by divine grace.

Throughout history Satan has worked through a series of earthly powers (represented by the waters of the abyss) in an effort to destroy the people of God and to establish his counterfeit religious system. Sometimes he has masterminded thoroughly pagan systems of religion and used great nations to foster them. On other occasions he has perverted God's truth by bringing to the fore a counterfeit in which there was a subtle intermingling of Bible truth and pagan error. The fifth trumpet (Rev. 9:1–12) depicts Satan's use of a historical earthly power to deceive and destroy professed Christians.

SMOKE AND FURNACE

"He opened the shaft of the bottomless pit, and from the shaft rose smoke like the smoke of a great furnace, and the sun and the air were darkened with the smoke from the shaft" (Rev. 9:2). The Greek word for "smoke" is *kapnos*. In the Septuagint, it represents iniquity, spiritual confusion, and destruction of the unfaithful. The wise man wrote, "As a sour grape is hurtful to the teeth, and smoke to the eyes, so iniquity hurts those who practice it" (Prov. 10:26, LXX; cf. Isa. 9:18). The Lord spoke through Joel of the destruction that will occur at the end of time: "I will shew wonders in heaven, and upon the earth, blood, and fire, and vapour of smoke. The sun shall be turned into darkness, and the moon into blood, before the great and glorious day of the LORD come" (Joel 2:30, 31, LXX; cf. Isa. 51:6). Isaiah uses smoke from the north as a symbol of the Babylonian invasion that would destroy Philistia. "Howl, ye gates of cities; let the cities be troubled and cry, even all the Philistines: for smoke is coming from the north, and there is no possibility of living" (Isa. 14:31, LXX). And Job 41:20 speaks of smoke coming from the nostrils of Leviathan.

The smoke that ascends from the shaft of the bottomless pit (Rev. 9:2) represents the deceptive and destructive designs of Satan. By his falsehoods Satan attempts to hide the truth (the sun and the air) from humankind.

LOCUSTS

"Then from the smoke came locusts on the earth" (Rev. 9:3). The Greek word translated "locusts" is *akris*. In the Septuagint, God sometimes allows a literal plague of locusts to fall upon apostate or pagan people. The eighth plague to fall upon Egypt was a plague of locusts (Exod. 10:4, 12–14, 19, LXX). God warned that His own people, Israel, would also suffer a plague of locusts if they turned away from Him (Deut. 28:38, LXX; cf. 2 Chron. 6:28; 7:13, 14). And, indeed, it happened; there were times when locust plagues devastated the land. "He gave their fruit to the canker worm, and their labours to the locust" (Ps. 78 [77]:46, LXX; cf. 104 [105]:34; Joel 1:4; 2:25).

Locusts are used figuratively sometimes, to symbolize destroying nations that God allowed to attack apostate or pagan nations. Israel's enemies and those of Egypt, Nineveh, and Babylon are referred to as locusts. The Midianites and Amalekites, who afflicted ancient Israel, were likened to locusts (Judg. 6:5, 6; 7:12, LXX). Nahum said Nineveh would be destroyed by an army that he compared to locusts (Nah. 3:15–17, LXX). God warned that the nations that destroyed His professed people would suffer the attacks of "spoilers" that He likened to locusts (Isa. 33:4, LXX). Jeremiah predicted that Nebuchadnezzar, the king of the north, would attack Egypt. "They shall cut down her forest, saith the LORD, for their number cannot at all be conjectured, for it exceeds the locust in multitude, and they are innumerable" (Jer. 26 [46]:23, LXX). Similarly, God said that the Medes, like a multitude of locusts, would destroy Babylon (Jer. 28 [51]:14, LXX).

The nations that the Lord allowed to destroy His apostate people were themselves subject to the judgments of God. He said,

> "Woe to you, destroyer, who yourself have not been destroyed; you treacherous one, with whom none has dealt treacherously! When you have ceased to destroy, you will be destroyed; and when you have made an end of dealing treacherously, you will be dealt with treacherously" (Isa. 33:1).

God punished unfaithful Israel by withdrawing His protection and allowing Satan to bring calamity upon them, but Israel's enemies would eventually suffer the same fate.

SCORPIONS

"And they were given power like the power of scorpions of the earth" (Rev. 9:3). The Greek word translated "scorpion" is *skorpios*.

Arndt and Gingrich comment: "*The scorpion*, a species of vermin (an arachnid, 4 to 5 inches long) common in southern latitudes, much feared because of its sting Rv 9:3, 5, 10. . . . Fig. as a type of extreme harmfulness."[6]

Through Moses, the Lord reminded ancient Israel that He had brought them "through that great and terrible wilderness, where is the biting serpent, and scorpion, and drought" (Deut. 8:15, LXX). The Lord instructed Ezekiel not to be afraid of the people, even though they were like scorpions.

> Thou, son of man, fear them not, nor be dismayed at their face; (for they will madden and will rise up against thee round about, and thou dwellest in the midst of scorpions): be not afraid of their words, nor be dismayed at their countenance, for it is a provoking house (Ezek. 2:6, LXX).

Jesus likened serpents and scorpions to evil spirits, whom Satan leads. When the seventy disciples returned from their evangelistic tour, they rejoiced, saying,

> "Lord, even the demons are subject to us in your name!" And he said to them, "I saw Satan fall like lightning from heaven. Behold, I have given you authority to tread upon serpents and scorpions, and over all the power of the enemy; and nothing shall hurt you. Nevertheless do not rejoice in this, that the spirits are subject to you; but rejoice that your names are written in heaven" (Luke 10:17–20).

Jesus wasn't referring to literal serpents and scorpions, even though He has power to protect from them (Acts 28:3–6). He was likening the evil spirits over whom His disciples had exercised His power to serpents and scorpions. This application enlightens our study of the fifth trumpet. The locusts with the sting of scorpions evidently represent human forces that will afflict the professed people of God. But even more significantly, they refer to demons who will torture the people of God for a time.[7] As we search for both a historical and an eschatological application of the prophecy, we must keep these facts in mind.

THE GRASS AND THE SEAL OF GOD

"They were told not to harm the grass of the earth or any green growth or any tree, but only those of mankind who have not the seal of God upon their foreheads" (Rev. 9:4). The grass, green growth, and trees represent the professed servants of God, professed Christians, whether they're genuine believers or apostate. (See the discussion of grass and trees in chapter 3 on the first trumpet.)

Translated literally from the Greek text, Revelation 9:4 says, "And it was said to them that they should not harm the grass of the earth, nor any green thing, nor any tree, *except* (*ei mē*) those men who do not have the seal of God upon their foreheads." Hence, the grass, green things, and trees represent all professed believers. Only those who have the seal of God upon their foreheads are to be protected from the sting of the locusts.

The seal of God may be viewed two ways. As soon as individuals accept Christ as Savior and Lord, they receive the initial seal of the Holy Spirit. Paul wrote to the Ephesians:

In him you also, who have heard the word of truth, the gospel of your salvation, and have believed in him, were sealed with the promised Holy Spirit, which is the guarantee of our inheritance until we acquire possession of it, to the praise of his glory (Eph. 1:13, 14; cf. 4:30; 2 Cor. 1:22).

However, in the book of Revelation, the seal of God refers to the end-time seal of the Spirit given to the faithful before the close of probation. Revelation 7 describes the 144,000, who are sealed shortly before the winds of strife are let loose on our world. These are the righteous who are living on the earth when Jesus comes the second time. After describing the Second Advent in Revelation 6:12–16, John asks the crucial question, "Who is able to stand?" (Rev. 6:17, NKJV). The answer is found in chapter 7: the 144,000 will stand and will fearlessly welcome their Lord as He appears with His holy angels.

The number 144,000 is symbolic of the multitude of believers who will be alive to welcome the return of our Lord. The number is embedded in a symbolic prophecy. The "four angels" of Revelation 7:1 are symbolic of all the angels who are working for humankind. The "four corners of the earth" denote the entire earth. The "earth," "sea," and "tree" symbolize people.

The seal of God isn't a literal mark; the phrase refers to the control the Holy Spirit has of the minds of those who have totally committed themselves to Jesus. This seal is identified in Revelation 14:1, which says that the 144,000 are those who have "his name [Christ's name] and his Father's name written on their foreheads." The names of Christ and the Father are symbolic of their character (Isa. 57:15), so the 144,000 are people upon whom the Holy Spirit has bestowed the character of Christ and of the Father (cf. John 14:17–23; Rom. 8:9, 10). They are the "great multitude" of Revelation 7:9.[8]

Verse 14 describes the 144,000 for us: "These are they who have come out of the great tribulation; they have washed their robes and made them white in the blood of the Lamb." "In their mouth no lie was found, for they are spotless" (Rev. 14:5).

Who passes through the great end-time tribulation? Those who conquer "the beast and its image and the number of its name" (Rev. 15:2). Those who pass through the great last-day time of trouble and stand as a people ready to welcome Jesus when He returns.

The mention of the "seal of God" in Revelation 9:4 clearly points us to an end-time application of the prophecy. It is quite possible to identify a historical power that attacked the people of God after the papacy assumed ecclesiastical supremacy. As we proceed, we'll try to identify that power. But the fact that scorpions denote evil spirits, and the fact that it is those who don't have the end-time seal of God who suffer at their hands strongly suggests that we can expect intense demonic torture of the professed people of God after the close of probation. Before we spell out what that torture involves, we must focus on the historical evil forces that were types or examples of the end-time evil forces that will afflict God's people.

THE PERSECUTION

> They were allowed to torture them for five months, but not to kill them, and their torture was like the torture of a scorpion, when it stings a man. And in those days men will seek death and will not find it; they will long to die, and death will fly from them (Rev. 9:5, 6).

Applying the day-for-a-year principle that emerges from the study of apocalyptic prophecy, we can see that five months of prophetic time signifies 150 years of actual time.[9] Daniel identified the period during which the little horn power would exercise ecclesiastical dominion as "a time, two times, and half a time" (Dan. 7:25; cf. 12:7). Revelation 11:2 identifies the period in which this same power "will trample over the holy city" as "forty-two months" (cf. Rev. 13:5). Those forty-two months are equal to 1,260 days (verse 3). In Rev. 12, the 1,260 days (verse 6) are referred to as "a time, and times, and half a time" (verse 14).

Since the same period is spoken of either as 1,260 days or forty-two months, we can conclude that one prophetic month comprises thirty days. Five months then equals 150 days. Additionally, to make sense of Daniel 7 and Revelation 11–13, the day-year principle must be applied. The 1,260 days that Daniel 7 says the little horn exercised its power represent 1,260 years. The period during which the great dragon of Revelation 12 persecuted the "woman," the true church, was not a mere 1,260 literal days, but 1,260 years (AD 538–1798). Applying the same day-year principle to Revelation 9:5, we can see that the five-month period during which professed Christians were to be tortured by the power symbolized by locusts with the power of scorpions represented a literal 150 years.

On the basis of our dual application of the trumpets, it would seem quite feasible to conclude that the persecuting forces spoken of in Revelation 9:1–12 represent a historic nation, one that attacked the world of people who claim to be Christians after the papacy achieved ecclesiastical predominance. The prophecy says this power would torture professed Christians for 150 years.

This historical power is a type or example of the evil forces of Satan that will attack professed Christians for a time after the close of probation. Only those who have the end-time seal of God will be protected (cf. Rev. 9:4 with Rev. 7). The torture won't result in the death of those attacked, but the attacks will be so fierce as to make them wish for death.

The point seems to be that Satan and his evil angels will so trouble professed Christians after the close of probation that those of them who don't have the seal of God will fall victim to despair and the desire for death (cf. Job 3:21; Jer. 8:3). Thus, Revelation 9:7–10 helps us identify the historic power represented by the locusts with the sting of scorpions.

1. It was a military power relying upon cavalry (Rev. 9:7; cf. verse 9).
2. The troops wore a distinctive headdress ("crowns of gold," verse 7).
3. The faces of the locusts "were like human faces" because they represent human soldiers (verse 7).
4. The soldiers had long hair (verse 8).
5. The prophecy says that the teeth of the locusts are like a lion's teeth (verse 8). These teeth, then, would seem to symbolize the destructiveness and rapacity of these warriors.
6. "They had scales like iron breastplates" (verse 9). The Greek word for breastplate (*thorax*) may also mean "the part of the body covered by the breastplate, the chest."[10] The sentence may read literally: "They had breastplates ["chests"] like breastplates of iron." These troops wore some kind of armor for the torso.
7. The "wings" (verse 9) would seem to symbolize their speed of conquest (cf. Jer. 4:13; 48:40; 49:22).
8. Revelation 9:10 says, "They have tails like scorpions, and stings, and their power of hurting men for five months lies in their tails." This verse seems to be about the weapons these warriors use.

THE TURK (HISTORICAL INTERPRETATION)

Early Adventist interpreters considered the fifth and sixth trumpets to be successive periods of Ottoman Turkish rule. They regarded the 150 years spoken of in the fifth trumpet as beginning on July 27, 1299, the date for the battle of Bapheum, the first attack of the Ottoman Turks on the Byzantine Empire. So the 150 years of the fifth trumpet would end and the time period spoken of in the sixth trumpet would begin on July 27, 1449.

We'll discuss the sixth trumpet in more detail later. For now it is important to note that the early Adventist interpreters deduced Revelation 9:15's "the hour, the day, the month, and the year" comprised another prophetic time period. Adventist interpreters believed an hour of prophetic time to represent 15 days; a day to symbolize a year; a month of 30 days to represent 30 years; and a year, or 360 days, to denote 360 years. So the time period in the sixth trumpet represented 391 years and 15 days.

Adventist interpreters believed this period extended from the beginning to the end of the sixth trumpet, which they considered to cover the life of the Ottoman Empire, which would lose its power as an independent entity at the end of that period. Adding the 391 years and 15 days to July 27, 1449, the date of the beginning of the sixth trumpet, then, would bring us to the end of that period—the end of the sixth trumpet. The *Seventh-day Adventist Bible Commentary* clearly states the interpretation at which the early Adventists arrived:

> In 1832 William Miller made a new approach to the dating of these trumpets by connecting them chronologically (in the fifth of a series of articles in the Vermont *Telegraph*). On the basis of the year-day principle (see on Dan. 7:25), Miller calculated the five months of the fifth trumpet (Rev. 9:5) to be 150 literal years, and the hour, day, month, and year of the sixth to be 391 years and 15 days. Many expositors before

Miller had adopted these same calculations, but they had not connected the two periods chronologically. Miller set forth the view that the time period of the sixth trumpet followed immediately upon that of the fifth, so as to make the entire period one of 541 years and 15 days. This period he dated from A.D. 1298, when he considered the first attack by the Ottoman Turks on the Byzantine Empire occurred, to 1839. Thus, according to his view, both trumpets represented the Ottoman Turks, the fifth, their rise and the sixth, their period of domination.

In 1838 Josiah Litch, one of Miller's associates in the second advent movement in America, revised Miller's dates to A.D. 1299 to 1449 for the fifth trumpet, and 1449 to 1840 for the sixth. Litch accepted the date July 27, 1299, for the battle of Bapheum, near Nicomedia, which he took as the first attack by the Ottoman Turks on the Byzantine Empire.[11] He saw the date 1449 as significant of the collapse of Byzantine power, for toward the end of 1448 a new Byzantine emperor, Constantine Palaeologus, had requested permission of the Turkish sultan Murad II before daring to ascend his throne, and he did not, in fact receive the crown until January 6, 1449, after such permission had been granted. Litch believed that this 150-year period constituted the time during which the Ottoman Turks "tormented" (see v. 5) the Byzantine Empire.

As already stated, Litch set 1299 as the beginning of the fifth trumpet, to be more exact, July 27, 1299, his date for the battle of Bapheum. He gave to this fifth trumpet a period of 150 years. This brought him to July 27, 1449, for the beginning of the sixth trumpet. Adding on 391 years brought him to July 27, 1840. The 15 days carried him over into the month of August of that year. He predicted that in that month the power of the Turkish Empire would be overthrown. However, at the outset he did not fix on a precise day in August. A short time before the expiration of this period he declared that the Turkish Empire would be broken August 11, which is exactly 15 days beyond July 27, 1840.

At that time world attention was directed to events taking place in the Turkish Empire. In June, 1839, Mohammed Ali, pasha of Egypt and nominally a vassal of the sultan, had rebelled against his overlord. He defeated the Turks and captured their navy. At this juncture Mahmud II, the sultan, died, and the ministers of his successor, Abdul Mejid, proposed a settlement to Mohammed Ali by which he would receive the hereditary pashalik of Egypt, and his son Ibrahim, the rulership of Syria. However, Britain, France, Austria, Prussia, and Russia, who all had interests in the Near East, intervened at this point and insisted that no agreement between the Turks and Mohammed Ali be made without their consultation. Negotiations were protracted until the summer of 1840, when, on July 15, Britain, Austria, Prussia, and Russia signed the Treaty of London, proposing to back with force the terms suggested the previous year by the Turks. It was about this time that Litch announced that he anticipated Turkish power to come to an end on August 11. On that day the Turkish emissary, Rifat Bey, arrived at Alexandria with the terms of the London Convention. On that day also the ambassadors of the four powers received a communication from the sultan inquiring as to what measures were to be taken in reference to a circumstance vitally affecting his empire. He was told that "provision had been made," but he could not know what it was. Litch interpreted these events as a recognition by the Turkish government that its independent power was gone.

These events, coming at the specified time of Litch's prediction, exercised a wide influence upon the thinking of those in America who were interested in the Millerite movement. Indeed, this prediction by Litch went far to give credence to other, as yet unfulfilled, time prophecies—particularly that of the 2300 days—which were being preached by the Millerites. Thus this occurrence in 1840 was a significant factor in building up the expectation of the second advent three years later. . . .

Generally speaking, the Seventh-day Adventist interpretation of the fifth and sixth trumpets, particularly as touching the time period involved, is essentially that of Josiah Litch.[12]

It is interesting to note that Ellen White accepted the validity of Litch's interpretation and prediction:

In the year 1840 another remarkable fulfillment of prophecy excited widespread interest. Two years before, Josiah Litch, one of the leading ministers preaching the second advent, published an exposition of Revelation 9, predicting the fall of the Ottoman Empire. According to his calculations, this power was to be overthrown "in A.D. 1840, sometime in the month of August;" and only a few days previous to its accomplishment he wrote: "Allowing the first period, 150 years, to have been exactly fulfilled before Deacozes ascended the throne by permission of the Turks, and that the 391 years, fifteen days, commenced at the close of the first period, it will end on the 11th of August, 1840, when the Ottoman power in Constantinople may be expected to be broken. And this, I believe, will be found to be the case."—Josiah Litch, in *Signs of the Times, and Expositor of Prophecy*, August 1, 1840.

When it became known, multitudes were convinced of the correctness of the principles of prophetic interpretation adopted by Miller and his associates, and a wonderful impetus was given to the advent movement. Men of learning and position united with Miller, both in preaching and in publishing his views, and from 1840 to 1844 the work rapidly extended.[13]

Islam began in the seventh century AD. The Ottoman Turks accepted the teachings of Mohammed, and in the fourteenth century they rose to power—by 1389 founding an empire of vassal principalities in the Balkans and Anatolia.

Holy War was intended not to destroy but to subdue the infidel world. . . . The Ottomans established their empire by uniting Muslim Anatolia and the Christian Balkans under their rule, and, although continuous Holy War was the fundamental principle of the state, the empire emerged, at the same time, as protector of the Orthodox Church and millions of Orthodox Christians. Islam guaranteed the lives and property of Christians and Jews, on the conditions of obedience and payment of a poll tax. It allowed them free exercise of their own religions and to live according to their own religious laws. Living in a frontier society and mixing freely with Christians, the Ottomans applied these principles of Islam with the greatest liberality and tolerance. During the early years of the empire the Ottomans pursued a policy of attempting to secure the voluntary submission and confidence of the Christians, before resorting to warfare.[14]

The appearance of the Ottoman troops as described in Revelation 9:7–10 matches that of observers of the time. "In appearance the locusts were like horses arrayed for battle" (verse 7). The Ottoman military depended to a great extent on the cavalry. "On their heads were what looked like crowns of gold; their faces were like human faces" (verse 7). The "crowns of gold" symbolize the turbans worn by the Ottoman horsemen. The faces of the locusts with the power of scorpions were like human faces because they represent the Ottoman army. "Their hair like women's hair" (verse 8) depicts the long hair of the cavalry troops. And "their teeth like lions' teeth" (verse 8) symbolizes the determined, destructive power of the Ottoman cavalry.

Verse 9 says, "They had scales like iron breastplates." Note what Bernard Lewis writes of the armor of the Ottoman troops.

> We have, surviving from the early Ayyubid period onwards, specimens of armour and mailed coats; these must have been preserved on account of their value to succeeding generations. The plain coat of mail survived in Islamic usage down to the XIII/19th century, lingering longest in peripheral regions like India and sub-Saharan Africa; but there were also to be found splint armour, that is, mailed coats reinforced by rectangular, overlapping splints, and the brigandine or short jerkin, a heavily padded or laminated jacket covered with velvet or satin and heavily studded with nails.[15]

Scripture says, "The noise of their wings was like the noise of many chariots with horses rushing into battle" (verse 9). This symbolism depicts the amazing speed of conquest of the Ottoman cavalry.

Revelation goes on to say, "They have tails like scorpions, and stings, and their power of hurting men for five months lies in their tails" (verse 10). Bernard Lewis observed:

> Already in the III/9th century, the author al-Jahiz of Basra commented that if one numbered a Turk's days at the end of his life, one would find that he had spent more time in the saddle than on the ground, that the Turks always carry with them two or three bows and their strings, and that they are such expert archers that their arrows shot backwards when retreating are as deadly as those shot forwards.[16]

TIME OF TROUBLE (END-TIME INTERPRETATION)

The historical events outlined in the fifth trumpet are types, examples, pre-enactments of similar events that will occur after the end-time close of probation. As we have seen, the trumpets are blown after our heavenly High Priest casts the intercessory censer onto the ground (Rev. 8:5). Then will come the most terrible time of trouble this world has ever known. Of it, Daniel wrote: "At that time shall arise Michael, the great prince who has charge of your people. And there shall be a time of trouble, such as never has been since there was a nation till that time; but at that time your people shall be delivered, every one whose name shall be found written in the book" (Dan. 12:1).

Jesus spoke of the same unprecedented time of trouble: "There will be great tribulation, such as has not been from the beginning of the world until now, no, and never will be" (Matt. 24:21; cf. Mark 13:19, 20). In the context of the passage, this tribulation may refer to the trouble and calamity preceding and surrounding the destruction of Jerusalem in AD 70.[17] It may also refer to the persecution of the people of God during the Middle Ages.[18] But those periods of tribulation were merely types of the quintessential time of trouble that will burst upon the world after the close of probation.[19]

> The records of the past,—the long procession of tumults, conflicts, and revolutions, the "battle of the warrior . . . with confused noise, and garments rolled in blood" (Isaiah 9:5),— what are these, in contrast with the terrors of that day when the restraining Spirit of God shall be wholly withdrawn from the wicked, no longer to hold in check the outburst of human passion and satanic wrath! The world will then behold, as never before, the results of Satan's rule.
>
> But in that day, as in the time of Jerusalem's destruction, God's people will be delivered, everyone that shall be found written among the living. Isaiah 4:3.[20]

The context of Jesus' prophecy about a time of trouble (Matt. 24:21–27) makes it perfectly clear that He is speaking of the end of time when the forces of evil will be extremely active to deceive the inhabitants of earth and to persecute and destroy those who don't accept their delusions. It is this end-time period of tribulation that is the subject of the fifth trumpet. Satan is "the star fallen from heaven to earth" (Rev. 9:1) who will envelop the world with the darkening smoke of his deceptions. The locusts with the power of scorpions (verse 3) are the evil demons in the employ of Satan who will torture the professed people of God for a period of time. As pointed out above, Jesus likened evil spirits to scorpions (Luke 10:17–20). These demons will possess the minds and bodies of unbelievers, motivating them to destroy God's professed people. They will also torture believers in Christ with the horrible thought that, because of their past sins—

which Satan, the tempter, knows all too well—they are certain to be lost for eternity. The excruciating pain that God's people will suffer at that time will be mental anguish caused by the demons of hell, who will do all in their power to discourage them.

Chapter 9:4 reveals that those professed Christians who do not have the seal of God will suffer at the hands of demons. But while Satan will attack those who have the seal of God, he won't be permitted to harm them. God will shelter those whom He has sealed (see Rev. 7:1–8).*

The historic period of five prophetic months (Rev. 9:5) is simply a type of an indefinable period of trial imposed by Satan and his demons upon the professed people of God after the end-time close of probation.

> When Christ shall cease his work as mediator in man's behalf, then this time of trouble will begin. Then the case of every soul will have been decided, and there will be no atoning blood to cleanse from sin. When Jesus leaves his position as man's intercessor before God, the solemn announcement is made, "He that is unjust, let him be unjust still; and he which is filthy, let him be filthy still, and he that is righteous, let him be righteous still; and he that is holy, let him be holy still." Then the restraining Spirit of God is withdrawn from the earth. As Jacob was threatened with death by his angry brother, so the people of God will be in peril from the wicked who are seeking to destroy them. And as the patriarch wrestled

---

* Ellen White spells out in no uncertain terms the cause of the tribulation, indicating that Satan will attack the people of God through human instrumentalities as well as through demonic deception. She notes that the anguish God's people suffer will be primarily spiritual and that to be prepared for that time of trouble we must have an especially close relationship with Jesus. See *The Great Controversy*, 615–623.

all night for deliverance from the hand of Esau, so the righteous will cry to God day and night for deliverance from the enemies that surround them.[21]

The fifth plague will be poured out in the midst of this final turmoil. "The fifth angel poured his bowl on the throne of the beast, and its kingdom was in darkness; men gnawed their tongues in anguish and cursed the God of heaven for their pain and sores, and did not repent of their deeds" (Rev. 16:10, 11).

The "beast" referred to is the first beast of Revelation 13:1–10. The specifications of the prophecy point clearly to the papacy as the fulfillment of this symbol. The "throne" of the beast evidently refers to Rome, the center of papal government, and "its kingdom" is Vatican City. Because the Roman Catholic Church chooses to adhere to non-biblical traditions, accepting satanic darkness, persecuting those who refuse to obey its ecclesiastical dictates, and cooperating with the forces of evil in attacking the believing people of God, the Lord will bring upon it the darkness, pain, and sores of the fifth plague. Satan's work of torturing the people of God, as predicted by the fifth trumpet, will be counteracted as God intervenes by bringing the fifth plague upon those who cooperate with evil demons.

Truly, trying days await us.

---

1. Francis Brown, S. R. Driver, and Charles A. Briggs, *A Hebrew and English Lexicon of the Old Testament* (Oxford: Clarendon Press, 1952), s.v. "אֲבַדּוֹן."
2. William F. Arndt and F. Wilbur Gingrich, *A Greek-English Lexicon of the New Testament and Other Early Christian Literature,* 4th ed. (Cambridge: University Press, 1957), s.v. "Ἀπολλύων."
3. Caird, *The Revelation of St. John the Divine,* 117, 118.
4. Arndt and Gingrich, *A Greek-English Lexicon,* s.v. "φρεαρ."
5. Ibid., s.v. "αβυσσος."
6. Ibid., s.v. "σκορπιος."
7. David E. Aune comments: "Since the angel of the abyss is their king (9:11),

this must be an army of demons. . . . The reason for the detailed description of demons in the form of locusts is to underline their evil origin. . . . A similar description is found in *Apoc. Zeph.* 4:1–4 of ugly angels whose task it is to carry off the souls of the unrighteous and cast them into their eternal punishment." *Revelation 6 – 16,* 495, 496.

8. White, *The Great Controversy,* 648, 649.

9. On the validity of the year-day principle, see William H. Shea, *Selected Studies on Prophetic Interpretation,* Daniel and Revelation Committee Series, vol. 1 (Washington, DC: Review and Herald®, 1982), 56–93.

10. Arndt and Gingrich, *A Greek-English Lexicon,* s.v. θωραξ.

11. The date was given by Edward Gibbon in *Decline and Fall of the Roman Empire* (New York: E. P. Dutton, 1910), 6:292: "It was on the twenty-seventh of July, in the year twelve hundred and ninety-nine of the Christian era, that Othman first invaded the territory of Nicomedia; and the singular accuracy of the date seems to disclose some foresight of the rapid and destructive growth of the monster."
Edwin R. Thiele quotes Possinius, a seventeenth-century historian who dated the battle of Bapheum on July 27, 1299: " 'Now, Pachymeres is very explicit in stating that these events took place in the immediate vicinity of Bapheum, not far from Nicomedia, on the 27th day of July. The year, we asseverate in our synopsis, comparing carefully the events, to have been the year of our Lord 1299.' " *Outline Studies in Revelation,* 175. Thiele is quoting Possinius, *Observationum Pachymerianarum,* Book III (Chronology), 8, Sec 5.

12. Nichol, ed., *Seventh-day Adventist Bible Commentary,* 7:795, 796.
For an alternative view of the fifth and sixth trumpets presented by an Adventist author, see Doukhan, *Secrets of Revelation,* 84–91. Doukhan does not identify the Ottoman Turkish incursions as the fulfillment of the fifth and sixth trumpets.

13. White, *The Great Controversy,* 334, 335.

14. Halil İnalcık, *The Ottoman Empire: The Classical Age 1300–1600* (London: Weidenfeld and Nicolson, 1973), 7.

15. Bernard Lewis, ed., *Islam and the Arab World: Faith, People, Culture* (New York: American Heritage, 1976), 208, 209.

16. Ibid., 205.

17. White, *The Great Controversy,* 25.

18. Ibid., 39, 266, 267, 393.

19. Ibid., 25, 36, 37.

20. Ibid, 36–37.

21. White, *Patriarchs and Prophets,* 201.

CHAPTER 8

THE SIXTH TRUMPET

We now come to the incredible warnings of the sixth trumpet:

Then the sixth angel blew his trumpet, and I heard a voice from the four horns of the golden altar before God, saying to the sixth angel who had the trumpet, "Release the four angels who are bound at the great river Euphra'tes." So the four angels were released, who had been held ready for the hour, the day, the month, and the year, to kill a third of mankind. The number of the troops of cavalry was twice ten thousand times ten thousand; I heard their number. And this was how I saw the horses in my vision: the riders wore breastplates the color of fire and of sapphire and of sulphur, and the heads of the horses were like lions' heads, and fire and smoke and sulphur issued from their mouths. By these three plagues a third of mankind was killed, by the fire and smoke and sulphur issuing from their mouths. For the power of the horses is in their mouths and in their tails; their tails are like serpents, with heads, and by means of them they wound. The rest of mankind, who were not killed by these plagues, did not repent of the works of their hands nor give up worshiping demons and idols of gold and silver and bronze and stone and wood, which cannot either see or hear or walk; nor did they repent of their murders or their sorceries or their immorality or their thefts (Rev. 9:13–21).

Revelation 8:3–5, as we saw, depicts Christ standing before the heavenly altar of incense offering His own merits mingled with the prayers of the saints. He throws the censer onto the earth to mark the end of mediation at the close of probation. The voice mentioned in Revelation 9:13, which gives the command quoted in verse 14, seems clearly to be the voice of Christ. Clearly, then, Satan does what he does only with divine permission.

THE EUPHRATES RIVER

"I heard a voice from the four horns of the golden altar before God saying to the sixth angel who had the trumpet, 'Release the four angels who are bound at the great river Euphrates' " (Rev. 9:13–14). God originally gave to the descendants of Abraham the land from Egypt and the Mediterranean Sea to the river Euphrates (Gen. 15:18; Deut. 1:7; 11:24; Josh. 1:4). Because the enemies of Israel often came from the area near the Euphrates and even east of it, the Euphrates became a symbol of God's judgments upon unfaithful Israel and upon her pagan enemies. The Assyrians and Babylonians came from that direction, and the Persians, whose homeland was farther east, gained control of the area around the Euphrates and from there invaded Palestine.

Isaiah wrote,

The LORD spoke to me again: "Because this people have refused the waters of Shilo'ah that flow gently, and melt in fear before Rezin and the son of Remali'ah; therefore, behold, the Lord is bringing up against them the waters of the River, mighty and many, the king of Assyria and all his glory; and it will rise over all its channels and go over all its banks; and it will sweep on into Judah, it will overflow and pass on, reaching even to the neck; and its outspread wings will fill the breadth of your land, O Imman'u-el" (Isa. 8:5–8). H. B. Swete comments:

The Euphrates was on the East "the ideal limit" of the land of Israel. . . . Beyond it lay the great heathen kingdoms of the East, Babylonia on the east bank of the river, the Assyrian Empire further to the N.E.; an invasion of Israel by these nations is likened to an overflow of the Great River in Isa. viii.7. . . . Thus the idea presented by the angels of vengeance bound on the banks of the Euphrates is that the day of vengeance was held back only till God's time has come. When at length they are loosed, the flood will burst its barriers, and ruin will follow.[1]

Hence, Revelation 9:14 seems clearly to be announcing the coming judgments of God in the form of His permitting evil powers to attack and destroy the apostate peoples of earth. The Euphrates symbolizes the powers of evil (whether earthly nations, evil spirits, or both) that God allows to slay the unfaithful. The "four angels" symbolize evil forces that in the past were restrained but that now are being let loose. God has finally allowed the forces of evil to punish and destroy those who have rejected His love, preferring idolatry, murder, sorcery, immorality, and theft (verses 20, 21).

The Ottoman again (historical interpretation)

Uriah Smith wrote that the four angels "are the four principal sultanies of which the Ottoman Empire was composed, located in the country watered by the Euphrates. These sultanies were situated at Aleppo, Iconium, Damascus, and Baghdad. Previously they had been restrained; but God commanded, and they were loosed."[2]

Josiah Litch agreed.[3] As we noted in the previous chapter, Litch considered July 27, 1299, the date of the battle of Bapheum, to be the beginning of the period under the fifth trumpet. That period ended on July 27, 1449; and the period of the sixth trumpet began immediately, ending 391 years and 15 days later, on August 11, 1840.[4]

The Ottoman Turks originated as a power in the late thirteenth century, when the Mongol hordes under Genghis Khan drove them out of central Asia and toward the west. They settled in Asia Minor and conquered territories ranging from Persia to Austria. The Balkan states, Greece, Anatolia, Syria, Palestine, Egypt, Cyrenaica, Tripolitania, and Algeria all came under their control.

"The number of the troops of cavalry was twice ten thousand times ten thousand: I heard their number" (Rev. 9:16). Literally, the Greek means "double myriads of myriads." Arndt and Gingrich comment: "The number given is twenty thousand times ten thousand. An indefinite number of incalculable immensity is indicated."[5] The number of the Turkish hordes that absorbed the Byzantine Empire and threatened the western Roman Empire is beyond computation.

And this was how I saw the horses in my vision: the riders wore breastplates the color of fire and of sapphire and of sulphur, and the heads of the horses were like lions' heads, and fire and smoke and sulphur issued from their mouths. By these three plagues a third of mankind was killed, by the fire and smoke and sulphur issuing from their mouths. For the power of the horses is in their mouths and in their tails; their tails are like serpents, with heads, and by means of them they wound (Rev. 9:17–19).

In our discussion of the fifth trumpet, we mentioned the armor and coats of mail worn by the Muslim cavalry. The heads of the horses, appearing to John like lions' heads with fire and smoke and sulphur issuing from their mouths, might well be a depiction of fire-arms, which the Ottoman Turks used.

That the Ottomans achieved such a position of military advantage in the centuries of the empire's florescence . . . was in fair measure due to the comparatively enthusiastic and expert way in which they took to the revolutionary new means of waging war: firearms. . . .

Hence, *naft*, originally white bitumen, was used first for saltpetre when this substance was introduced into the Islamic world (probably from China) in the early VII/13th century, and then for gunpowder. . . .

The hand gun appears in the shape of the cumbersome arquebus in the 1440s, the time of Murad's Hungarian wars, but may well have been known two or three decades previously. . . . The fame of the Turkish gunners was such throughout the Islamic world that we hear of Turks assisting the Safavids, and the Ottomans supplied technical experts as far afield as to Muslim India, where Turkish-manned guns helped to repel the Portuguese from the shores of Bombay and Gujerat in the X/16th century. They further sent firearms to the Crimean Tartars and to the Muslim leader in Ethiopia against the Christians, Ahmad Gran, enabling the latter in 949/1542 to win a victory over the Emperor of Ethiopia's Portuguese auxiliaries. Some Ottoman artillerymen even found their way to distant Atcheh in Sumatra, and cannon cast by them were used against the Portuguese at Malacca.[6]

John's description of the power of the horses being "in their mouths and in their tails" seems to be a reference to the ability of the Ottoman cavalry to fire both forwards and backwards—guns they could shoot both when attacking the enemy and when retreating.

MODERN BABYLON (END-TIME INTERPRETATION)

From the perspective of twenty-first-century readers, the eschatological interpretation is more relevant. Introducing the sixth trumpet, Revelation 9:13 points us back to the events described in chapter 8:3–5. The angel offering incense is a symbol of Christ our heavenly High Priest (cf. Heb. 8:1, 2). Christ ministers in heaven by mingling the merits of His intercession with the prayers of His believing people. But verse 5 tells us that eventually He takes the censer and casts it onto the earth, thus ending probationary time. At that point the trumpets are sounded and the events they depict unfold.

When the sixth trumpet sounds, Christ's voice is heard from the vicinity of the "golden altar before God," the altar of incense (Rev. 9:13). The command He gives comes after He throws the censer down. In other words, the sixth trumpet depicts events that occur after the close of probation. The historical application of the symbolism—applying it to the devastation caused by the Ottoman Turks up to the middle of the nineteenth century—is undoubtedly correct. But history will be repeated—and on a more universal scale. The Turkish incursions symbolize the final onslaught when, just before Jesus returns, Satan, working through the human beings he controls, makes war upon the professed people of God. At that time, evil spirits and human beings who have turned from God will unite in a concerted, worldwide effort to wipe out His last-day church.

The scourge described under the sixth trumpet comes from "the great river Euphrates" (Rev. 9:14). The Euphrates River was the life support for the city of Babylon—which makes it an appropriate symbol of the peoples who supported ancient Babylon, and particularly of those end-time peoples who support antitypical Babylon.

When the Lord planned to punish ancient Israel by permitting the Babylonians to invade Palestine, He instructed Jeremiah to act out a prophecy. Jeremiah says the Lord told him to

> "go and buy a linen waistcloth, and put it on your loins, and do not dip it in water." So I bought a waistcloth according to the word of the Lord, and put it on my loins. And the word of the Lord came to me a second time, "Take the waistcloth which you have bought, which is upon your loins, and arise, go to the Euphra'tes, and hide it there in a cleft of the rock." So I went, and hid it by the Euphra'tes, as the Lord commanded me. And after many days the Lord said to me, "Arise, go to the Euphra'tes, and take from there the waistcloth which I commanded you to hide there." Then I went to the Euphra'tes, and dug, and I took the waistcloth from the place where I had hidden it. And behold, the waistcloth was spoiled; it was good for nothing. Then the word of the Lord came to me: "Thus says the Lord: Even so will I spoil the pride of Judah and the great pride of Jerusalem. This evil people, who refuse to hear my words, who stubbornly follow

their own heart and have gone after other gods to serve them and worship them, shall be like this waistcloth, which is good for nothing. For as the waistcloth clings to the loins of a man, so I made the whole house of Israel and the whole house of Judah cling to me, says the LORD, that they might be for me a people, a name, a praise, and a glory, but they would not listen" (Jer. 13:1–11).

The point is that the Euphrates symbolized the Babylonians whom God allowed to invade Palestine and take His apostate people captive. Those who survived were like Jeremiah, Daniel, and Ezekiel, for these men served God despite the attacks upon their people.

The book of Revelation contains similar symbolism. It portrays antitypical Babylon in chapter 17.

Then one of the seven angels who had the seven bowls came and said to me, "Come, I will show you the judgment of the great harlot who is seated upon many waters, with whom the kings of the earth have committed fornication, and with the wine of whose fornication the dwellers on earth have become drunk." And he carried me away in the Spirit into a wilderness, and I saw a woman sitting on a scarlet beast which was full of blasphemous names, and it had seven heads and ten horns. The woman was arrayed in purple and scarlet, and bedecked with gold and jewels and pearls, holding in her hand a golden cup full of abominations and the impurities of her fornication; and on her forehead was written a name of mystery: "Babylon the great, mother of harlots and of earth's abominations." And I saw the woman, drunk with the blood of the saints and the blood of the martyrs of Jesus (Rev. 17:1–6).

Ancient Babylon was situated on the river Euphrates. The woman named Babylon whom John saw in vision was "seated upon many waters" (verse 1). An angel told John, "The waters that you saw, where the harlot is seated, are peoples and multitudes and nations and tongues" (verse 15). Applying that symbolism to Revelation 9:14, we can conclude that the "great river Euphrates" that is the source of the scourge of the sixth trumpet represents "peoples and multitudes and nations and tongues" who are supporting antitypical Babylon.

The message seems clearly to be that the hordes of the Ottoman Turks who so devastated the eastern and western Mediterranean world and threatened Western Europe from 1449 to 1840 were types of the multitudes of evil demons and their human subjects who will attack the professed people of God with unprecedented fury after the close of probation and shortly before the second coming of Jesus.

As we shall see in the next chapter, under the sixth plague, "the great river Euphrates, and its water" will be dried up "to prepare the way for the kings from the east" (Rev. 16:12). The kings from the east who destroyed ancient Babylon were the Medo-Persians led by Cyrus. Christ and His angels are depicted here as the antitype of Cyrus and the Medo-Persians. Just as Cyrus and the Persians delivered the Jews from their Babylonian oppressors, so Jesus will deliver His people from antitypical Babylon by His return to earth.

Revelation 16:12 tells us that at some point prior to the Second Coming, the multitudes supporting antitypical Babylon will recognize that she has deceived them and dry up their support. John tells us about those who supported Babylon prior to this event. He says that he saw "three foul spirits like frogs" coming from "the mouth of the dragon and from the mouth of the beast and from the mouth of the false prophet" (Rev. 16:13). John says these were "demonic spirits" who performed signs (miracles), and "who go abroad to the kings of the whole world, to assemble them for the battle on the great day of God the Almighty" (Rev. 16:14).

The "dragon" is Satan (Rev. 12:4, 9). The "beast" is the first beast of Revelation 13, the papacy. The "false prophet" is the second beast of Revelation 13. It symbolizes apostate Protestantism, which supports the first beast, making an image of the beast "so that the image of the beast should even speak," and these powers will seek to "cause those who would not worship the image of the beast to be slain" (Rev. 13:15). Babylon's support, which is represented by the Euphrates River, consists of those who give allegiance to Satan, the papacy, and apostate Protestantism.[7]

Here is the antitype of the Ottoman rule that is brought to view under the sixth trumpet. Multitudes of demons and their human allies will attack the professed people of God, torturing many and destroying all that they can. The ones who suffer most are those of God's professed people who, because they didn't make the necessary spiritual preparation before the close of probation, have not been sealed. While those who have the end-time seal of God will suffer too, God will shelter them from the full extent of the attack (cf. Rev. 9:4).

The cosmic nature of the attack upon the professed people of God is emphasized by the final words of Revelation 9.

> The rest of mankind, who were not killed by these plagues, did not repent of the works of their hands nor give up worshiping demons and idols of gold and silver and bronze and stone and wood, which cannot either see or hear or walk; nor did they repent of their murders or their sorceries or their immorality or their thefts (Rev. 9:20–21).

"The rest of mankind" means all the followers of antitypical Babylon who, because of their allegiance to her, will survive her attacks upon the professed people of God. They save their skin by their loyalty to false religious systems. However, because of their failure to repent, they will suffer the seven last plagues (Rev. 16) and will ultimately be destroyed along with the dragon, the beast, and the false prophet (Rev. 19:20, 21; 20:10).

Like John, Ellen White foresaw Satan's final attack upon the people of God:

> When the irrevocable decision of the sanctuary has been pronounced and the destiny of the world has been forever fixed, the inhabitants of the earth will know it not. The forms of religion will be continued by a people from whom the Spirit of God has been finally withdrawn; and the satanic zeal with which the prince of evil will inspire them for the accomplishment of his malignant designs, will bear the semblance of zeal for God.[8]

> The wrath of Satan increases as his time grows short, and his work of deceit and destruction will reach its culmination in the time of trouble.

> Fearful sights of a supernatural character will soon be revealed in the heavens, in token of the power of miracle-working demons. The spirits of devils will go forth to the kings of the earth and to the whole world, to fasten them in deception, and urge them on to unite with Satan in his last struggle against the government of heaven. By these agencies, rulers and subjects will be alike deceived.[9]

As the decree issued by the various rulers of Christendom against the commandment keepers shall withdraw the protection of government and abandon them to those who desire their destruction, the people of God will flee from the cities and villages and associate together in companies, dwelling in the most desolate and solitary places. Many will find refuge in the strongholds of the mountains. Like the Christians of the Piedmont valleys, they will make the high places of the earth their sanctuaries and will thank God for "the munitions of rocks." Isaiah 33:16. But many of all nations and of all classes, high and low, rich and poor, black and white, will be cast into the most unjust and cruel bondage. The beloved of God pass weary days, bound in chains, shut in by prison bars, sentenced to be slain, some apparently left to die of starvation in dark and loathsome dungeons. No human ear is open to hear their moans; no human hand is ready to lend them help.[10]

In that day, multitudes will desire the shelter of God's mercy which they have so long despised. . . . The people of God will not be free from suffering; but while persecuted and distressed, while they endure privation and suffer for want of food they will not be left to perish. That God who cared for Elijah will not pass by one of His self-sacrificing children. . . . While the wicked are dying from hunger and pestilence, angels will shield the righteous and supply their wants.[11]

To human sight it will appear that the people of God must soon seal their testimony with their blood as did the martyrs before them. They themselves begin to fear that the Lord has left them to fall by the hand of their enemies. It is a time of fearful agony. Day and night they cry unto God for deliverance. The wicked exult, and the jeering cry is heard: "Where now is your faith? Why does not God deliver you out of our hands if you are indeed His people?" . . .

Could men see with heavenly vision, they would behold companies of angels that excel in strength stationed about those who have kept the word of Christ's patience.[12]

When the protection of human laws shall be withdrawn from those who honor the law of God, there will be, in different lands, a simultaneous movement for their destruction. As the time appointed in the decree draws near, the people will conspire to root out the hated sect. It will be determined to strike in one night a decisive blow, which shall utterly silence the voice of dissent and reproof.

The people of God—some in prison cells, some hidden in solitary retreats in the forests and the mountains—still plead for divine protection, while in every quarter companies of armed men, urged on by hosts of evil angels, are preparing for the work of death. It is now, in the hour of utmost extremity, that the God of Israel will interpose for the deliverance of His chosen.[13]

Because the sixth plague is so significant, the chapter that follows is also devoted to its consideration.

1. Swete, *The Apocalypse of St. John,* 121.
2. Uriah Smith, *The Prophecies of Daniel and the Revelation* (Nashville, TN: Southern Publishing Association, 1944), 506.
3. Josiah Litch, "Dissertation on the Fall of the Ottoman Empire: the 11th of August, 1840," *Second Advent Tracts,* no. XI (1841), 7.
4. Maxwell revises Josiah Litch's dating of the fifth and sixth trumpets. See *God Cares,* 2:256.
5. Arndt and Gingrich, *A Greek-English Lexicon,* s.v. "δισμυριας."
6. Lewis, ed., *Islam and the Arab World,* 210, 211.
7. In the next chapter, evidence is given identifying the papacy as the "beast" of Revelation 13:1–10 and apostate Protestantism as the second beast brought to view in Revelation 13:11–17.
8. Ellen G. White, *The Great Controversy,* 615.
9. Ibid., 623, 624.
10. Ibid., 626.
11. Ibid., 629.
12. Ibid., 630.
13. Ibid., 635.

CHAPTER 9

THE SIXTH PLAGUE

In this chapter we will look at the sixth plague, and what it means for the overall message of the trumpets.

> The sixth angel poured his bowl on the great river Euphra'tes, and its water was dried up, to prepare the way for the kings from the east. And I saw, issuing from the mouth of the dragon and from the mouth of the beast and from the mouth of the false prophet, three foul spirits like frogs; for they are demonic spirits, performing signs, who go abroad to the kings of the whole world, to assemble them for battle on the great day of God the Almighty. ("Lo, I am coming like a thief! Blessed is he who is awake, keeping his garments that he may not go naked and be seen exposed!") And they assembled them at the place which is called in Hebrew Armaged'don (Rev. 16:12–16).

God intended that the Euphrates should be the northern border of the Promised Land. Except briefly during the reigns of David and Solomon, it rarely was (2 Sam. 8:3; 1 Chron. 18:3; 1 Kings 4:21,

24). The territory around the Euphrates was taken over by the Assyrians and later by the Babylonians (2 Kings 23:29; Jer. 46:2, 6, 10).

Jeremiah prophesied that Babylon would "sink to rise no more" (Jer. 51:64), and he dramatized his prophecy by having his assistant tie a stone to the scroll containing the prophecy and then throw it into the Euphrates River when he went to Babylon (verses 59–63). This prophecy offered hope to the Israelites who had been taken captive in the Babylonian invasions in the time of Nebuchadnezzar (605, 597, and 586 BC). The captives could obey God's call for them to come out of Babylon (Jer. 50:8–10; Isa. 48:20) when Cyrus and the Medes and Persians conquered the city in 539 BC.

Way back in the eighth century BC the prophet Isaiah recorded God's revelation of Cyrus's successful conquest:

> Thus says the LORD, your Redeemer, who formed you from the womb: "I am the LORD, who made all things, who stretched out the heavens alone, who spread out the earth, . . . who says of Cyrus, 'He is my shepherd, and he shall fulfil all my purpose'; saying of Jerusalem, 'She shall be built,' and of the temple, 'Your foundation shall be laid.' "
>
> Thus says the LORD to his anointed, to Cyrus, whose right hand I have grasped, to subdue nations before him and ungird the loins of kings, to open doors before him that gates may not be closed: "I will go before you and level the mountains, I will break in pieces the doors of bronze and cut asunder the bars of iron, I will give you the treasures of darkness and the hoards in secret places, that you may know that it is I, the LORD, the God of Israel, who call you by your name. For the sake of my servant Jacob, and Israel my chosen, I call you by your name, I surname you, though you do not know

me. I am the LORD, and there is no other, besides me there is no God; I gird you, though you do not know me, that men may know, from the rising of the sun and from the west, that there is none besides me; I am the LORD, and there is no other" (Isa. 44:24, 28–45:6).

In the sixth century BC, Daniel recorded the fulfillment of the prophecy. As narrated in Daniel 5, Belshazzar and his lords and his concubines were feasting in the royal palace in Babylon when "the fingers of a man's hand appeared and wrote on the plaster of the wall of the king's palace" (Dan. 5:5). Overcome with fear, the king offered great rewards to any wise man who could decipher the writing, but no one could. At this point the queen mother entered the banqueting hall and suggested that Daniel, who had interpreted dreams in the time of Nebuchadnezzar, would be able to read the inscription. So, Daniel was called, and, sure enough, he was able to decipher the writing on the wall.

The writing on the wall said,

"MENE, God has numbered the days of your kingdom and brought it to an end; TEKEL, you have been weighed in the balances and found wanting; PERES, your kingdom is divided and given to the Medes and Persians." Then Belshaz'zar commanded, and Daniel was clothed with purple, a chain of gold was put about his neck, and proclamation was made concerning him, that he should be the third ruler in the kingdom. That very night Belshaz'zar the Chalde'an king was slain. And Darius the Mede received the kingdom, being about sixty-two years old (Dan. 5:26–31).

How did Cyrus's Medes and Persians conquer Babylon, surrounded as it was by a massive wall and stocked with supplies that were sufficient to withstand a lengthy siege?

Some commentators are convinced that the queen mother who advised that Daniel be called to read the writing on the wall was none other than Queen Nitocris, a daughter of Nebuchadnezzar and most likely the mother of Belshazzar.[1] If Herodotus's *Histories* is to be believed, Queen Nitocris unwittingly prepared the way for the Persians to enter Babylon and take it captive.[2]

> She changed the course of the Euphrates, which flows through Babylon. Its course was originally straight, but by cutting channels higher upstream she made it wind about with so many twists and turns that now it actually passes a certain Assyrian village called Ardericca three separate times. . . . In addition to this she constructed embankments on both sides of the river of remarkable strength and height, and a long way above the city, close beside the river, dug a basin for a lake some forty-seven miles in circumference. . . . When the basin was finished, the queen had stone brought to the place and built up the edge of it the whole way round. The purpose both of the excavation and of the diversion of the river was to cause the frequent bends to reduce the speed of the current, and to prevent a direct voyage downstream to the city. A boat would be faced with a devious course, and at the end of her trip she would have to make the tedious circuit of the lake. Moreover, these works lay in the neighbourhood of the approaches to Assyria and on the direct route to Media, and the intention of the queen was to discourage the Medes from mixing with the peoples of Babylon and thus getting to know what was going on there.[3]

In fact, Nitocris's basin made it possible for the Medes and Persians to gain access to the city and to destroy the Neo-Babylonian Empire:

The siege dragged on and no progress was made by the besieging army. Cyrus was beginning to despair of success when somebody suggested to him a way out of the deadlock. The plan (which may, indeed, have been his own) was as follows: he stationed part of his force at the point where the Euphrates flows into the city and another contingent at the opposite end where it flows out, with orders to both [cohorts] to force an entrance along the river-bed as soon as they saw that the water was shallow enough. Then, taking with him all his noncombatant troops, he withdrew to the spot where Nitocris had excavated the lake, and proceeded to repeat the operation which the queen had previously performed: by means of a cutting he diverted the river into the lake (which was then a marsh) and in this way so greatly reduced the depth of water in the actual bed of the river that it became fordable, and the Persian army, which had been left at Babylon for the purpose, entered the river, now only deep enough to reach about the middle of a man's thigh, and, making their way along it, got into the town. If the Babylonians had learnt what Cyrus was doing or had seen it for themselves in time, they could have let the Persians enter and then, by shutting all the gates which led to the waterside and manning the walls on either side of the river, they could have caught them in a trap and wiped them out. But as it was they were taken by surprise. The Babylonians themselves say that owing to the great size of the city the outskirts were captured without the people in the centre knowing anything about it; there was a festival going on, and even while the city was falling they continued to dance and enjoy themselves, until hard facts brought them to their senses. That, then, is the story of the first capture of Babylon.[4]

Ezra 1 records the decree of Cyrus, passed in 537 BC, for the return of the Jews to their own land and for the rebuilding of the temple in Jerusalem. Thus Cyrus and the Medes and Persians were kings from the east who were responsible for drying up the river Euphrates and for the release of God's people from captivity.

THE PAPACY

This whole historical scenario is the background for the sixth plague, which is presented in one verse, Revelation 16:12. God designed this plague to counteract the work of Satan in the sixth trumpet. Under the sixth trumpet, evil demons are released "at the great river Euphrates" (Rev. 9:14). These demons are then responsible for untold devastation as they motivate the torture and persecution practiced by the Ottoman Turks. But the Ottoman Turks are types of the evil demons and humans who, after the close of probation, will launch a final attack upon the professed people of God. This attack is outlined in Revelation 16:13, 14:

And I saw, issuing from the mouth of the dragon and from the mouth of the beast and from the mouth of the false prophet, three foul spirits like frogs; for they are demonic spirits, performing signs [*semeia,* "miracles"] who go abroad to the kings of the whole world, to assemble them for the battle on the great day of God the Almighty.

The work of these demonic spirits is the work of the four evil angels who were released at the great river Euphrates. Their work is "to kill a third of mankind" (Rev. 9:15). The point is that Revelation 16:13, 14 is parallel to chapter 9:13–21. The Revelation 16 passage gives us the end-time application of the sixth trumpet. The Ottomans were symbols or types of the demonic forces that, after the close of probation, prepare for "the battle on the great day of God the Almighty," which is the battle of Armageddon (Rev. 16:14, 16).

These demons work through human agencies. John saw in vision "three foul spirits like frogs" issuing "from the mouth of the dragon and from the mouth of the beast and from the mouth of the false prophet" (Rev. 16:13). The dragon is Satan himself (Rev. 12:3, 4, 7–9). The dragon and his demons are the "demonic spirits" spoken of in Revelation 16:14. But these evil spirits work through the beast and the false prophet. The beast is the papacy, whose corrupt work is outlined in Revelation 13:1–10. There are seven reasons why we apply these verses to the papacy.

1. It is a blasphemous power (Rev. 13:6; cf. 2 Thess. 2:4; Dan. 7:25). It is blasphemy for a mere human being to claim to be God (John 10:33); and it is blasphemy when human priests claim to be able to forgive sins (Luke 5:21).
2. The papacy is a persecuting power (Rev. 13:7; cf. 2 Thess. 2:4, 10–12; Dan. 7:25).
3. For a set time the papacy was given ecclesiastical supremacy over a good portion of Western Europe (Rev. 13:5; cf. Dan. 7:25; 12:7; Rev. 11:2, 3; 12:6, 14). This period of forty-two prophetic months, or 1,260 literal years, began in AD 538 and reached to 1798.
4. The papacy rose out of the pagan Roman Empire. It was the

recognition the emperors gave to the popes that supported the rise of the papacy (Rev. 13:2; 2 Thess. 2:7; Dan. 7:7, 8). "To it [the first beast of Revelation 13, the papacy] the dragon gave his power and his throne and great authority" (Rev. 13:2). As we have seen, the dragon of Revelation 12 is primarily Satan, but Satan worked through pagan Rome in an attempt to destroy Christ as soon as He was born (Rev. 12:4). Pagan Rome gave the papacy the center of its government (Rome) and the power that it exercised in Western Europe.

5. The papacy does the work of Satan, opposing the will and law of God (Rev. 13:8; 2 Thess. 2:9; Dan. 7:25). The papacy has added the second commandment of the ten to the first, making them one. Then, so that God's law has ten commandments again, it split the tenth commandment. The fourth commandment is called the third, and the Sabbath is said to be Sunday now, because it was the first day of Creation week and the day of Christ's resurrection. Thus the seventh-day Sabbath of both Old and New Testaments is set aside.

6. The papacy was a world power and is becoming such again (Rev. 13:7; 2 Thess. 2:9; Dan. 7:20–25).

7. The papacy and those who give allegiance to it will be destroyed at the second coming of Jesus (Rev. 13:10; 19:20; 20:10; 2 Thess. 2:8; Dan. 7:26).

The point is that "the demonic spirits, performing signs [miracles]" (Rev. 16:14) will employ the papacy to unite the world against the teaching of Scripture, against the God of the Bible, and the result will be that the world will turn against the people of God in one last terrible attempt to annihilate them from the earth. These events culminate in the great battle of Armageddon, the final battle between the armies of heaven and earth, in which Christ and His angels will prevail (see Rev. 17:13, 14).

THE UNITED STATES

The demonic spirits of Revelation 16:14 also work through "the false prophet." Who is this false prophet?

The false prophet is the second beast power of Revelation 13 (see verses 11–18). This power gives homage to the first beast (the papacy) and forces the whole world to worship according to the dictates of the papacy (Rev. 13:12–14). Those who resist will be forbidden to buy or sell (verse 17) and will ultimately be condemned to death (verse 15). John says the first beast rose out of the sea, but this second beast rises "out of the earth" (verse 11). Since water often represents multitudes of people (Rev. 17:15; cf. Dan. 7:2, 3), the second beast's rising from the earth, in contrast to coming up from the "sea," represents a power that rises from a relatively unpopulated area, which suggests that this second beast is none other than the United States of America.

The United States is the power that emerged in the New World toward the end of the period of papal supremacy. This great country began with "two horns like a lamb." In Scripture, horns symbolize power (Ps. 75:10; Amos 6:13, KJV; Dan. 7). The power of the U.S. government resides in the fact that it is based on democracy and religious liberty. But the prophecy tells us it will eventually speak "like a dragon" as it forms an image to the papacy and obliges the whole world to worship as the papacy dictates.

The issue is that Protestantism within the United States will turn from its commitment to the Bible and the Bible only as the rule of faith and practice, and it will pressure the government to pass laws stipulating a day of worship and a mode of worship that is acceptable to the papacy but unacceptable to God. These are the forces used by "demonic spirits" both before and after the close of probation to bring the whole world into unity against the government of God and against total commitment to Jesus Christ and obedience to His Word.

DRYING OF THE RIVER

The sixth plague, however, puts a stop to the work of these demonic spirits. When the sixth angel poured his bowl on the great river Euphrates, "its water was dried up" (Rev. 16:12). As we have seen, the demonic spirits of the sixth trumpet came from the territory of the river Euphrates. Now the water of the Euphrates is dried up. The Euphrates was the lifeline of the ancient city of Babylon. To conquer Babylon, Cyrus, in a sense, dried up the river by diverting its water into the lake created by Queen Nitocris. Since the water on which the harlot Babylon is seated represents "peoples and multitudes and nations and tongues," the drying up of the waters of the Euphrates symbolizes the withdrawal of the support for antitypical Babylon that the multitudes had previously provided.

So, the peoples of earth will ultimately turn against the dragon, the beast, and the false prophet. But since this happens after the close of probation, it happens too late for those who have chosen Babylon in preference to the God of the Bible. Babylon will lose its support, but the multitudes who gave her their allegiance will suffer with her by losing eternal life.

Ellen G. White dramatically describes this judgment against modern, antitypical Babylon:

"Her sins have reached unto heaven, and God hath remembered her iniquities. . . . In the cup which she hath filled fill to her double. How much she hath glorified herself, and lived deliciously, so much torment and sorrow give her: for she saith in her heart, I sit a queen, and am no widow, and shall see no sorrow. Therefore shall her plagues come in one day, death, and mourning, and famine; and she shall be utterly burned with fire: for strong is the Lord God who judgeth her. And the kings of the earth, who have committed fornication and lived deliciously with her, shall bewail her, and lament for her, . . . saying, Alas, alas that great city Babylon, that mighty city! for in one hour is thy judgment come." Revelation 18:5–10.

"The merchants of the earth," that have "waxed rich through the abundance of her delicacies," "shall stand afar off for the fear of her torment, weeping and wailing, and saying, Alas, alas that great city, that was clothed in fine linen, and purple, and scarlet, and decked with gold, and precious stones, and pearls! For in one hour so great riches is come to nought." Revelation 18:11, 3, 15–17.

Such are the judgments that fall upon Babylon in the day of the visitation of God's wrath. She has filled up the measure of her iniquity; her time has come; she is ripe for destruction.

When the voice of God turns the captivity of His people, there is a terrible awakening of those who have lost all in the great conflict of life. While probation continued they were blinded by Satan's deceptions, and they justified their course of sin. The rich prided themselves upon their superiority to those who were less favored; but they had obtained their riches by violation of the law of God. They had neglected to feed the hungry, to clothe the naked, to deal justly, and to love mercy. They had sought to exalt themselves and to obtain the homage of their fellow creatures. Now they are stripped of all that made them great and are left destitute and defenseless. They look with terror upon the destruction of the idols which they preferred before their Maker. They have sold their souls for earthly riches and enjoyments, and have not sought to become rich toward God. The result is, their lives are a failure; their pleasures are now turned to gall, their treasures to corruption. The gain of a lifetime is swept away in a moment. The rich bemoan the destruction of their grand houses, the scattering of their gold and silver. But their lamentations are silenced by the fear that they themselves are to perish with their idols.

The wicked are filled with regret, not because of their sinful neglect of God and their fellow men, but because God has conquered. They lament that the result is what it is; but they do not repent of their wickedness. They would leave no means untried to conquer if they could.

The world see the very class whom they have mocked and derided, and desired to exterminate, pass unharmed through pestilence, tempest, and earthquake. He who is to the transgressors of His law a devouring fire, is to His people a safe pavilion.

The minister who has sacrificed truth to gain the favor of men now discerns the character and influence of his teachings. It is apparent that the omniscient eye was following him as he stood in the desk, as he walked the streets, as he mingled with men in the various scenes of life. Every emotion of the soul, every line written, every word uttered, every act that led men to rest in a refuge of falsehood, has been scattering seed; and now, in the wretched, lost souls around him, he beholds the harvest. . . . Jeremiah 8:11; Ezekiel 13:22. . . . Jeremiah 23:1, 2; 25:34, 35. . . .

Ministers and people see that they have not sustained the right relation to God. They see that they have rebelled against the Author of all just and righteous law. The setting aside of the divine precepts gave rise to thousands of springs of evil, discord, hatred, iniquity, until the earth became one vast field of strife, one sink of corruption. This is the view that now appears to those who rejected truth and chose to cherish error. No language can express the longing which the disobedient and disloyal feel for that which they have lost forever— eternal life. Men whom the world has worshiped for their talents and eloquence now see these things in their true light. They realize what they have forfeited by transgression, and they fall at the feet of those whose fidelity they have despised and derided, and confess that God has loved them.

The people see that they have been deluded. They accuse one another of having led them to destruction; but all unite in heaping their bitterest condemnation upon the ministers. Unfaithful pastors have prophesied smooth things; they have led their hearers to make void the law of God and to persecute those who would keep it holy. Now, in their despair, these teachers confess before the world their work of deception. The multitudes are filled with fury. "We are lost!" they cry, "and you are the cause of our ruin;" and they turn upon the false shepherds. The very ones that once admired them most will pronounce the most dreadful curses upon them. The very hands that once crowned them with laurels will be raised for their destruction. The swords which were to slay God's people are now employed to destroy their enemies. Everywhere there is strife and bloodshed.

"A noise shall come even to the ends of the earth; for the Lord hath a controversy with the nations, He will plead with all flesh; He will give them that are wicked to the sword." Jeremiah 25:31. For six thousand years the great controversy has been in progress; the Son of God and His heavenly messengers have been in conflict with the power of the evil one, to warn, enlighten, and save the children of men. Now all have made their decisions; the wicked have fully united with Satan in his warfare against God. The time has come for God to vindicate the authority of His downtrodden law. Now the controversy is not alone with Satan, but with men. "The Lord hath a controversy with the nations;" "He will give them that are wicked to the sword."[5]

THE KINGS OF THE EAST

The water of the Euphrates is dried up "to prepare the way for the kings from the east" (Rev. 16:12).

Who are the kings from the east? The Greek phrase (*anatolēs hēliou*) literally means "from the rising of the sun." The word *anatolē* means "rising," "east," "orient."[6] The following facts are relevant to the phrase "kings from the east" in Revelation 16:12:

1. The Israelite wilderness sanctuary, the later Solomonic temple, and the temple of Ezekiel's vision all faced east (Exod. 38:13–15; 2 Chron. 29:4; Ezek. 11:1; 47:1, 8).
2. In the wilderness period the tribe of Judah, into which Jesus was born, encamped "on the east side toward the sunrise" (Num. 2:3).

3. Moses and Aaron, who were types of Christ, encamped "before the tabernacle on the east, before the tent of meeting toward the sunrise" (Num. 3:38).

4. Cyrus and the Medes and Persians were the literal kings from the east who conquered ancient Babylon in 539 BC. God used Cyrus to defeat Babylon "that men may know, from the rising of the sun and from the west, that there is none besides me; I am the LORD, and there is no other" (Isa. 45:6).

5. The Messiah symbolized by Cyrus is depicted as coming from the east and the north (Isa. 41:2, 25; 46:11; Ezek. 43:1–9).

6. The Septuagint uses *anatolē* to translate a Hebrew word that means "branch" (Hebrew *tsemach:* "the growing," "growth," "the sprout"; Zech. 3:9 [8], LXX; 6:12, LXX; Jer. 23:5, LXX). This translation may reflect the tradition that the Messiah would come (spring up, sprout) from the east. And Zechariah, the father of John the Baptist, spoke of "the tender mercy of our God, with which the Sunrise [*anatolē*] from on high will visit us" (Luke 1:78, NASB).

7. The "east wind" is depicted as destroying the wicked (Job 27:21; 38:24; Ps. 48:7; Isa. 27:8; Jer. 18:17; Ezek. 19:12; Hosea 13:15).

8. In the New Testament, the star seen by the wise men rose in the east (Matt. 2:2, 9); the sealing angel of Revelation 7:2 comes from the east, "the rising of the sun" (*anatolēs hēliou*); and Christ will come from the east (Matt. 24:27).

The major point is that usage of the word *east* in both the Old and the New Testaments suggests that Christ and His angels are "the kings from the east" (Rev. 16:12). They are the antitypical Cyrus and his Medes and Persians, and just as Cyrus and his forces overthrew Babylon and released the captive Jews, so Christ and His heavenly army will overthrow antitypical Babylon and release His captive people. (Cf. Rev. 17:14; 18:9, 17, 20, 21; 19:1–6.)

Ellen G. White speaks of Christ coming the second time from the east:

> Soon there appears in the east a small black cloud, about half the size of a man's hand. It is the cloud which surrounds the Saviour and which seems in the distance to be shrouded in darkness. The people of God know this to be the sign of the Son of Man. In solemn silence they gaze upon it as it draws nearer the earth, becoming lighter and more glorious, until it is a great white cloud, its base a glory like consuming fire, and above it the rainbow of the covenant. Jesus rides forth as a mighty conqueror.[7]

SIXTH PLAGUE AND SIXTH TRUMPET

The picture that has emerged from our study of the trumpets and plagues is that the trumpets picture Satan's work—his work both in the past (the historical fulfillment) and in the period following the end-time close of probation (the eschatological fulfillment). The plagues, on the other hand, represent what God does after the end-time close of probation to counteract Satan's efforts.

The angel who blows the sixth trumpet symbolically releases "the four angels who are bound at the great river Euphrates" (Rev. 9:14). These destroying angels (verse 15) represent the evil spirits who are responsible for inspiring the final attack on the professed people of God. Satan will lead evil spirits and lost, unsealed humans to join forces and attempt to destroy all the saints. They won't succeed in killing God's people, but their attack will result in the death of many professed Christians who didn't make the necessary spiritual preparation prior to the close of probation (Rev. 8:5; 9:15, 18).

The sixth plague is presented in only one verse: Revelation 16:12. The drying up of the river Euphrates is God's counteracting work, designed to protect His people from the fierce attack made by the combined forces of the demons and antitypical Babylon. Because of God's intervention, the peoples of earth will see through Babylon's claims and turn against their religious and political leaders. Their actions result in massive conflict among the ranks of lost humanity.

So, the sixth trumpet pictures the work of Babylon, while the sixth plague portrays the collapse of Babylon, which is brought about by God's intervention immediately before the Second Advent.

Revelation 16:13–16 parallels the sixth trumpet. These verses outline Satan's work of combining the forces of spiritualism, the papacy, and apostate Protestantism in preparation for the final clash with the forces of God. It is the drying up of the river Euphrates (verse 12) that frustrates Satan's plans. He will have successfully united the world under his banner in preparation for Armageddon (verse 16), but at the point of his greatest ascendancy, when it seems that he and his supporters (Babylon) are about to annihilate the true believers, God intervenes, metaphorically drying up the Euphrates. He makes it apparent to lost humanity that they have been victims of wholesale deception. Then the forces of evil, hopelessly divided, throw themselves into the battle of Armageddon (Rev. 16:16). This battle is the subject of the seventh trumpet and the seventh plague.

1. See Ulrike Unruh, "Daniel Five: Who Was Belshazzar?" in *Studies in the Book of Daniel,* http://dedication.www3.50megs.com/dan/belshazzar.html.

2. Aubrey de Sélincourt, trans., *Herodotus, the Histories* (Baltimore, MD: Penguin Books, 1954), 87–89.

3. Ibid., 87, 88.

4. Ibid., 90, 91.

5. White, *The Great Controversy*, 653–656.

6. Arndt and Gingrich, *A Greek-English Lexicon,* s.v. "ανατολή."

7. White, *The Great Controversy,* 640, 641; see also White, *Early Writings,* 15, 16; Ellen G. White, *Maranatha: The Lord Is Coming* (Washington, DC: Review and Herald®, 1976), 287.

CHAPTER 10

TIME NO LONGER

Revelation 10:1–11:14 is a parenthesis or interlude between the sixth and seventh trumpets. This passage explains for us the events that will occur between the sixth trumpet and the seventh, which announces that "the kingdom of the world has become the kingdom of our Lord and of his Christ, and he shall reign for ever and ever" (Rev. 11:15).

Revelation 10 says,

> Then I saw another mighty angel coming down from heaven, wrapped in a cloud, with a rainbow over his head, and his face was like the sun, and his legs like pillars of fire. He had a little scroll open in his hand. And he set his right foot on the sea, and his left foot on the land, and called out with a loud voice, like a lion roaring; when he called out, the seven thunders sounded. And when the seven thunders had sounded, I was about to write, but I heard a voice from heaven saying, "Seal up what the seven thunders have said, and do not write it down." And the angel who I saw standing on sea and land lifted up his right hand to heaven and swore by him

who lives for ever and ever, who created heaven and what is in it, the earth and what is in it, and the sea and what is in it, that there should be no more delay, but that in the days of the trumpet call to be sounded by the seventh angel, the mystery of God, as he announced to his servants the prophets, should be fulfilled.

Then the voice which I had heard from heaven spoke to me again saying, "Go, take the scroll which is open in the hand of the angel who is standing on the sea and on the land." So I went to the angel and told him to give me the little scroll; and he said to me, "Take it and eat; it will be bitter to your stomach, but sweet as honey in your mouth." And I took the little scroll from the hand of the angel and ate it; it was sweet as honey in my mouth, but when I had eaten it my stomach was made bitter. And I was told, "You must again prophesy about many peoples and nations and tongues and kings" (Rev. 10:1–11).

HISTORY REPEATED

Like the six trumpets that we have already examined, Revelation 10 has a dual application. And the close of probation, as depicted in Revelation 8:5, happens twice too—first for ancient Israel in AD 34, and again, universally this time, shortly before the coming of Jesus. Hence, the trumpets have both a historical and an end-time application. History will be repeated. What has happened in the past provides a typological forecast of what will happen after the close of probation.

Considered historically, Revelation 10:1–11 is a forecast of the events that were to occur between the end of the sixth trumpet, on August 11, 1840, when the Ottoman Empire became dependent on the great powers of Europe, and the great disappointment the Millerite Adventists suffered on October 22, 1844. Considered eschatologically, this passage provides a preview of Christ's intervention when Satan, his demons, and the hosts of human beings who align themselves with them begin their final, great attack upon Christ's beleaguered people.

We will first consider the historical application of these verses, and then we'll outline, as far as possible, the eschatological application.

JESUS AND THE SCROLL

"Then I saw another mighty angel coming down from heaven" (Rev. 10:1). The evidence reveals that this angel is Christ. He is sometimes referred to in Scripture as an angel. Jacob spoke of God as "the angel who has redeemed me from all evil" (Gen. 48:16). "The angel of the Lord" who appeared to Moses in the burning bush was none other than God Himself (Exod. 3:2–6; cf. Acts 7:30–33; Exod. 14:19; 23:20–24; 1 Cor. 10:4; Judg. 2:1–4; 6:11–24).

John writes that the angel was "wrapped in a cloud" (Rev. 10:1). In Scripture, the Lord is often depicted as surrounded by a cloud (Exod. 16:10; 19:9; Lev. 16:2; Ezek. 1:4, 28; Dan. 7:13; Matt. 17:5; Acts 1:9; 1 Cor. 10:1–4; Rev. 1:7; 14:14–16). Just as "one like a son of man" (Dan. 7:13) came "with the clouds of heaven" to the Father as the Advocate in the pre-Advent judgment, so the same Christ is depicted by John as the source of the message that between 1840 and 1844 announced the commencement of that judgment. This point will become clearer as we proceed.

This angel has "a rainbow over his head" (Rev. 10:1). The rainbow is a symbol that never again will there be a universal flood (Gen. 9:13–16). The rainbow is a sign of God's everlasting covenant with His believing people (cf. Isa. 54:9, 10). Ezekiel saw a rainbow surrounding the throne of God: "Like the appearance of the bow that is in the cloud on the day of rain, so was the appearance of the brightness round about" (Ezek. 1:28). And in an earlier vision, John had seen "a rainbow that looked like an emerald" (Rev. 4:3) surrounding God's throne.

Ellen White wrote,

> The rainbow spanning the heavens with its arch of light is a token of "the everlasting covenant between God and every living creature." Genesis 9:16. And the rainbow encircling the throne on high is also a token to God's children of His covenant of peace.
>
> As the bow in the cloud results from the union of sunshine and shower, so the bow above God's throne represents the union of His mercy and His justice. To the sinful but repentant soul God says, Live thou; "I have found a ransom." Job 33:24.[1]

"And his face was like the sun" (Rev. 10:1). The appearance of the Deity is often associated with the glory of the sun. For example, "The LORD God is a sun and a shield" (Ps. 84:11). "The sun shall be no more your light by day, nor for brightness shall the moon give light to you by night; but the LORD will be your everlasting light, and your God will be your glory" (Isa. 60:19; cf. Rev. 21:23; 22:5). "For you who fear my name the sun of righteousness shall rise, with healing in its wings" (Mal. 4:2). "And he [Jesus] was transfigured before them, and his face shone like the sun, and his garments became white as light" (Matt. 17:2). Paul saw "a light from heaven, brighter than the sun" (Acts 26:13). When Christ first appeared to John on Patmos, "his face was like the sun shining in full strength" (Rev. 1:16).

The evidence indicates that Christ is the One whose face shines like the sun, which is a symbol of His perfect righteousness. "God makes His sun to shine on the just and on the unjust, and this sun represents Christ, the Sun of Righteousness, who shines as the light of the world, giving His blessings and mercies, seen and unseen, to rich and poor alike."[2]

"And his legs like pillars of fire" (Rev. 10:1). The Greek word translated "legs" in the Revised Standard Version is *podes,* the plural of *pous,* which may mean "foot" or "leg." The depiction reminds us of what Christ looked like when He first revealed Himself to John on Patmos. "His feet were like burnished bronze, refined as in a furnace" (Rev. 1:15; cf. 2:18).

Because of the similarity of the descriptions in Daniel and Revelation, we can assume that it was Christ who appeared to Daniel when he was standing on the bank of the Tigris:

> I lifted up my eyes and looked, and behold, a man clothed in linen, whose loins were girded with gold of Uphaz. His body was like beryl, his face like the appearance of lightning, his eyes like flaming torches, *his arms and legs like the gleam of burnished bronze,* and the sound of his words like the noise of a multitude (Dan. 10:5, 6; italics added).

> The mighty angel who instructed John was no less a personage than Jesus Christ. Setting His right foot on the sea, and His left upon the dry land, shows the part which He is acting in the closing scenes of the great controversy with Satan. This position denotes His supreme power and authority over the whole earth.[3]

"He had a little scroll open in his hand" (Rev. 10:2). The Greek word translated "little scroll" is *biblaridion*. This is a diminutive of *biblos,* which means "book," or of *biblion,* which means "book" or "scroll." Ranko Stefanovic comments:

> A careful analysis of *biblos, biblion,* and *biblaridion* in Revelation shows that John the revelator does not have a consistent pattern in using these words. For instance, in Revelation 20 *biblos* and *biblion* are used interchangeably for the book of life; in 20:12 it is the *biblion* of life (cf. 13:8; 17:8; 21:27), but in 20:15 it is the *biblos* of life (cf. 3:5). Especially interesting is that in Revelation 10:2 the little scroll is called *biblaridion,* and in verse 8 it is called *biblion.* This shows clearly that in Revelation there is no consistent or purposeful use of one or the other form of the word for the scroll.[4]

The book has been opened and now stands open (*ēneōgménon,* a perfect passive participle of *anoigō*). This would imply that the book had been closed (not understood), but now its message is to be revealed. Bible prophecy refers to two books that originally were sealed but that later were to be understood. The first was the book of Daniel. God instructed Daniel: "But you, Daniel, shut up the words, and seal the book, until the time of the end" (Dan. 12:4). According to the following verses, the time of the end was to begin at the conclusion of "a time, two times, and half a time" (Dan. 12:7). The passage implies that the part of the book of Daniel that concerns the end time would be sealed until "the time of the end." The "time, two times, and half a time" refer to the 1,260 years of papal ecclesiastical supremacy that began in AD 538 and extended until 1798.

Hence, from 1798 on, we would expect to see an increase in people's understanding of the end-time prophecies of the book of Daniel. This is precisely what took place. People's understanding of Daniel's prophecies increased greatly after that year; and the growth in their understanding was particularly apparent between 1840 and 1844. William Miller and his associates interpreted the 2,300 day/year prophecy of Daniel 8:14 correctly regarding the time spans involved (primarily, 457 BC to AD 1844). Their principles of interpretation were correct—what they mistook was the event that was to take place at the end of the 2,300 years.

Understanding Jesus' ministry in the sanctuary in heaven is the key to understanding the book of Daniel. That wasn't fully grasped until after 1844. In fact, we are yet to see all that this prophetic book has to tell us. In other words, the unsealing of the book of Daniel wasn't a one-time operation. It was a process that began after 1798, was given great impetus after 1844, and still goes on today.

The other book (scroll, actually) that was sealed and is not to be understood until it is unsealed is the scroll of Revelation 5. Since it is a scroll and it has been sealed with seven seals, its contents cannot be known until the breaking of the seventh seal at the second coming of Jesus (Rev. 8:1). This scroll isn't about the events that occur at the breaking of each seal. Those are historical events that occur prior to the coming of Jesus. When Jesus returns, the seventh seal will be broken and the contents of the scroll will become known. (We'll discuss the relationship between this scroll and the message of Revelation 10 when we consider the eschatological application of this chapter.)

"And he set his right foot on the sea, and his left foot on the land" (Rev. 10:2). The vision dramatizes the universal sovereignty of the Lord Jesus Christ. Because of Calvary, Jesus has wrested from Satan the rulership that he has claimed. Satan is no longer "the prince of this world" (John 12:31, KJV; 14:30; 16:11). Instead, Jesus is "the

Prince of life, whom God hath raised from the dead" (Acts 3:15, KJV). He is "a Prince and a Saviour, for to give repentance to Israel, and forgiveness of sins" (Acts 5:31, KJV). He is "the prince of the kings of the earth" (Rev. 1:5, KJV) who has "the keys of Death and Hades" (Rev. 1:18). He is "King of kings and Lord of lords" (Rev. 19:16). His placement of "his right foot on the sea, and his left foot on the land" demonstrates the universal nature of His dominion.

Moreover, the symbolism suggests the worldwide extent of the message He is about to proclaim. "The angel's position, with one foot on the sea, the other on the land, signifies the wide extent of the proclamation of the message. It will cross the broad waters and be proclaimed in other countries, even to all the world."[5]

TIME SHALL BE NO LONGER

> And [he] called out with a loud voice, like a lion roaring; when he called out, the seven thunders sounded. And when the seven thunders had sounded, I was about to write, but I heard a voice from heaven saying, "Seal up what the seven thunders have said, and do not write it down" (Rev. 10:3, 4).

"Loud" or "great" voices are frequently heard in the book of Revelation (Rev. 1:10; 5:2, 12; 6:10; 7:2, 10). God intends the message to be heard. Christ is the "Lion of the tribe of Judah" (Rev. 5:5); hence, He proclaims His message in lionlike tones.

But the message of the "seven thunders" was not to be immediately promulgated. John heard what the thunders had to say, but he was instructed not to record it. When God thunders from heaven, He does so to intervene on behalf of His people or to proclaim a special message for His people (1 Sam. 2:10; 7:10; 2 Sam. 22:14; Job

26:14; 37:4, 5; 40:9; Ps. 18:13; Isa. 29:5, 6). The thunders in Revelation sometimes represent the voice of God and sometimes the voices of angels or of redeemed human beings (Rev. 4:5; 6:1; 8:5; 11:19; 14:2; 16:18; 19:6). We can deduce the message of the seven thunders of Revelation 10:3, 4 only in the context of the rest of the chapter.

> The angel whom I saw standing upon the sea and upon the earth raised his right hand to heaven and swore by the One who lives for ever and ever, who created the heaven and the things in it, and the earth and the things in it, and the sea and the things in it, that there shall be time no longer. But in the days of the voice of the seventh angel, when he should be about to blow the trumpet, then the mystery of God was finished as He preached [announced] to His servants the prophets (Rev. 10:5–7).[6]

The proclamation is Christ's. The authority of His oath is based on the everlasting nature of the Deity and on the fact that He is the Creator of all things. Translated literally, the announcement says "time no longer shall be" or "there shall be time no longer" (Rev. 10:6). The Greek language has two words for "time." The word used here is *chronos,* which means "*time, mostly in the sense of a period of time . . . a long time.*" [7] The other Greek word for time is *kairos,* which means "*time, i.e. point of time as well as period of time.*"[8]

The proclamation reminds us of the cry of the dead martyrs recorded in Revelation 6:9–11. Their blood cries out from the grave as did that of Abel (Gen. 4:10), "O Sovereign Lord, holy and true, how long before thou wilt judge and avenge our blood on those who dwell upon the earth?" (Rev. 6:10). The answer comes from the Lord. "They were each given a white robe, and it was said to them that they should rest yet a little time [*chronon*] until their fellow servants and their brethren who are about to be killed as they were might be made complete."[9]

Revelation 10:6, 7 proclaims that the little time of waiting has expired, and no more time shall elapse before the righteous dead are judged and vindicated. When the seventh angel blows his trumpet, "the kingdom of the world" becomes "the kingdom of our Lord and of his Christ" (Rev. 11:15). "The nations raged, but thy wrath came, and the time for the dead to be judged, for rewarding thy servants, the prophets and saints, and those who fear thy name, both small and great" (verse 18).

According to Daniel 7, Christ receives His kingdom in the pre-Advent judgment (verses 9–14). In this judgment the Son of man is "given dominion and glory and kingdom, that all peoples, nations, and languages should serve him; his dominion is an everlasting dominion, which shall not pass away, and his kingdom one that shall not be destroyed" (Dan. 7:14). In this judgment, "the kingdom and the dominion and the greatness of the kingdoms under the whole heaven shall be given to the people of the saints of the Most High; their kingdom shall be an everlasting kingdom, and all dominions shall serve and obey them" (verse 27; see also verse 22). Hence, in effect, prophetic time ceases when the pre-Advent judgment commences. Then Christ receives His kingdom in the sense that the heavenly judgment decides who are eternally His and who will be eternally lost.

The next chapter of Daniel informs us when the pre-Advent judgment began. Daniel 8:14 is parallel to Daniel 7:9–14. The 2,300 days/years began at the same time as the seventy weeks of years (490 years) of Daniel 9:24: "From the going forth of the commandment to restore and to build Jerusalem . . ." (verse 25, KJV). Ezra 6:14

indicates that God's commandment for the rebuilding of Jerusalem, the restoration of the temple and its services, and the reestablishment of the Jewish state was put into effect by the decrees of three Persian monarchs: Cyrus, Darius, and Artaxerxes. Cyrus's decree for the return of the Jews was probably made in 537 BC. That of Darius I was passed about 519 or 518 BC. The decree of Artaxerxes I Longimanus went into effect in the autumn of 457 BC.[10]

Since God's command for the rebuilding of Jerusalem and the restoration of the ancient Israelite state was put into operation by three human decrees, we must use the third date, 457 BC. Twenty-three hundred years from 457 BC brings us to 1844. Since the decree of Artaxerxes was put into effect in the autumn of 457 BC, it follows that the cleansing of the sanctuary, the heavenly pre-Advent judgment spoken of in Daniel 8:14, began 2,300 years later, in the autumn of 1844. None of the time prophecies of Scripture extend beyond that date. So, prophetic time ended in 1844, and Revelation 10:6, 7 was fulfilled.[11]

Interpreting the prophecy historically, Ellen White wrote:

> This time, which the angel declares with a solemn oath, is not the end of this world's history, neither of probationary time, but of prophetic time, which should precede the advent of our Lord. That is, the people will not have another message upon definite time. After this period of time, reaching from 1842 to 1844, there can be no definite tracing of the prophetic time. The longest reckoning reaches to the autumn of 1844.[12]

> There will never again be a message for the people of God that will be based on time. We are not to know the definite

time either for the outpouring of the Holy Spirit or for the coming of Christ.[13]

THE MYSTERY OF GOD

"But in the days of the voice of the seventh angel, when he should be about to blow the trumpet, then the mystery of God was finished as He preached [announced] to His servants the prophets" (Rev. 10:5–7).[14] H. B. Swete comments:

> "So far from further delays supervening, as soon as the days of the Seventh Trumpet have come, at the moment when the Seventh Angel is about to blow, then . . . the secret of God is finished." The clause as a whole corrects the impression that χρονος ουκετι εσται [chronos ouketi estai] implies an immediate end.[15]

What is "the mystery of God"? In the Gospels, the mysteries of the kingdom of heaven are the spiritual truths that Jesus gave to those who believed in Him but withheld from those who refused to believe (Matt. 13:11; Mark 4:11, 12; Luke 8:10).

In the epistles of Paul, the mystery of the gospel is the message of salvation by faith in Christ for those who believe in Him as Savior and Lord. This mystery is a revelation to those who believe. It was, indeed, a mystery for ages, not in the sense that Old Testament people couldn't be saved, but in the sense that the greater light revealed by the life and death of Christ amounted to a blaze of divine glory by comparison with the partial revelation of God in the Old Testament era.[16]

The mystery of God is completed in the pre-Advent judgment in the sense that this event decides who shall be saved and who will be lost. In a very personal, individual sense, the mystery of God is revealed for each individual as the heavenly court (Dan. 7:9–14) decides who has received the righteousness of Christ and who has not.

BITTER IN THE STOMACH

> Then the voice which I had heard from heaven spoke to me again saying, "Go, take the scroll which is open in the hand of the angel who is standing on the sea and on the land." So I went to the angel and told him to give me the little scroll; and he said to me, "Take it and eat; it will be bitter to your stomach, but sweet as honey in your mouth." And I took the little scroll from the hand of the angel and ate it; it was sweet as honey in my mouth, but when I had eaten it my stomach was made bitter (Rev. 10:8–10).

The word of the Lord is sweet to the believer. "How sweet are thy words to my taste, sweeter than honey to my mouth!" (Ps. 119:103). Jeremiah testified to the fact: "Thy words were found, and I ate them, and thy words became to me a joy and the delight of my heart; for I am called by thy name, O LORD, God of hosts" (Jer. 15:16). But the people to whom Jeremiah preached refused the word of the Lord, and the sweetness of his initial experience was made bitter (Jer. 15:17–21).

The sweet experience of receiving the Word of God may, at times, result in bitterness. Ezekiel 2:8–3:21 pictures God giving Ezekiel a scroll and telling him to eat it. He was to digest the message of the scroll. Ezekiel obeyed. He testified: "Then I ate it; and it was in my mouth as sweet as honey" (Ezek. 3:3). God instructed Ezekiel to speak His words to the house of Israel (verse 4). This was the source of a bitter experience. The people weren't willing to listen; they despised

God's message. The joy Ezekiel had in absorbing the words of God was turned to gall as he tried to impart the message.

John's taking the scroll and eating it represents the new understandings of the book of Daniel that were revealed to God's people between 1798 and 1844.[17] The meaning of this previously closed book was especially clarified between 1831 and 1844. During this period, though the Millerites didn't understand the message of the heavenly sanctuary and that its cleansing was to begin in 1844, they were interpreting the time prophecies accurately.

The new understanding of Daniel was exciting, and the Millerites looked forward with joyous expectancy to the coming of the Lord in 1844. The message of Christ's advent was wonderfully sweet. What a disappointment ensued! It is hard to imagine the sorrow that swept over their souls as October 22, 1844, passed, and Christ had not come.

No one who attended these meetings [the Millerite meetings] can ever forget those scenes of deepest interest.

Those who sincerely love Jesus can appreciate the feelings of those who watched with the most intense longing for the coming of their Saviour. The point of expectation was nearing. The time when we hoped to meet Him was close at hand. We approached this hour with calm solemnity. The true believers rested in a sweet communion with God—an earnest of the peace that was to be theirs in the bright hereafter. None who experienced this hope and trust can ever forget those precious hours of waiting.

Worldly business was for the most part laid aside for a few weeks. We carefully examined every thought and emotion of our hearts, as if upon our deathbeds, and in a few hours to close our eyes forever upon earthly scenes. There was no making of "ascension robes" for the great event; we felt the need of internal evidence that we were prepared to meet Christ, and our white robes were purity of soul, character cleansed from sin by the atoning blood of our Saviour.

But the time of expectation passed. This was the first close test brought to bear upon those who believed and hoped that Jesus would come in the clouds of heaven. The disappointment of God's waiting people was great. The scoffers were triumphant, and won the weak and cowardly to their ranks. Some who had appeared to possess true faith seemed to have been influenced only by fear; and now their courage returned with the passing of the time, and they boldly united with the scoffers, declaring that they had never been duped to really believe the doctrine of Miller, who was a mad fanatic. Others, naturally yielding or vacillating, quietly deserted the cause.

We were perplexed and disappointed, yet did not renounce our faith.[18]

The comprehension of truth, the glad reception of the message, is represented in the eating of the little book. The truth in regard to the time of the advent of our Lord was a precious message to our souls.[19]

Since the book of Daniel was not really digested by God's people until after the disappointment of 1844,[20] the bittersweet experience of the prophet would also seem to symbolize the joy and then sorrow that come to God's servants who, like Ezekiel, gladly receive the truth themselves and then attempt to present it to an unbelieving world. The sweetness of the scroll may be seen as a symbol of the joyous reception of the message and the thrill of seeing others accept it too.

The bitterness may be seen as the sorrow and heartache suffered by the messenger whose message is rejected. The knowledge of the pre-Advent judgment as presented in Daniel and Revelation is a source of great joy to the one who believes, but it is also, to the believer, a source of genuine concern and sorrow in view of other people's rejection of God's forgiveness, cleansing, and vindication.

The bittersweet experience of John was also a symbol of the spiritual trial through which God's people must pass during the pre-Advent judgment (1844 to the end), so that their lives may be brought into harmony with God's will.[21]

THE SEVEN THUNDERS

The seven thunders revealed the bittersweet experience through which God's people were to pass between 1840 and 1844. Revealing ahead of time the events to occur would destroy the effectiveness of the test that God had designed for them. God gave to the Millerites great truth about the teachings of the book of Daniel, but He withheld the truth about the heavenly sanctuary and its cleansing. This enabled Him to test the sincerity of those who were professing to believe the Bible message—that's why God told John not to write down the words of the seven thunders.

> After these seven thunders uttered their voices, the injunction comes to John as to Daniel in regard to the little book: "Seal up those things which the seven thunders uttered." These relate to future events which will be disclosed in their order. Daniel shall stand in his lot at the end of the days. John sees the little book unsealed. Then Daniel's prophecies have their proper place in the first, second, and third angels' message to be given to the world. The unsealing of the

little book was the message in relation to time.

The books of Daniel and the Revelation are one. One is a prophecy, the other a revelation; one a book sealed, the other a book opened. John heard the mysteries which the thunders uttered, but he was commanded not to write them.

The special light given to John which was expressed in the seven thunders was a delineation of events which would transpire under the first and second angels' messages. It was not best for the people to know these things, for their faith must necessarily be tested. In the order of God, most wonderful and advanced truths would be proclaimed. The first and second angels' messages were to be proclaimed, but no further light was to be revealed before these messages had done their specific work. This is represented by the angel standing with one foot on the sea, proclaiming with a most solemn oath that time should be no longer.[22]

"And I was told, 'You must again prophesy about many peoples and nations and tongues and kings' " (Rev. 10:11).

After the sweet-bitter experience involved in the great disappointment of 1844, God's faithful people were given a special commission. This was, in effect, a repetition of the Great Commission Jesus gave His disciples before His ascension (Matt. 28:19, 20). Once again God's people were to harness their spiritual resources by total dependence upon Christ's power and take the message of salvation to the world. With a new understanding of Daniel 8:14 and the cleansing of the heavenly sanctuary, they were empowered to proclaim the positive message of the pre-Advent judgment and the soon coming of Jesus.

Were God's people to prophesy "*before* many peoples, and nations, and tongues, and kings" (Rev. 10:11; italics added), as the King James

Version puts it, or *about* them, as the Revised Standard Version has it? Or is it both? The answer hinges on the meaning of the Greek preposition *epi.* Greek prepositions can mean different things in different contexts. Followed by the dative, for instance, *epi* may mean "on," "in," "above," "upon," "against," "at," "near," "by," "over," "to," or "in addition to."[23] Greek grammarians indicate that *epi* followed by the dative may also mean either "before" or "about."[24]

After 1844, God's people were instructed to "prophesy" both "before" and "about" peoples and nations. An expanded work is yet to be done. The gospel of salvation must go to the whole world before Jesus can come. "This gospel of the kingdom will be preached throughout the whole world, as a testimony to all nations; and then the end will come" (Matt. 24:14).

> The people whom God has made the depositaries of His law are not to permit their light to be hidden. The truth must be proclaimed in the dark places of the earth. Obstacles must be met and surmounted. A great work is to be done, and this work has been entrusted to those who know the truth.[25]

> A great work is to be done, and those who know the truth should make mighty intercession for help. The love of Christ must fill their own hearts. The Spirit of Christ must be poured out upon them, and they must be making ready to stand in the judgment. As they consecrate themselves to God, a convincing power will attend their efforts to present the truth to others. We must no longer sleep on Satan's enchanted ground, but call into requisition all our resources, availing ourselves of every facility with which Providence has furnished us. The last warning is to be proclaimed before

"many peoples, and nations, and tongues, and kings," and the promise is given, "Lo, I am with you alway, even unto the end of the world." Revelation 10:11; Matt. 28:20.[26]

End-time interpretation

As we have seen, the sixth plague will be the drying up of the river Euphrates (Rev. 16:12); literally, the withdrawal by multitudes of people of their support for Babylon. But they recognize too late that they have been misled by their preachers and teachers of religion, and they react in anger at the deception that has been imposed upon them.

This drying up of the river will come at the end of the final great attack upon the people of God by those who have aligned themselves with Satan and Babylon (Rev. 9:13–21; 16:13–16). At earth's darkest midnight, when it appears to God's people that they are about to be wiped out by their persecutors, Jesus intervenes on their behalf. He is the "mighty angel coming down from heaven, wrapped in a cloud, with a rainbow over his head, and his face . . . like the sun, and his legs like pillars of fire" (Rev. 10:1).

This depiction of Christ with "his right foot on the sea, and his left foot on the land" symbolizes His intervention on behalf of His people in 1844. The righteous dead had been crying out for judgment and vindication (Rev. 6:9–11). Then the judgment began, and "the time for the dead to be judged" (Rev. 11:18). But Christ's intervention in 1844 was a type or example of His ultimate intervention for His persecuted people shortly before His second advent. The righteous dead were told to rest "yet a little time, until their fellow servants and their brethren who were about to be killed as they were might be made complete" (Rev. 6:11, my translation).

The making complete or spiritually victorious of the living believers occupies the period from the beginning of the judgment to Christ's intervention on behalf of believers after the close of probation. Before the close of probation, God's people are given victory over sin (Rev. 22:11; 1 Cor. 1:8; 1 Thess. 3:11–13; 2 Pet. 3:14), but after the close of probation God allows them to pass through a time of terrible trouble to purge their dross and purify their gold.

Jacob's history is also an assurance that God will not cast off those who have been deceived and tempted and betrayed into sin, but who have returned unto Him with true repentance. While Satan seeks to destroy this class, God will send His angels to comfort and protect them in the time of peril. The assaults of Satan are fierce and determined, his delusions are terrible; but the Lord's eye is upon His people, and His ear listens to their cries. Their affliction is great, the flames of the furnace seem about to consume them; but the Refiner will bring them forth as gold tried in the fire. God's love for His children during the period of their severest trial is as strong and tender as in the days of their sunniest prosperity; but it is needful for them to be placed in the furnace of fire; their earthliness must be consumed, that the image of Christ may be perfectly reflected.[27]

When this purifying work is complete, then Christ intervenes to deliver His suffering people. This intervention is symbolized in Revelation 10:1 by the mighty angel who comes down from heaven. Christ is that mighty Angel, and when the situation of His people is the most desperate, He demonstrates that He is the world's Sovereign who will bring them relief, protection, and reassurance.

With shouts of triumph, jeering, and imprecation, throngs

of evil men are about to rush upon their prey, when, lo, a dense blackness, deeper than the darkness of the night, falls upon the earth. Then a rainbow, shining with the glory from the throne of God, spans the heavens and seems to encircle each praying company. The angry multitudes are suddenly arrested. Their mocking cries die away. The objects of their murderous rage are forgotten. With fearful forebodings they gaze upon the symbol of God's covenant and long to be shielded from its overpowering brightness.

By the people of God a voice, clear and melodious, is heard, saying, "Look up," and lifting their eyes to the heavens, they behold the bow of promise. The black, angry clouds that covered the firmament are parted, and like Stephen they look up steadfastly into heaven and see the glory of God and the Son of man seated upon His throne. In His divine form they discern the marks of His humiliation; and from His lips they hear the request presented before His Father and the holy angels: "I will that they also, whom Thou hast given Me, be with Me where I am." John 17:24. Again a voice, musical and triumphant, is heard, saying: "They come! they come! holy, harmless, and undefiled. They have kept the word of My patience; they shall walk among the angels;" and the pale quivering lips of those who have held fast their faith utter a shout of victory.

It is at midnight that God manifests His power for the deliverance of His people. The sun appears, shining in its strength. Signs and wonders follow in quick succession. The wicked look with terror and amazement upon the scene, while the righteous behold with solemn joy the tokens of their deliverance.[28]

According to my very literal translation of Revelation 10:2, Christ holds in His hand a little scroll that "has been opened and is standing open." As we have observed, Bible prophecy mentions two books that at first were sealed but later were to be understood. The first is the book of Daniel, which we have already discussed. The second is the scroll of Revelation 5. This scroll is sealed with seven seals, the seventh of which cannot be broken until the coming of Christ (Rev. 8:1). Hence, the content of the book cannot be known until the book is opened at the Second Advent.

This book records the verdict of the heavenly court regarding who is to be saved and who lost.[29] Revelation 4 and 5 portray a pre-Advent judgment scene that is parallel to the one in Daniel 7:9–14. Revelation 5:4 tells us that John wept because no one was qualified to open this book. Then he was told that the Lamb could break the seals and open the book because He "has conquered" (verse 5). He is worthy to open the book because He "was slain" and by His blood He ransomed "men for God from every tribe and tongue and people and nation" (verse 9).

If the little book of Revelation 10:2 is the book of Revelation 5, how can it be represented as open prior to the coming of Christ spoken of in Revelation 8:1?

The point is that the book is open *in Christ's hand*. Probation has closed (Rev. 8:5), and *Christ* knows who is saved and who is lost. John, as the representative of God's people, doesn't understand the book's contents until he takes it from the hand of Christ and eats it (Rev. 10:8–10). He isn't told to do this until he has heard the proclamation that is to be made at the beginning of the seventh trumpet: "There should be time no longer" (Rev. 10:6). Just as the book of Daniel was partially understood prior to 1844, but not fully understood until after that date, so the contents of the book of Revelation 5 are partially grasped prior to the Second Advent, but not fully realized until that event. The seven last plagues reveal in part the verdict of the heavenly court because the lost suffer the plagues, while the saved do not. But not until Jesus actually comes to reign is the verdict fully known.

REVELATION 10

The message of Revelation 10, like that of the trumpets generally, has a historical and an eschatological application. The events immediately prior to and just after 1844 are types of the end-time events immediately prior to and associated with the second coming of Jesus. Moreover, since the book of Daniel was unsealed by the understanding and proclamation of the three angels' messages, it was the breaking of the seals of the Revelation 5 book that unsealed the book of Daniel. This is so because the first three seals (Rev. 6:1–6) parallel the three angels' messages of Revelation 14:6–12. The contents of the seals (Rev. 6) explain the contents of the book of Daniel.

The breaking of John's seven seals (Rev. 5:1–8:1) is the fulfillment of the end-time message of the book of Daniel. The revealing of the contents of the Revelation 5 book is possible only when the end-time events predicted by Daniel and John are fulfilled. At the beginning of the pre-Advent judgment in 1844 (Dan. 7:9–14; Rev. 4; 5), the end-time message of the book of Daniel was understood as never before. This is represented in Revelation 10:8–10 by John's eating the little book. In that sense, the little book open in the hand of Christ (Rev. 10:2) represents the book of Daniel.

At the end of the pre-Advent judgment, probation will close (Rev. 8:2–5), and the verdict of the heavenly court (the contents of the Revelation 5 book) will be partially known when the wicked suffer the seven last plagues (Rev. 16). The book open in the hand of Christ also represents this verdict of the heavenly court, which is fully known to the universe and after probation's close becomes increasingly apparent to the peoples of earth. The events surrounding the Second Advent will fully reveal to humankind the contents of the little book. This revelation is also represented by John's taking the book from Christ's hand and eating it.

There is a close relationship between the book of Daniel and the scroll of Revelation 5. The portion of Daniel sealed and not fully understood until after 1844 concerned the pre-Advent judgment, a court session designed to determine who is to be saved and who will be lost. The scroll of Revelation 5 reveals the verdict of that judgment and therefore contains the record of who is to be saved and who will be lost. Hence, it isn't unreasonable to conclude that the scroll of Revelation 10:2 represents both the book of Daniel and the scroll of Revelation 5.

In summary, we can say that the scroll of Revelation 10:2 represents (1) the pre-Advent judgment message of the book of Daniel; and (2) the verdict of the pre-Advent judgment for both saved and lost as contained in the Revelation 5 scroll. After 1798, and especially after 1844, people's understanding of Daniel's message about the heavenly court began to grow. The verdict of the heavenly court will become increasingly known after the close of probation and will become fully known at the second coming of Jesus.

"When he called out, the seven thunders sounded" (Rev. 10:3). Between the end of the historical sixth trumpet in 1840 and 1844 (Rev. 9:13–21), God's people passed through a bittersweet experience that they were not to know about ahead of time. This was a terrible time of testing. Similarly, in the period just prior to and during the beginning of Christ's intervening on their behalf, God's end-time people will endure a terrible test. They will be hunted and haunted by evil demons and malicious human beings who are bent upon their destruction. No one can anticipate the intensity of the suffering involved, and it has not been revealed ahead of time. John was told not to write what the thunders proclaimed.

But Christ will interpose. There is both great bitterness and sweetness in the experience. The suffering prior to His intervention will be terrible, but when He manifests His power on behalf of God's people, the sweetness of the event will be tarnished by the bitterness of seeing multitudes, including some of their loved ones and friends, fleeing in terror from the heavenly "signs and wonders" that "follow in quick succession."[30] There can be no unmitigated joy for the believers while they see "that everything in nature seems turned out of its course."[31] But by faith they will look up to their Redeemer and praise Him for His merciful solicitude on their behalf.

"THERE SHALL BE TIME NO LONGER"

The blood of the martyrs cries out from their graves: "O Sovereign Lord, holy and true, how long before thou wilt judge and avenge our blood on those who dwell upon the earth?" (Rev. 6:10). "Then they were each given a white robe, and it was said to them that they should rest yet a little time, until their fellow servants and their brethren who are about to be killed as they were might be made complete" (verse 11).

The waiting for judgment and vindication ended when the 1844 pre-Advent judgment began. The righteous dead were given white robes at that time in the sense that they were vindicated in that judgment. But they continue to rest until their living brothers and sisters who are under attack have been made complete in Christ. That won't happen until Christ intervenes on behalf of those suffering the final attack Satan and the wicked make upon them. Only then will it be true that the righteous dead need wait no longer.

Eschatologically, the proclamation of "time no longer" refers to Christ's announcement immediately prior to His advent. Applying the announcement historically, Ellen White wrote that "the time which the angel declares with a solemn oath is not the end of this world's history, neither of probationary time, but of prophetic time, which should precede the advent of our Lord."[32]   Since this statement is made in the context of a discussion that applies the message of Revelation 10 to the events surrounding 1844, it fits. In that context, the proclamation of "time no longer" doesn't refer to the end of human history but to the end of *prophetic* time. Even so, this application doesn't rule out the possibility of a secondary, eschatological application of the prophecy. Such an eschatological application in no way contradicts Ellen White's statement that the proclamation in 1844 of "time no longer" didn't refer to the end of human history.

Revelation 10:7 makes it clear that the proclamation of "time no longer" occurs "in the days of the trumpet call to be sounded by the seventh angel." When the seventh angel blows his trumpet, the announcement is made that "the kingdom of the world has become the kingdom of our Lord and of his Christ, and he shall reign for ever and ever" (Rev. 11:15). Then the twenty-four elders who are in the presence of God fall down and worship him, saying, "We give thanks to thee, Lord God Almighty, who art and who wast, that thou hast taken thy great power and begun to reign" (verse 17). Thus, the proclamation of "time no longer" clearly means that Christ's eternal reign has begun. The righteous dead and the persecuted living need wait no longer. Christ has now intervened to exert His authority over the entire world as "King of kings, and Lord of lords" (Rev. 19:16).

Furthermore, when the proclamation of "time no longer" is made, "the mystery of God as he announced to his servants the prophets, should be fulfilled" (Rev. 10:7). As we have pointed out above, the mystery of God is the message and experience of salvation through Christ. In a very real sense, this mystery is fulfilled for believers who are vindicated in the pre-Advent judgment. It won't reach its ultimate fulfillment until Christ declares His power from above when He intervenes to turn the captivity of His people. Then the wait for ultimate redemption is over, and the time has come "for rewarding thy servants, the prophets and saints, and those who fear thy name, both small and great, and for destroying the destroyers of the earth" (Rev. 11:18).

1. Ellen G. White, *Education* (Mountain View, CA: Pacific Press®, 1903), 115.
2. White, *Testimonies to Ministers,* 280.
3. Nichol, ed., *Seventh-day Adventist Bible Commentary,* 7:971.
4. Stefanovic, *Revelation of Jesus Christ,* 318, 319.
5. Nichol, ed., *Seventh-day Adventist Bible Commentary,* 7:971.
6. My translation, emphasizing the literal meaning of the text.
7. Arndt and Gingrich, *A Greek-Hebrew Lexicon,* s.v. "χρονος."
8. Ibid., s.v. "καιρος."
9. Literal translation.
10. See Siegfried H. Horn and Lynn H. Wood, *The Chronology of Ezra 7* (Washington, DC: Review and Herald®, 1953, 1970).
11. On the issue of the pre-Advent judgment, see "How, When, and Why Does God Judge His People?" in Gane, *You Ask, God Answers,* 177–198.
12. Nichol, ed., *Seventh-day Adventist Bible Commentary,* 7:971.
13. Ellen G. White, *Selected Messages* (Washington, DC: Review and Herald®, 1958), 1:188.
14. My literal translation.
15. Swete, *The Apocalypse of St. John,* 129.
16. On the mystery of God in the writings of Paul, see Rom. 16:25, 26; 1 Cor. 2:7; 4:1; Eph. 1:9; 3:3–5, 9; 6:19; Col. 1:26, 27; 2:2, 3; 4:3; 1 Tim. 3:9, 16.
17. Jacques B. Doukhan comments: "Eagerly Yohanan takes the 'scroll that lies open in the hand of the angel,' and eats it (Rev. 10:8, 9). The word is thus assimilated and digested. 'The scroll that lies open' represents the book of Daniel, previously sealed but now accessible to all. . . . The insights of Daniel and of the Apocalypse converge into a revelation of the 'time of the end.' Daniel compares it to Kippur, to a time of trembling expectation of judgment and recreation. The Apocalypse portrays this period through the vision of the 'open scroll' with the bittersweet taste, evocative of the dual message of judgment and recreation that characterizes the nature of Kippur." *Secrets of Revelation,* 92, 93.

18. Ellen G. White, *Life Sketches of Ellen G. White* (Mountain View, CA: Pacific Press®, 1915), 56, 57.

19. Nichol, ed., *Seventh-day Adventist Bible Commentary,* 7:971.

20. White, *The Great Controversy,* 429–432.

21. White, *Early Writings,* 243.

22. Nichol, ed., *Seventh-day Adventist Bible Commentary,* 7:971.

23. Arndt and Gingrich, *A Greek-English Lexicon,* s.v. "επι."

24. See H. E. Dana and Julius R. Mantey, *A Manual Grammar of the Greek New Testament* (New York: Macmillan, 1927, 1960), 106; J. H. Moulton, *A Grammar of New Testament Greek,* vol. 3, *Syntax,* Nigel Turner, ed. (Edinburgh: T. & T. Clark, 1963), 271, 272; Friedrich Blass and A. Debrunner, *A Greek Grammar of the New Testament and Other Early Christian Literature* (Chicago: University of Chicago Press, 1961), 123; Swete, *The Apocalypse of St. John,* 132.

25. White, *Testimonies for the Church,* 5:454.

26. Ibid., 9:123.

27. White, *The Great Controversy,* 621.

28. Ibid., 635, 636.

29. See Gane, *Heaven's Open Door,* 42–46; White, *Christ's Object Lessons,* 294; *Testimonies for the Church,* 8:159; ibid., 9:266, 267.

30. White, *The Great Controversy,* 636.

31. Ibid.

32. "Ellen G. White Comments," *Seventh-day Adventist Bible Commentary,* 7:971.

CHAPTER 11

THE MEASURING OF THE TEMPLE AND THE PEOPLE

Revelation 11:1–14 is a continuation of the interlude between the sixth and seventh trumpets. This section follows on naturally and logically from Revelation 10, which concluded with the injunction that believers must "again prophesy about [and before] many peoples and nations and tongues and kings" (Rev. 10:11).

What is to be the subject of their proclamation? Revelation 11:1–14 has the answer. They are to teach about God's temple and the altar and those who worship in the temple (verse 1). They are also to promote the messages of the two witnesses whose messages were blunted for forty-two months or 1,260 days (verses 2, 3). Now that period has come to an end, and the messages of the two witnesses can be proclaimed with revitalized power.

THE MEASURING ROD

John writes, "Then I was given a measuring rod like a staff, and I was told: 'Rise and measure the temple of God and the altar and those who worship there' " (Rev. 11:1). Literally translated, the first part of verse 1 reads: "And there was given to me a reed like a rod." The word *reed* translates from the Greek word *kalamos,* which also means "stalk," "staff," "measuring rod," and the word translated "rod" is *hrabdo;* it means "staff" or "stick." The *kalamos* was a plant that grew in the Jordan Valley; its stalk worked well as a measuring rod. So John tells us that he was given something used for measurement.

Then John says he was instructed to rise and measure the temple of God and the altar and those who are worshiping in it (Rev. 11:1). In the Greek original, the word *measure* is the imperative form of the verb *metreō.* This verb means to take the dimensions of, "give out, deal out, apportion . . . something to someone."[1] The word is used in the Greek Old Testament in the sense of measuring quantities of produce (Exod. 16:18, LXX; cf. Ruth 3:15). It was also used in contexts that speak of measuring real estate (Num. 35:5, LXX).

Ezekiel saw in vision "a man, whose appearance was like bronze, with a line of flax and a measuring reed in his hand" (Ezek. 40:3). Ezekiel 40–48 describes the angel measuring the entire temple complex. The measuring represented the restoration of the temple and its services after the Israelites returned to Jerusalem following the Babylonian captivity. The daily and Day of Atonement sacrifices were to be restored, and the annual feasts practiced once more (cf. Zech. 2:1–7).

In speaking of His power and majesty, God asks, "Who has measured the water in his hand, and the heaven with a span, and all the earth in a handful? Who has weighed the mountains in scales, and the forests in a balance?" (Isa. 40:12, LXX). God is the One who measures both physical and spiritual phenomena.

At times in the Septuagint, the Greek verb "to measure" is used in contexts that speak of judgment. For example, "David smote Moab, and measured them out with lines, having laid them down on the ground: and there were two lines for slaying, and two lines he kept alive: and Moab became servants to David, yielding tribute" (Kings II [2 Sam.] 8:2, LXX). Thus, David's measuring the Moabites involved judging them as worthy of life or death. God also measured or judged the Babylonians in the time of Belshazzar. Daniel interpreted the handwriting on the wall of the palace as saying, "*Mane;* God has measured thy kingdom, and finished it" (Dan. 5:26, LXX). God had judged the Babylonians and found them guilty and worthy of death.

Again, in the New Testament, measuring people involves their being judged by their works. Jesus said, "Judge not, that you be not judged. For with the judgment you pronounce you will be judged, and the measure you give will be the measure you get" (Matt. 7:1, 2; cf. Mark 4:24; Luke 6:38). Jesus is the Judge (Acts 10:42); He determines what measure should be given to those who practice good or evil.

The Corinthians were making the mistake of judging themselves in comparison to other people rather than by God's standard of righteousness. Paul warned, "When they measure themselves by one another, and compare themselves with one another, they are without understanding" (2 Cor. 10:12).

Revelation 21 describes John's vision of an angel with a measuring rod who measured the Holy City, the New Jerusalem and its gates and walls (Rev. 21:15). As Ezekiel saw the temple complex measured as a sign of its restoration, so John saw the New Jerusalem measured as a surety that it would be a perfect structure for the indwelling of a perfected people (Rev. 21:9–21).

The command to John to "measure" quite evidently involved both restoration of the temple message and judgment of those who worship in the temple. Measuring included restoration and judgment. As we shall see, there is a close relationship between the temple and judgment.

MEASURING THE TEMPLE, ALTAR, AND WORSHIPERS

John was then told, "Rise and measure the temple of God" (Rev. 11:1). The Greek word translated "temple" in this verse is *naos*. In the Septuagint, this word often refers to the temple structure as a whole (Kings I [1 Sam.] 1:9, LXX; Kings II [2 Sam.] 22:7, LXX; Kings III [1 Kings] 6:17, LXX). But the temple structure, the *naos,* is represented as distinct from the court. For example, Solomon "built the inner court, three rows of hewn stones, and a row of wrought cedar round about, and he made the curtain of the court of the porch of the house that was in front of the temple" (Kings III [1 Kings] 6:36, LXX). The court is depicted as separate from the temple (*naos*). The court containing the altar of burnt offering was distinct from the *naos*. "Solomon offered up to the Lord whole-burnt-offerings on the altar which he had built to the Lord before the temple" (2 Chron. 8:12, LXX; cf. 2 Chron. 15:8, LXX). But the altar of incense was located within the temple (*naos*). Ozias (Uzziah) transgressed against God by going into the "temple of the Lord to burn incense on the altar of incense" (2 Chron. 26:16, LXX).

Likewise, in the New Testament, the temple (*naos*) often refers to the entire temple structure (Matt. 23:16, 17, 21). But the temple structure itself is distinguished from the court containing the altar of burnt offering. Jesus said that those who claimed to be God's people yet who persecuted the righteous people He sent to warn them were guilty of "all the righteous blood shed on earth, from the blood of innocent Abel to the blood of Zechari'ah the son of Barachi'ah, whom you murdered *between the sanctuary* [naos] *and the altar*" (Matt. 23:35; italics added). The altar in this verse is the altar of burnt offering in the court, which is depicted as distinct from the temple or sanctuary. On the other hand, the place where the altar of incense stood was within the structure called the *naos*. Zechariah, the father of John the Baptist, entered "the temple [*naos*] of the Lord" to burn incense (Luke 1:9; cf. verse 21).

Revelation 11:19 speaks of "God's temple [*naos*] in heaven," and it depicts His throne as being within that temple (*naos;* Rev. 7:15). The reference is to the heavenly temple, in which the saved will worship God after the second coming of Jesus. (See also Rev. 14:15, 17; 15:5, 6, 8; 16:1, 17.)

By contrast, another word for temple, *hieron,* not used in the book of Revelation, refers to the temple complex as a whole, including the court. "Jesus entered the temple of God and drove out all who sold and bought in the temple, and he overturned the tables of the money-changers and the seats of those who sold pigeons" (Matt. 21:12; cf. verse 15). The word for "temple" used here is *hieron.* This word referred to the entire temple complex, including the court, because it was there that the money-changers did their business, so it was from the court of the temple that Jesus cast them out. When those who wrote the Gospels speak of Jesus teaching in the temple (*hieron*), it's the court of the temple they have in mind (Matt. 21:23; cf. 26:55; Mark 11:11, 15; 12:35).

The point is clear, then, that when John was told to "measure the temple [*naos*] of God" (Rev. 11:1), he was to measure the part of the heavenly temple that contains God's throne. The earthly temple was destroyed by the Romans in AD 70, long before John was writing the book of Revelation. As Ezekiel saw the angel measuring the earthly temple complex as a sign that the Jerusalem temple was to be rebuilt, so John's measuring the heavenly temple represents the restoration of the heavenly sanctuary message after the Revelation 10 disappointment. This heavenly temple (*naos*) does not include the court containing the altar of burnt offering, but it does include the altar of incense.

John was told to "measure the temple of God *and the altar*" (Rev. 11:1; italics added). The Greek word for "altar" in this verse is *thusiastērion*. In the New Testament, this word is used for both the altar of burnt offering in the court of the temple (Matt. 5:23, 24; 23:18 20, 35; 1 Cor. 9:13; 2 Cor. 10:18; Rev. 6:9) and the altar of incense in the Holy Place of the temple itself (Luke 1:11; Rev. 8:3, 5; 9:13; 14:17, 18; 16:7). The "altar" of Revelation 11:1 is the altar of incense in the heavenly temple.

The altar of burnt offering in the court was the place where all the animal sacrifices were to be made (Lev. 17:1–8; cf. Exod. 29:38–46). This altar symbolized Calvary, where Jesus offered the only sacrifice valuable enough to stand in place of all humankind. Every animal sacrifice offered at the altar of burnt offering pointed forward to the all-atoning sacrifice of the Messiah (Heb. 8:1–7; 9:6–14; 10:1–14).

John was told to measure not only the temple of God and the altar, but also "those who worship there" (Rev. 11:1); in other words, God's professed people. They worship in the heavenly temple in the sense that they appeal to Christ in His role as Mediator in the heavenly temple. They look to Him for forgiveness of their sins and for power to serve Him faithfully by obeying His law.[2]

THE CLEANSING OF THE EARTHLY SANCTUARY

Revelation 11:1 tells us that the disappointment of 1844 was to be followed by a recovery of the truth taught by the heavenly sanctuary. But the measuring of the temple, of the altar of incense, and of the people also involves a judgment in heaven that is the antitype of the Day of Atonement judgment of ancient Israel. Kenneth Strand posits that the Day of Atonement judgment described in Leviticus 16 is the Old Testament background to the measuring of the temple, the altar, and the people pictured in Revelation 11:1.[3]

Leviticus 16 describes a judgment/measuring of the "holy place" (the Most Holy Place), the "tent of meeting" (the Holy Place, which contains the altar of incense), and the altar of burnt offering in the court (Lev. 16:14–19). God's instruction was that Aaron should "make atonement for the sanctuary [the Most Holy Place], and he shall make atonement for the tent of meeting [the Holy Place, including the altar of incense] and for the altar [the altar of burnt offering in the court], and he shall make atonement for the priests and for all the people of the assembly" (Lev. 16:33). The purpose was the cleansing of the sanctuary from all the sins that had been transferred to it in the daily services during the year (see Lev. 4–6). The purpose was also the spiritual cleansing of the people, who on this day were to put away all sin from their lives.[4] "On this day shall atonement be made for you, to cleanse you; from all your sins you shall be clean before the Lord" (Lev. 16:30).

Thus the Day of Atonement was a judgment day specifically designed to measure (set right, restore) the sanctuary itself and to measure (judge) the people by having them put away all sin. The parallel with Revelation 11:1 is dramatic. After the disappointment of 1844 (Rev. 10), there was to be a measuring, a judgment involving the setting right of the heavenly sanctuary, and a judgment of God's professed people, who during this time are to put away all sin.

The book of Daniel provides the antitype of the Leviticus 16 Day of Atonement. Daniel 7:9–14 predicts a pre-Advent judgment (cf. verses 22, 26). It involves thrones being placed in heaven and "the ancient of days," the heavenly Father, occupying His throne (Dan. 7:9), surrounded by myriads of the heavenly hosts (verse 10). And "the court sat in judgment, and the books were opened" (verse 10)—this is a judgment based on books of record. One like "a son of man" comes into the court, "and to him was given dominion and glory and kingdom" (verse 14). Thus the people are measured by the heavenly records, and the decision is made as to who should be saved in the kingdom of the Son of man.

The prophecy of Daniel 8 parallels that of Daniel 7. Daniel 8:14 parallels Daniel 7:9–14 and provides the antitype of the Leviticus 16 judgment that takes place on the Day of Atonement. The scholars who produced the Revised Standard Version translated Daniel 8:14 this way: "And he said to him, 'For two thousand and three hundred evenings and mornings; then the sanctuary shall be restored to its rightful state' " (Dan. 8:14). The word translated "restored to its rightful state" is *nitsdaq*—a word derived from the Hebrew *tsadaq*, which scholars have translated in several ways but primarily as meaning *justified*.

In several versions, the translators have used instead the word "cleansed"; among them, the version of the Jewish Publication Society: "He answered me, 'For twenty-three hundred evenings and mornings; then the sanctuary shall be *cleansed*' " (italics added).[5] Similarly, the King James Version has: "then shall the sanctuary be cleansed"; and the Douay Version: "the sanctuary shall be cleansed." And the Jewish scholars of old who produced the Septuagint translated the Hebrew *nitsdaq* with the Greek word *katharisthēsetai*, which means to make clean, cleanse, purify. Thus they also recognized the text as speaking of the *cleansing* of the sanctuary.

If *nitsdaq* means to "justify," why have so many competent scholars translated it as "cleansed" in Daniel 8:14? The answer is simply that while this word has other connotations as well, in several places in the Old Testament it clearly does have the connotation of cleansing. In the Old Testament, as in the New, when God justifies a person, He declares that person righteous. It is a true-to-fact declaration. God never declares anyone righteous whom He has not made righteous because of that person's covenant fellowship with Him. Because Old Testament believers responded in faith to God's mercy and grace, He was able to declare them to be what He had made them: clean, pure, righteous people. (See Gen. 15:6 [cf. Rom. 4:3–8, 19–25; Gal. 3:3–14]; 1 Kings 8:30–32; Exod. 23:7; Prov. 17:15; Isa. 53:11.)

In the Old Testament, various forms of *tsadaq* are used synonymously with words meaning "to cleanse." For example, consider Job 4:17: "Shall mortal man be more just [*tsadaq*] than God? Shall a man be more pure [*taher*] than his maker" (KJV). In this verse, *tsadaq* is used synonymously with *taher,* which means "to cleanse," "to purify." The two statements in the text are parallel. In other words, to be justified is to be clean or pure.

Job 4:17 establishes a linguistic connection between Daniel 8:14 and Leviticus 16:19, 30. Leviticus 16 uses the verb *taher* ("to cleanse") in speaking of the cleansing of the sanctuary and the people on the Day of Atonement. Daniel 8 uses the verb *tsadaq* ("to justify") in speaking of God's work in the sanctuary. But according to Job 4:17, the verb *to justify* means *to cleanse, to purify.* In Job 4:17, *tsadaq* and *taher* are synonymous. So it is appropriate for Bible translators to render *nitsdaq* by "cleanse" in Daniel 8:14.

When the Old Testament portrays believers as being justified, it declares that they are righteous because God has cleansed them. The verb *to justify* includes the idea of cleansing. This is why the ancient rabbis who translated the Septuagint translated the verb *to justify* in Daniel 8:14 by the Greek verb meaning *to cleanse.* And it is why so many other translators have done the same thing.

A second linguistic link between Daniel 8:14 and Leviticus 16 is the fact that both passages use the same Hebrew word for the sanctuary. The Hebrew word translated "sanctuary" in Daniel 8:14 is *qodesh.*

This word is used seven times in Leviticus 16 (verses 2, 3, 16, 20, 23, 27, 33), and in every instance, it refers to the Most Holy Place of the earthly sanctuary. In Leviticus 16, the Holy Place is spoken of as "the tabernacle of the congregation" (KJV) or "the tent of meeting" (RSV). Hence, *qodesh* refers to the special judgment ministry carried on in the Most Holy Place of the earthly sanctuary by the high priest on the Day of Atonement, the tenth day of the seventh month of the Israelite religious year.

Daniel 8:14, though, refers to the heavenly *qodesh* (Heb. 8:1, 2; 9:1–14), so we can conclude that in this verse Daniel was referring to a judgment in the Most Holy Place of the heavenly sanctuary. As there was a cleansing on earth, so there is a cleansing in heaven.

This message of the pre-Advent judgment or cleansing of the heavenly sanctuary was discovered after the disappointment of 1844. At that point, the founders of the Seventh-day Adventist Church understood that Daniel 8:14 speaks of the cleansing of the *heavenly* sanctuary, not the cleansing of the earth by fire. They realized that the heavenly sanctuary is cleansed in the sense that the books of record are examined to determine who has experienced justification and who has not, and who continues to enjoy the blessings of justification.

The same pre-Advent judgment message—the measuring of God's temple, the altar, and the people—is spoken of in Revelation 14:6, 7.[6] The message that "the hour of his judgment has come" has gone forth since the truth of the heavenly sanctuary was discovered after 1844, and it will continue to be proclaimed until all "those who dwell on earth . . . every nation and tribe and tongue and people" have had an opportunity to hear it and respond to it—until probation closes when Jesus casts the censer into the earth (Rev. 8:5).

The grand judgment is taking place, and has been going on for some time. Now the Lord says, Measure the temple and the worshipers thereof. Remember when you are walking the streets about your business, God is measuring you; when you are attending your household duties, when you engage in conversation, God is measuring you. Remember that your words and actions are being daguerreotyped [photographed] in the books of heaven, as the face is reproduced by the artist on the polished plate. . . .

Here is the work going on, measuring the temple and its worshipers to see who will stand in the last days. Those who stand fast shall have an abundant entrance into the kingdom of our Lord and Saviour Jesus Christ. When we are doing our work remember there is One that is watching the spirit in which we are doing it. Shall we not bring the Saviour into our everyday lives, into our secular work and domestic duties? Then in the name of God we want to leave behind everything that is not necessary, all gossiping or unprofitable visiting, and present ourselves as servants of the living God.[6]

The time has come when everything is to be shaken that can be shaken, that those things which cannot be shaken may remain. Every case is coming in review before God; He is measuring the temple and the worshipers therein.[7]

END-TIME JUDGMENT

God's temple, the altar, and His people are measured (Rev. 11:1) after the close of probation, when God intervenes to save His persecuted people. "The time for the dead to be judged" (Rev. 11:18) began in 1844, but the ultimate time for the dead and the living to be judged is when God begins to execute the sentence of the heavenly court upon the saved and lost after the close of probation and especially in the dramatic events that will immediately precede Jesus' advent. John describes the scene in the past tense, but what he saw will occur in the future. "The nations raged, but thy wrath came, and the time for the dead to be judged [measured], for rewarding thy servants, the prophets and saints, and those who fear thy name, both small and great, and for destroying the destroyers of the earth" (Rev. 11:18).

Those erstwhile believers who have identified themselves with unbelievers will suffer the agony of rejection that is to be the portion of unbelievers. Because they can't face the Savior, who comes in glory, they will cry out for the mountains and rocks to fall on them (Rev. 6:15, 16). They have been judged in the pre-Advent judgment, and now they are measured as the Babylonians were measured when the Medes and Persians attacked them in 539 BC. Daniel announced: "God has measured thy kingdom, and finished it" (Dan. 5:26, LXX).

By contrast, God's faithful ones who were sealed prior to the close of probation (Rev. 7:1–8) will welcome their returning Lord, who will take them to the heavenly kingdom (Rev. 7:13–17). They were "measured" (judged) in the pre-Advent judgment and found worthy of eternal life. Now they are measured in the sense of being delivered from their satanic and human enemies and transported to the home of the saved. Because they have "conquered the beast and its image and the number of its name," they are permitted to stand on "the sea of glass with harps of God in their hands" singing the song of Moses and the Lamb (Rev. 15:2, 3). By contrast, the unfaithful who professed to believe but were not clothed with the righteousness of Christ, will suffer the seven last plagues (Rev. 16) and will ultimately perish at the second coming of Jesus. True believers rejoice that they are given the robe of Christ's righteousness during the "marriage of the Lamb," the pre-Advent judgment (Rev. 19:7, 8). Those who are unprepared will be destroyed along with "the beast" and "the false prophet" (Rev. 19:11–21).

After the second coming of Jesus, those judged "blessed and holy" will "reign with him a thousand years" (Rev. 20:6). But those who once believed but did not prove true will remain in their graves to be raised at the end of the thousand years to face the ultimate measuring when the books are finally opened, and they are confronted by the record of their sins (Rev. 20:11–14; cf. Matt. 25:31–40).

The point is that the ultimate measuring of the faithful and the unfaithful takes place after the close of probation. Ellen White dramatically describes the final scenes in the great controversy between Christ and Satan in the final three chapters of her book *The Great Controversy*. The ultimate measuring begins just before Jesus appears.

Prison walls are rent asunder, and God's people, who have been held in bondage for their faith, are set free.

Graves are opened, and "many of them that sleep in the dust of the earth . . . awake, some to everlasting life, and some to shame and everlasting contempt." Daniel 12:2. All who have died in the faith of the third angel's message come forth from the tomb glorified, to hear God's covenant of peace with those who have kept His law. "They also which pierced Him" (Rev. 1:7), those that mocked and derided Christ's dying agonies, and the most violent opposers of His truth and His people, are raised to behold Him in His glory and to see the honor placed upon the loyal and obedient.

Thick clouds still cover the sky; yet the sun now and then breaks through, appearing like the avenging eye of Jehovah.

Fierce lightnings leap from the heavens, enveloping the earth in a sheet of flame. Above the terrific roar of thunder, voices, mysterious and awful, declare the doom of the wicked. The words spoken are not comprehended by all; but they are distinctly understood by the false teachers. Those who a little before were so reckless, so boastful and defiant, so exultant in their cruelty to God's commandment-keeping people, are now overwhelmed with consternation and shuddering in fear. Their wails are heard above the sound of the elements. Demons acknowledge the deity of Christ and tremble before His power, while men are supplicating for mercy and groveling in abject terror.

Said the prophets of old, as they beheld in holy vision the day of God: "Howl ye; for the day of the Lord is at hand; it shall come as a destruction from the Almighty." Isaiah 13:6. "Enter into the rock, and hide thee in the dust, for fear of the Lord, and for the glory of His majesty. The lofty looks of man shall be humbled, and the haughtiness of men shall be bowed down, and the Lord alone shall be exalted in that day. For the day of the Lord of hosts shall be upon everyone that is proud and lofty, and upon everyone that is lifted up; and he shall be brought low." "In that day a man shall cast the idols of his silver, and the idols of his gold, which they made each one for himself to worship, to the moles and to the bats; to go into the clefts of the rocks, and into the tops of the ragged rocks, for fear of the Lord, and for the glory of His majesty, when He ariseth to shake terribly the earth." Isaiah 2:10-12, 20, 21.

Through a rift in the clouds there beams a star whose brilliancy is increased fourfold in contrast with the darkness. It speaks hope and joy to the faithful, but severity and wrath to the transgressors of God's law. Those who have sacrificed all for Christ are now secure, hidden as in the secret of the Lord's pavilion. They have been tested, and before the world and the despisers of truth they have evinced their fidelity to Him who died for them. A marvelous change has come over those who have held fast their integrity in the very face of death. They have been suddenly delivered from the dark and terrible tyranny of men transformed to demons. Their faces, so lately pale, anxious, and haggard, are now aglow with wonder, faith, and love. Their voices rise in triumphant song: "God is our refuge and strength, a very present help in trouble. Therefore will not we fear, though the earth be removed, and though the mountains be carried into the midst of the sea; though the waters thereof roar and be troubled, though the mountains shake with the swelling thereof." Psalm 46:1-3.[8]

Thus professed people of God are measured; some are vindicated, and some are condemned, while all are made aware that God is on His throne and that He will judge righteously.

---

1. Arndt and Gingrich, *A Greek-English Lexicon*, s.v. "μετρέω."
2. David E. Aune comments significantly: "The act of measuring signifies *preservation*. Thus vv 1-2, part of the larger unit in vv 1-13 that is placed between the sixth and seventh trumpets, emphasizes preservation just as the first part of 7:1-17 (placed between the sixth and seventh seals) emphasizes the preservation of the 144,000 through their sealing. In this new context, the worshipers represent the divinely protected remnant of Christians who will survive until the arrival of the eschaton." *Revelation 6–16*, Word Biblical Commentary, vol. 52B (Nashville: Thomas Nelson, 1998), 630.
3. Kenneth A. Strand, "An Overlooked Old-Testament Background to Revelation 11:1," *Andrews University Seminary Studies* 22 (Autumn 1984): 322–325.

4. As Roy Gane has pointed out, cleansing the people was accomplished by cleansing the sanctuary. See *Altar Call* (Berrien Springs, MI: Diadem, 1999), 238–246.

5. *Tanakh: the Holy Scriptures. The New JPS [the Jewish Publication Society] Translation According to the Traditional Hebrew Text* (New York: Jewish Publication Society, 1985), s.v. "Daniel 8:14."

6. Significantly, David E. Aune comments: "Thus the worshipers in the temple of God, in my view, are analogous to the 144,000 whom God has sealed (7:3–8; see Form/Structure/Setting on Rev 7:1–17), for they too are divinely protected against the divine punitive plagues as well as the murderous intent of the enemies of God." *Revelation 6–16,* Word Biblical Commentary, vol. 52B (Nashville: Thomas Nelson, 1998), 598.

7. "Ellen G. White Comments," *SDA Bible Commentary,* 7:972.

8. White, *The Great Controversy,* 637–639; White, *Testimonies for the Church,* 7:219.

CHAPTER 12
GOD'S TWO WITNESSES

After the dramatic end-time scenes we've already considered, the prophecy says, "Do not measure the court outside the temple; leave that out, for it is given over to the nations, and they will trample over the holy city for forty-two months" (Rev. 11:2).

What is going on here? How are we to understand this text?

In the first place, the Greek word translated "court" in this verse is *aulē*. This is the word used in the Septuagint to speak of the court of the wilderness tabernacle (Exod. 27:9, 16, LXX). The altar of burnt offering upon which all the sacrifices were to be offered stood in this court (Exod. 27:1–8; 29:38–43; 38:1–7). The same Greek word is used in the Septuagint for the court of Solomon's temple: "He [Solomon] built the inner court, three rows of hewn stones, and a row of wrought cedar round about, and he made the curtain of the court of the porch of the house that was in front of the temple" (3 Kings [1 Kings] 6:36 LXX). The existence of an inner court presupposes the existence of an outer court. Second Kings 21:5 mentions "the two courts of the house of the LORD." (Cf. 2 Kings 23:12.) And 2 Chronicles 4:9 tells us that Solomon "made the court of the priests, and the great court." The court of the priests contained the altar of burnt offering (2 Chron. 4:1–6) and ten lavers (1 Kings 7: 38).

The temple of Jesus' day, called Herod's temple, had four courts: (1) the court of the Gentiles, open to everyone regardless of race or religion; (2) the court of the women, open to all Jews, regardless of age or sex, but forbidden to everyone else; (3) the court of Israel, open only to male Jews; and (4) the court of the priests, which only they could enter and within which the sacrifices were offered.

A popular interpretation of Revelation 11:2 suggests that it must have been the court outside the temple, the court of the Gentiles, that was not to be measured, because the Gentiles trampled over the city of Jerusalem for forty-two months (1,260 years)—and so they were excluded from the judgment described in Revelation 11:1.[1] Another interpretation that seems more to the point is that the court referred to in Revelation 11:2 is the court that contained the altar of burnt offering where all the sacrifices were offered. This altar symbolized Calvary, where Jesus provided the ultimate sacrifice for our sins. Every sacrifice offered on the altar of burnt offering symbolized the death of Jesus Christ (Heb. 7–10).

The nations of Gentiles are said to "trample over the holy city for forty-two months." The forty-two months are equated in the next verse with the 1,260 years of papal supremacy. Not only did the little horn power of Dan. 7 and 8 persecute the faithful people of God (Dan. 7:25), but this power also took away the "continual" (the *tamid;* Dan. 8:11)—the antitype of the daily rituals of the earthly temple. These daily rituals pointed forward to the once-for-all sacrifice of Jesus (Heb. 7:27; 9:28; 10:12). The sacrifices offered on the altar of burnt offering and the priestly sprinkling of blood on the horns of the altar (Lev. 4) typified His sacrificial and mediatorial ministries.

The papacy, by teaching that in each celebration of the Mass,

Christ is sacrificed again, diminished the significance of His once-for-all sacrifice on Calvary. It also blinded people to the realization that by virtue of Christ's sacrifice, their sins could be forgiven immediately, without the mediation of an earthly confessor (though Christ's ministry in the heavenly sanctuary continued despite this misunderstanding).

The message of Revelation 11:1, 2 is that though the ministry of Christ in the heavenly sanctuary was generally misunderstood by humankind during the period of papal supremacy, it was grasped anew in the years leading up to 1844. On one hand, the truth that Christ's sacrificial work in the court of the temple—in other words, on this earth—had made immediate access to God and immediate forgiveness possible was to a great extent uncovered following the French Revolution, when the papal spell over Europe was broken. And on the other hand, the increased understanding of the benefits of the sacrificial atonement began with the Reformation (AD 1517 and after) and greatly increased in Europe following the French Revolution. And since this restoration of the court took place before 1844, there was no need for the court to be measured at that time.

At this point, one might say, "Revelation 10 and 11:1 predict the beginning of the pre-Advent judgment in 1844. Why then does Revelation 11:2–14 take us back to the 1,260-year period of papal supremacy and to the events of the late eighteenth century?"

The historical answer, I believe, is that these verses explain why "the court outside the temple" was not to be measured in 1844. The events occurring during the period of papal supremacy and in the French Revolution, which ended that supremacy in 1798, were followed by the restoration of Bible truth—specifically, the sacrificial and mediatorial ministry of Jesus Christ. It was this restoration that prepared the way for the judgment-hour message that people began to preach in 1844.

Daniel also foresaw this historical development. Chapter 7 of his book focuses on the work of the little horn power, and chapter 8 pictures the beginning in 1844 of the pre-Advent judgment—the cleansing of the heavenly sanctuary. The French Revolution broke the stranglehold that the papacy had on Western Europe, and the consequent freedom opened the way for a great missionary movement that spanned the globe. It was this movement, associated with renewed study of the prophecies concerning the second coming of Jesus, that prepared the way for the message of the pre-Advent judgment to be proclaimed after 1844. Both Daniel and Revelation recognize the historical significance of 1798 in relation to 1844.

The eschatological answer to the question posed above is, I believe, that Revelation 11:2–14 takes us back to the events of the third and fourth trumpets, which forecast Satan's great deception after the close of probation and the resulting worldwide spiritual and theological darkness. Just as the dissemination of God's Word after 1798 made possible a renewed understanding of the gospel, so, after the close of probation, the current cosmic spiritual darkness will finally be dispelled by Christ's intervention on behalf of His persecuted people. Just before His second coming, dramatic divine events displayed in the heavens will exonerate the Word of God, which has been set at naught by the multitudes of earth.

TWO WITNESSES

"They will trample over *the holy city* for forty-two months" (Rev. 11:2; italics added). The literal "holy city" is Jerusalem (Neh. 11:1; Isa. 48:2; Matt. 4:5; 27:53). Of what then is literal Jerusalem a symbol? What did Gentiles trample underfoot for 1,260 years?

During the papacy's long ecclesiastical rule (AD 538–1798), it not only withheld the truth regarding Christ's sacrifice and ministry (in "the court"), but it also persecuted the faithful people of God. The Reformation broke the power of the papacy in some countries of Europe, but others were under its dominance until the French Revolution, and evangelical Christians continued to suffer persecution in those countries. So, Jerusalem represents God's persecuted church (cf. Dan. 7:25; 8:13; Matt. 24:15–22). Jesus used Daniel's predictions regarding the destruction of Jerusalem as a type of the persecution of His people in the Middle Ages and at the end of time. Hence, Jerusalem is a type of the true church of God, which was a victim of the papacy during its period of supremacy and which the antitypical Babylon will subject to persecution in the final days of earth's history.

> The suppression of the Scriptures under the dominion of Rome, the terrible results of that suppression, and the final exaltation of the word of God, are vividly portrayed by the prophetic pencil. To John the exile on lonely Patmos was given a view of the 1260 years during which the papal power was permitted to trample upon God's word and oppress his people. Said the angel of the Lord: "The holy city [the true church] shall they tread under foot forty and two months."[2]

Two witnesses are mentioned in Revelation 11:3, 4: " 'And I will grant my two witnesses power to prophesy for one thousand two hundred and sixty days, clothed in sackcloth.' These are the two olive trees and the two lampstands which stand before the Lord of the earth." Who or what were the two witnesses that prophesied for the 1,260 years of papal supremacy "clothed in sackcloth"?

In the Old Testament, the word *witness* may refer to

1. God, as a witness between people or in favor of His own truthfulness: Gen. 31:50; Isa. 55:4; Jer. 29:23; 42:5; Mic. 1:2; Mal. 2:14; 3:5.

2. God's people, who are witnesses to His love, power, and Deity: Josh. 24:22; Isa. 43:10, 12; 44:8.

3. A memorial in stone that witnesses a covenant between two parties: Josh. 24:27.

4. A book (or deed) that testifies to land ownership. (See, e.g., Jer. 32:6–15, 42–44, where the deed that Jeremiah signed and had witnessed testified to the fact that God would restore His people from captivity.)

5. The Ten Commandment law of God, which was the "witness" or "testimony" deposited in the ark and kept in the Most Holy Place of "the tabernacle of witness": Exod. 25:16, 21, 22; 40:20; cf. Jer. 44:23; Acts 7:44; Rev. 15:5.

6. Legal witnesses at a trial. Two witnesses were required (see Deut. 17:6, 7; 19:15).

WITNESS IN THE NEW TESTAMENT

In the New Testament, the word *witness* may refer to

1. Witnesses at a court trial or in a disagreement between people: Matt. 18:16; 2 Cor. 13:1; 1 Tim. 5:19; Matt. 26:59, 62.

2. The gospel: Matt. 24:14.

3. Prophets, such as John, Peter, Paul, and the Old Testament prophets: John 1:7; Acts 10:42, 43; 22:15; Rom. 3:21; 1 Pet. 5:1; 1 John 1:2.

4. Jesus and His works: John 3:11; 5:36; 10:25; Rom. 1:5.

5. The Father: John 5:32; 8:18; Rom. 1:9.

6. The Holy Spirit: Rom. 8:16; Heb. 10:15–18 (quoting Jer. 31:33, 34).

7. Christ's people: John 3:28; 15:27; Acts 1:8; 4:33.

8. The Old Testament tabernacle and temple: Acts 7:44.

We know the two witnesses in Revelation 11:3 don't symbolize the Deity, since God speaks of them as entities other than Himself. The two witnesses are His witnesses, external to Him. Since they are symbolized by "the two olive trees, and the two lampstands which stand before the Lord of the earth" (verse 4), they cannot refer to a Member of the Deity. Nor can they be regarded as human beings, because human beings don't "stand before the Lord of the earth." Mortals can attack these two witnesses, but the witnesses are able to defend themselves (verse 5). They have power to produce calamities and plagues (verse 6). They prophesy (verse 6). In fact, they are "two prophets" (verse 10). They can be killed (verses 7, 8); but they will be resurrected (verse 11). And when they are resurrected, they are taken up to heaven in the sight of all their enemies (verse 12).

God presented His will through Old and New Testament prophets. He foreshadowed the gospel through the sanctuary and temple services. He presented His law as the testimony of His will for humanity. He speaks His Word through His Son, Jesus Christ, and through His people. The same Holy Spirit of God who gave to the Old Testament prophets the messages they were commissioned to deliver also gave messages that the apostles of the New Testament were to deliver.[3] God's two witnesses live in His presence while simultaneously being attacked on earth. Since they prophesy (verses 6, 10) and produce retributive punishments (verses 5, 6), they must represent some aspect of God's rule. So, it seems most reasonable to conclude that Revelation 11:3's two witnesses are God's Word, the Old and New Testaments. This interpretation is the only one that fits all the specifications given in Revelation 11, and it is quite consistent with the manner in which the word *witness* is used in both Old and New Testaments. The prophets of both Testaments are God's witnesses. In a special sense, God's law, as expressed in both

Testaments, is His witness to us of His divine will for us. God's righteousness is witnessed to by "the law and the prophets" (Rom. 3:21) and is manifested in the life of those who have faith in Christ.

Concerning the two witnesses the prophet declares further: "These are the two olive trees, and the two candlesticks standing before the God of the earth." "Thy word," said the psalmist, "is a lamp unto my feet, and a light unto my path." Revelation 11:4; Psalm 119:105. The two witnesses represent the Scriptures of the Old and the New Testament. Both are important testimonies to the origin and perpetuity of the law of God. Both are witnesses also to the plan of salvation. The types, sacrifices, and prophecies of the Old Testament point forward to a Saviour to come. The Gospels and Epistles of the New Testament tell of a Saviour who has come in the exact manner foretold by type and prophecy.[4]

OLIVE TREES AND LAMPSTANDS

"These are the two olive trees and the two lampstands which stand before the Lord of the earth" (Rev. 11:4). The allusion is to the prophecy of Zechariah 4. In vision, Zechariah saw two olive trees standing by the seven-branched lampstand (the *menorah*). The olive trees were the source of the oil that burned in the seven lamps, providing the light for the sanctuary. Then Zechariah was given a message for Zerubbabel, the governor: "Not by might, nor by power, but by My Spirit, says the LORD of hosts" (Zech. 4:6). Hence, the oil that provided light for the sanctuary symbolized the Holy Spirit, and the olive trees were the source of the oil. Three times Zechariah asked the angel what the olive trees represented, and eventually the answer came: "These are the two anointed who stand by the Lord of the whole earth" (Zech. 4:14).

Significantly, in the Most Holy Place of the earthly sanctuary, there were likenesses of angels on either end of the ark of the covenant. God commanded Moses:

> "And you shall make two cherubim of gold; of hammered work shall you make them, on the two ends of the mercy seat. Make one cherub on the one end, and one cherub on the other end; of one piece with the mercy seat shall you make the cherubim on its two ends. The cherubim shall spread out their wings above, overshadowing the mercy seat with their wings, their faces one to another; toward the mercy seat shall the faces of the cherubim be. And you shall put the mercy seat on the top of the ark; and in the ark you shall put the testimony that I shall give you. There I will meet with you, and from above the mercy seat, from between the two cherubim that are upon the ark of the testimony, I will speak with you of all that I will give you in commandment for the people of Israel" (Exod. 25:18–22).

Clearly the two cherubim represented angels who live in God's presence but who also minister to humanity. "Are they not all ministering spirits sent forth to serve, for the sake of those who are to obtain salvation?" (Heb.1:14).

Zechariah was told that the two olive trees on either side of the seven-branched lampstand "are the two anointed *who stand by the Lord of the whole earth*" (Zech. 4:14; italics added). John was told that God's two witnesses "are the two olive trees and the two lampstands *which stand before the Lord of the earth*" (Rev. 11:4; italics added).

The exciting truth is that heaven's angels cooperate with the Holy Spirit in bringing God's Word to His people. The oil from the olive trees represents the Holy Spirit; the lampstands are the cherubim, "the two anointed who stand by the Lord of the whole earth."[5] By the inspiration of the Holy Spirit and the ministry of heaven's angels, God's Word becomes a lamp to our feet and a light to our path (Ps. 119:105).

> From the two olive trees, the golden oil was emptied through golden pipes into the bowl of the candlestick and thence into the golden lamps that gave light to the sanctuary. So from the holy ones that stand in God's presence, His Spirit is imparted to human instrumentalities that are consecrated to His service. The mission of the two anointed ones is to communicate light and power to God's people. It is to receive blessing for us that they stand in God's presence. As the olive trees empty themselves into the golden pipes, so the heavenly messengers seek to communicate all that they receive from God. The whole heavenly treasure awaits our demand and reception; and as we receive the blessing, we in our turn are to impart it. Thus it is that the holy lamps are fed, and the church becomes a light bearer in the world.[6]

WITNESSES CLOTHED IN SACKCLOTH

God's two witnesses, the Old and New Testaments, prophesied for 1,260 days/years "clothed in sackcloth" (Rev. 11:3). Sackcloth was a symbol of mourning (Gen. 37:34; 2 Sam. 3:31; 1 Kings 20:31, 32; Esther 4:1–4; Jer. 4:8). The apostasy from the truths that Scripture teaches and the subjugation of the Scriptures during the medieval period brought sorrow to God's heart and to the heavenly host. The witnesses clothed in sackcloth symbolize the restriction of the testimony that God's Word sought to bear during the period of papal supremacy. Various popes ruled that the laity should not have the Bible in the language they spoke. The Vulgate was the official version of the Bible, but it was in Latin, which most people didn't speak or understand. The church taught that popes and priests were to be obeyed implicitly and that their interpretation of the Bible was to be accepted as the Word of God. The result was that spiritual and theological ignorance prevailed for centuries.

John VIII in 880 permitted, after the reading of the Latin gospel, a translation into Slavonic; but Gregory VII in a letter to Duke Vratislav of Bohemia in 1080 characterized the custom as unwise, bold, and forbidden. . . . This was a formal prohibition, not of Bible reading in general, but of divine service in the vernacular.

With the appearance, in the twelfth and thirteenth centuries, of the Albigenses and Waldenses, who appealed to the Bible in all their disputes with the Church, the hierarchy was furnished with a reason for shutting up the Word of God. The Synod of Toulouse in 1229 forbade the laity to have in their possession any copy of the books of the Old and the New Testament except the Psalter and such other portions as are contained in the Breviary or the Hours of the Blessed Mary. "We most strictly forbid these works in the vulgar tongue." . . . The Synod of Tarragona (1234) ordered all vernacular versions to be brought to the bishop to be burned. James I renewed this decision of the Tarragona synod in 1276. The synod held there in 1317 under Archbishop Ximenes prohibited to Beghards, Beguines, and tertiaries of the Franciscans the possession of theological books in the vernacular. . . . The order of James I was renewed by later kings and confirmed by Paul II (1464–71). Ferdinand and Isabella (1474–1516) prohibited the translation of the Bible into the vernacular or the possession of such translations. . . .

In England Wyclif's Bible-translation caused the resolution passed by the third Synod of Oxford (1408): "No one shall henceforth of his own authority translate any text of Scripture into English; and no part of any such book or treatise composed in the time of John Wycliffe or later shall be read in public or private, under pain of excommunication." . . . In Germany, Charles IV issued in 1369 an edict to four inquisitors against the translating and the reading of Scripture in the German language. . . . In 1485 and 1486, Berthold, archbishop of Mainz, issued an edict against the printing of religious books in German, giving among other reasons the singular one that the German language was unadapted to convey correctly religious ideas, and therefore they would be profaned. . . .

Luther's translation of the Bible and its propagation could not but influence the Roman Catholic Church. . . .

At last the Council of Trent took the matter in hand, and in its fourth session (Apr. 18, 1546) adopted the *Decretum de editione et usu librorum sacrorum*, which enacted the following. "This synod ordains and decrees that henceforth sacred Scripture, and especially the aforesaid old and vulgate edition, be printed in the most correct manner possible; and that it shall not be lawful for any one to print, or cause to be printed, any books whatever on sacred matters without the name of the author; or in future to sell them, or even to possess them, unless they shall have been first examined and approved of by the ordinary." . . .

The first index published by a pope (Paul IV), in 1559, prohibited under the title of *Biblia prohibita* a number of Latin editions as well as the publication and possession of translations of the Bible in German, French, Spanish, Italian, English, or Dutch, without the permission of the sacred office of the Roman Inquisition.[7]

The history of the Roman Church's efforts to keep the Bible from the laity provides a telling testimony to the truth of John's prediction that for 1,260 years God's two witnesses would prophesy "clothed in sackcloth" (Rev. 11:3).

During the greater part of this period [the 1,260 years of papal supremacy], God's witnesses remained in a state of obscurity. The papal power sought to hide from the people the word of truth, and set before them false witnesses to contradict its testimony. . . . When the Bible was proscribed by religious and secular authority; when its testimony was perverted, and every effort made that men and demons could invent to turn the minds of the people from it; when those who dared proclaim its sacred truths were hunted, betrayed, tortured, buried in dungeon cells, martyred for their faith, or compelled to flee to mountain fastnesses, and to dens and caves of the earth— then the faithful witnesses prophesied in sackcloth. Yet they continued their testimony throughout the entire period of 1260 years. In the darkest times there were faithful men who loved God's Word and were jealous for His honor. To these loyal servants were given wisdom, power, and authority to declare His truth during the whole of this time.[8]

APOSTASY AND JUDGMENT

> And if any one would harm them, fire pours from their mouth and consumes their foes; if any one would harm them, thus he is doomed to be killed. They have power to shut the sky, that no rain may fall during the days of their prophesying, and they have power over the waters to turn them into blood, and to smite the earth with every plague, as often as they desire (Rev. 11:5, 6).

God's Word is invincible—history vindicates that claim. Fire was rained down on Sodom and Gomorrah (Gen. 19:24). Egypt suffered fire and hail sent by God (Exod. 9:23, 24). Fire from God's presence devoured Nadab and Abihu (Lev. 10:1, 2; cf. Num. 11:1; 16:34, 35). In the time of Elijah, the Lord withheld rain for three and a half years (1 Kings 17:1; Luke 4:25). When Moses lifted up his rod and struck the waters of the Nile, the Lord turned the water to blood (Exod. 7:20; Ps. 105:29). When the second and third plagues are poured out after the close of probation, sea water and river water will be turned to blood (Rev. 16:3).

This passage was a warning to those who, in the Middle Ages, withheld the Bible from the people and kept them in spiritual and theological darkness. It also is a fearful warning to those who, before and after the close of probation, dare to deny the truths of God's Word and persecute those who proclaim them. The seven last plagues recorded in Revelation 16 will be a fearful testimony to the power of God's Word. In fact, the final warning the Bible gives is to those who would dare to change or contradict the Word of the Lord.

"I warn every one who hears the words of the prophecy of

this book: if any one adds to them, God will add to him the plagues described in this book, and if any one takes away from the words of the book of this prophecy, God will take away his share in the tree of life and in the holy city, which are described in this book" (Rev. 22:18, 19).

"And when they have finished their testimony, the beast that ascends from the bottomless pit will make war upon them and conquer them and kill them" (Rev. 11:7). A literal translation of the first phrase reads: "And when they are finishing their testimony . . ."[9]

The prophecy says the two witnesses were to be "clothed in sackcloth" for 1,260 years—that is, until 1798. In the final years of this time of restricted witness, a violent attack would be made upon the Bible. The Greek grammarians justify Ellen White's interpretation of the text:

> "When they shall have finished [are finishing] their testimony." The period when the two witnesses were to prophesy clothed in sackcloth, ended in 1798. As they were approaching the termination of their work in obscurity, war was to be made upon them by the power represented as "the beast that ascendeth out of the bottomless pit." In many of the nations of Europe the powers that ruled in church and state had for centuries been controlled by Satan through the medium of the papacy. But here is brought to view a new manifestation of satanic power.[10]

The line "the beast that ascends from the bottomless pit" is an obvious reference to Satan. Revelation 9:1's "star fallen from heaven to earth" who was given "the key of the shaft of the bottomless pit" is to be identified as Satan. He is the one who darkens the earth with the smoke of unbelief and infidelity. He is the king over the forces that emerge from the bottomless pit. He is "the angel of the bottomless pit; his name in Hebrew is Abad'don, and in Greek he is called Apol'lyon" (Rev. 9:11). As we have seen in a previous chapter, he is the great destroyer.

Satan often works through various ones of earth's nations to perpetrate his attacks upon God's truth and people (see Dan. 7, 8; Rev. 9). He is the dragon of Revelation 12:3, 9. He provides the power and authority of the earthly organization represented in chapter 13 by the leopardlike beast (Rev. 13:1, 2). Revelation 11:7 indicates that it was Satan who attacked the Bible in the years just prior to 1798. But Satan employed a specific earthly power to carry out this attack—to destroy Scripture's influence. That power was revolutionary France.

Revelation 11:7 and the verses that follow refer to the dechristianization program that was carried out in revolutionary France from the fall of 1793 until mid-1797. For a period of three and a half years the Christianity of the Bible was replaced—first by an atheistic worship of Reason, and then by the application in France of the implications of a deistic concept of the Supreme Being based on Rousseau's understanding of the state. Prior to the events of November 1793, the Constituent Assembly passed a series of measures designed to break the power of the papal church over state affairs. Then, because of the identification of the papal church with anti-republican sentiments, the French decided that the non-Christian religion of the *philosophes* (the intellectual leaders, such as Rousseau) was more in sympathy with the Revolution than was Christianity. Hence, they threw out the baby (the Christianity of the Bible) with the bathwater (papalism). The experiment failed, and gradually, Christian worship, of both the Roman Catholic and the Protestant variety, crept back into France.[11]

"And their dead bodies will lie in the street of the great city which is allegorically called Sodom and Egypt, where their Lord was crucified" (Rev. 11:8). The "great city" here seems to be a symbol of the country that, toward the end of the period of papal supremacy (538–1798), rejected the Bible and its God. This was revolutionary France. The spiritual and moral states of Sodom and Egypt were singularly appropriate analogies of the spiritual and moral depravity that was characteristic of revolutionary France. The great sins of Sodom were immorality and violence (Gen. 19:4–11; Jer. 23:14), and immorality and violence were rampant in revolutionary France. In the Old Testament, God's unfaithful people are likened to the people of Sodom (Isa. 1:9–11; Lam. 4:6; Ezek. 16:46–52). In the Old Testament, literal and spiritual immorality are symbolized by Sodom and Gomorrah.

Egypt appropriately symbolizes France in this revolutionary era because of its persecution of the faithful, its defiance of the God of the Bible, and its idolatry. The sin of Pharaoh was defiance of the Lord, whose existence he denied. He declared to Moses: "Who is the LORD, that I should heed his voice and let Israel go? I do not know the LORD, and moreover I will not let Israel go" (Exod. 5:2). Idolatry and spiritism were also characteristic of Egypt (Isa. 19:1–4; cf. Jer. 43:12, 13; 44:8).

The Lord of the Bible was metaphorically crucified in both Sodom and Egypt. Between 1793 and 1797, He was also metaphorically crucified by the government and people of the new French Republic.

THE FRENCH REVOLUTION

For three days and a half men from the peoples and tribes and tongues and nations gaze at their dead bodies and refuse to let them be placed in a tomb, and those who dwell on the earth will rejoice over them and make merry and exchange presents, because these two prophets had been a torment to those who dwell on the earth (Rev. 11:9, 10).

Taking a day in apocalyptic prophecy to represent a literal year, the "three days and a half" day refers to the three-and-a-half-year period from the fall of 1793 until mid-1797, during which time the Bible was denigrated in France. The refusal to allow the "dead bodies" of God's two witnesses to be placed in a tomb symbolizes the great scorn and disrespect exhibited toward the Word of God. In ancient times, refusal to bury the body of an enemy was an act of utmost loathing (1 Kings 21:24; Jer. 8:1, 2; 14:15, 16); so the French and others who condoned this act manifested the greatest possible scorn for the Bible, the gospel of Christ, and the Christian religion in general. People rejoiced over the official rejection of Christianity because their sins were condemned by the Christian gospel. Now they thought themselves free to practice their ungodly lifestyle. But sin is not destroyed by attempts to eliminate the law of God. His will still stands, and lawbreakers are under the most fearful condemnation (Rom. 1:21–32).

On August 30, 1792, France made it legal to "divorce . . . by simple declaration only, and on Sept. 20 by common agreement."[12] From March to December 1793, the Convention passed a series of decrees instituting punishment for priests who remained loyal to Rome.

The period of September and October 1793 saw the beginning of the movement for the destruction of Christianity. This movement began in the provinces. "Thus Fouché at Nevers, in a proclamation of 26th September 1793, falsely claimed to be authorized by the Convention 'to substitute the religion of the Republic and natural morality for the superstitious and hypocritical cults to which the people are still so unfortunately devoted."[13] On October 10, Fouché proscribed all the religious emblems in cemeteries and ordered an inscription above the cemetery gates stating "Death is eternal sleep." On October 16, the Commune of Paris approved this decree in principle. At Rochefort, the parish church was turned into a "Temple of Truth," and on October 31, a ceremony was held in which eight Catholic priests and one Protestant minister abdicated their posts. The Paris Commune decreed that no minister of any religion whatever should appear out of doors in anything other than civilian attire.

On August 10, in the first of the purely civic national festivals, Nature was deified and a statue was honored with libations. And on October 5–7, 1793, the republican calendar was substituted for the Gregorian.[14] This was a political move, but it was also anti-religious.

> To substitute other dates and other festivals for the usual ones, to abolish Sunday and substitute the tenth day, to replace the names of the saints by those "of objects which constitute true national wealth," was to tear from Catholicism a part of its adornments and prestige, nay, to drive it violently out of the ordinary life of the nation. This decree horrified foreigners: they thought France had already destroyed Christianity within its borders.[15]

Tragically, not only was Catholicism denigrated, but Christianity in general was rejected. On November 5, 1793, the religion of the Fatherland was substituted for Catholicism. The Convention's Committee of Public Instruction produced propaganda against Catholicism. One member stated, "This infamous religion must be crushed."

The committee decreed that in the future, no ecclesiastic or nun could be appointed as a teacher in a school.

On the fifteenth Brumaire of the Year II, the Convention applauded and published a speech in which Marie-Joseph Chenier, in the name of the committee, proposed the substitution of the religion of the fatherland in place of Catholicism:

> "Wrench," he said, "the sons of the Republic from the yoke of theocracy which now weighs upon them. . . . Then, freed from prejudice and worthy to represent the French nation, you will be able, on the ruins of fallen superstitions, to found the one universal religion, which has neither secrets nor mysteries, whose one dogma is equality, whose orators are the laws, whose pontiffs are the magistrates, which asks no incense from the great human family to burn save before the altar of our country, our mother, and our deity."[16]

THE WORSHIP OF REASON

The worship of Reason was initiated in the autumn of 1793. A motion was passed in the convention providing for a religious ceremony in honor of Reason to be celebrated in the metropolitan church three days later. On a rock placed in Notre Dame, a circular temple was erected dedicated to "philosophy." On the morning of November 10, in the presence of members of the Commune, a procession of girls marched up and down past the rock, saluting the Flame of Truth. An actress from the Opera came out of the temple and was seated on a grass-covered throne. Dressed in white and wearing an azure cloak and red bonnet, she represented the goddess of Reason, and the other girls chanted a hymn to her. Then she was carried on the shoulders of four citizens to the Convention, where a member by the name of Chaumette addressed the assembly. "Fanaticism has lost its grip," he said. "Its shifty eyes have not been able to stand the brightness of enlightenment and it has given way to Justice and Truth. We will have no priests and no other gods but those that Nature herself offers us."[17]

It was then decreed that the metropolitan church should be renamed the "Temple of Reason and Liberty." The president kissed the goddess, and the members of the Convention returned to Notre Dame, where the ceremony was repeated. "Similar ceremonies took place in various places all over the country where many churches had been converted into temples of Reason."[18]

The dechristianization movement swept over in Paris. Most of the citizens—Protestant as well as Catholic—renounced religion, and the parish churches were reopened as Temples of Reason. No religion other than that of Liberty and Equality was to be tolerated. In Paris, the chapels of the Calvinists were deserted, and the Calvinists transferred whatever services they still conducted from Sunday to the tenth day. And the Lutherans did the same.[19]

Thus France rejected both Catholic and Protestant Christian worship, along with the Christianity of the Bible. In May 1794, Robespierre initiated the worship of the Supreme Being, "under which the attacks on Christianity went on and which was in truth only a continuation of the worship of Reason under another form."[20] But "it was the fatherland that was worshiped more and more, whether under the name of the Supreme Being or of Reason, and very soon the two cults, which the people could not distinguish one from another, became lost and merged in patriotism."[21]

Ellen White's account says,

According to the words of the prophet, . . . a little before the year 1798 some power of satanic origin and character would rise to make war upon the Bible. And in the land where the testimony of God's two witnesses should thus be silenced, there would be manifest the atheism of the Pharaoh and the licentiousness of Sodom.

This prophecy has received a most exact and striking fulfillment in the history of France. During the Revolution, in 1793, "the world for the first time heard an assembly of men, born and educated in civilization, and assuming the right to govern one of the finest of the European nations, uplift their united voice to deny the most solemn truth which man's soul receives, and renounce unanimously the belief and worship of a Deity."—Sir Walter Scott, *Life of Napoleon*, vol. 1, ch. 17. "France is the only nation in the world concerning which the authentic record survives, that as a nation she lifted her hand in open rebellion against the Author of the universe. Plenty of blasphemers, plenty of infidels, there have been, and still continue to be, in England, Germany, Spain, and elsewhere; but France stands apart in the world's history as the single state which, by the decree of her Legislative Assembly, pronounced that there was no God, and of which the entire population of the capital, and a vast majority elsewhere, women as well as men, danced and sang with joy in accepting the announcement."—*Blackwood's Magazine*, November, 1870.

France presented also the characteristics which especially distinguished Sodom. During the Revolution there was manifest a state of moral debasement and corruption similar to that which brought destruction upon the cities of the plain. And the historian presents together the atheism and the licentiousness of France, as given in the prophecy: "Intimately connected with these laws affecting religion, was that which reduced the union of marriage—the most sacred engagement which human beings can form, and the permanence of which leads most strongly to the consolidation of society—to the state of a mere civil contract of a transitory character, which any two persons might engage in and cast loose at pleasure. . . . If fiends had set themselves to work to discover a mode of most effectually destroying whatever is venerable, graceful, or permanent in domestic life, and of obtaining at the same time an assurance that the mischief which it was their object to create should be perpetuated from one generation to another, they could not have invented a more effectual plan than the degradation of marriage. . . . Sophie Arnoult, an actress famous for the witty things she said, described the republican marriage as 'the sacrament of adultery.' "—Scott, vol. 1, ch. 17.[22]

"But after the three and a half days a breath of life from God entered them, and they stood up on their feet, and great fear fell on those who saw them" (Rev. 11:11). Toward the end of 1795, the situation began to improve somewhat. The constitution of August 22, 1795, granted freedom in matters of religion to all who submitted to the law. But the denigration of religion continued. In October 1795, the convention threatened with death all exiled clergy who returned to France. "But the lot of the religious was making advance toward betterment during the year 1796 and the first part of 1797."[23] "On June 17, 1797, Camille Jordan, deputy from Lyons, delivered an address in favor of the priests and calling for a revision of the laws respecting religion. On

June 24 the directorium reported to the Five Hundred that, in consequence of the more favorable outlook in religious affairs, a large number of priests had returned and many religious organizations were asking freedom of worship. Finally a decree was passed to restore to the priests their civil rights."[24]

"It was in 1793 that the decrees which abolished the Christian religion and set aside the Bible passed the French Assembly. Three years and a half later a resolution rescinding these decrees, thus granting toleration to the Scriptures, was adopted by the same body."[25]

RESURGENCE

"Then they heard a loud voice from heaven saying to them, 'Come up hither!' And in the sight of their foes they went up to heaven in a cloud" (Rev. 11:12).[26] After the French Revolution there was an enormous resurgence of interest in the Christian gospel and in the dissemination of Bible knowledge around the world. John Dillenberger and Claude Welch describe this movement in some detail:

> The nineteenth century was the period of the greatest geographic spread of Christianity. The foremost American historian of the expansion of Christianity, Kenneth Scott Latourette, has asserted that, "Never had any other set of ideas, religious or secular, been propagated over so wide an area by so many professional agents maintained by the unconstrained donations of so many millions of individuals. . . . For sheer magnitude it has been without parallel in human history." In this process the Protestant churches, and especially the British and American churches, provided the chief impetus and the bulk of the resources.[27]

Toward the end of the eighteenth century, new missionary societies sprang up. In 1793, the Baptist Missionary Society was organized. Three years later the Scottish Missionary Society and the Glasgow Missionary Society were formed, and about that time the General Assembly of the Church in Scotland adopted an official policy covering missionary endeavors in India. Shortly before the turn of the century, the Church of England created the Church Missionary Society to direct the efforts of its members, and the London Missionary Society was established to direct cooperative work by various denominations. In the late eighteenth century, the Methodists also began to support foreign missions actively.[28]

> "Protestant circles on the European continent also saw an awakening of the missionary spirit. A society was founded in the Netherlands in 1797, reflecting the influence of the work in Britain, and missionary interest began to develop strongly in Germany and Switzerland after 1825. . . .
> " . . . In America, interest in missions closely paralleled the development in England, and eventually the United States supplied the majority of the missionaries and over half the financial support for Protestant missions."[29]

Even before the French Revolution, people had begun to develop Bible societies designed to spread the Word as widely as possible. In Britain, the Book Society for Promoting Religious Knowledge among the Poor was established in 1750. The Naval and Military Bible Society came into being in 1780, the Society for the Support and Encouragement of Sunday Schools in 1785, the Association for Discountenancing Vice and Promoting the Knowledge and Practice of the Christian Religion in 1792 (in Dublin), and the Religious Tract Society in London in 1799.[30]

Thus, while the Bible was being denigrated in France, it was being promoted elsewhere, and this trend grew even stronger in the early nineteenth century. In Scotland, the Edinburgh Bible Society was formed in 1809, the Glasgow Bible Society in 1812, the Glasgow Auxiliary Bible Society in 1821, and the National Bible Society in 1858. The British and Foreign Bible Society was created in 1804, and in 1812, encouraged by the British, Bible societies sprang up in Germany, Switzerland, Russia, and other European countries.[31]

In America, the first Bible Society was organized in Philadelphia in 1808. The next year societies were organized in Connecticut, Massachusetts, New York, and New Jersey. In 1816, the American Bible Society was established, and soon that year there were 128 such societies in America.[32]

Not only did Bible societies emerge after the French Revolution, but missionary societies became prevalent.

For the fifty years preceding 1792, little attention was given to the work of foreign missions. No new societies were formed, and there were but few churches that made any effort for the spread of Christianity in heathen lands. But toward the close of the eighteenth century a great change took place. Men became dissatisfied with the results of rationalism and realized the necessity of divine revelation and experimental religion. From this time the work of foreign missions attained an unprecedented growth.

The improvements in printing have given an impetus to the work of circulating the Bible. The increased facilities for communication between different countries, the breaking down of ancient barriers of prejudice and national exclusiveness, and the loss of secular power by the pontiff of Rome have opened the way for the entrance of the word of God. For some years the Bible has been sold without restraint in the streets of Rome, and it has now been carried to every part of the habitable globe.[33]

It was this great missionary outreach of the late eighteenth and early nineteenth centuries that made possible the preaching of the approaching second advent of Christ and especially the sermons of Miller and others who saw 1844 as a vital date in prophecy. And the soon coming of Jesus was proclaimed in Europe and other lands as well as in the New World. The French Revolution and the events that followed paved the way for the judgment-hour message of 1844 and the developments that followed.

OPPOSITION

Revelation 11:2–12 outlines the events that led up to Christ's proclamation that "there shall be time no longer" (Rev. 10:6, ERV), at which point the "temple in heaven was opened" (Rev. 11:19), and the measuring of God's temple and people began (Rev. 11:1).

The events of Revelation 11:1 occurred after the initial sounding of the seventh trumpet (Rev. 11:15–19). Revelation 11:2–13 is a parenthetical section designed to explain the historical situation that led up to the sounding of the seventh trumpet in 1844, when the pre-Advent judgment began.

"And in the sight of their foes they went up to heaven in a cloud" (Rev. 11:12). Despite opposition, the gospel message was disseminated widely in the late eighteenth and early nineteenth centuries. Since the Bible was being distributed in an unprecedented manner, it isn't surprising that opposition would come from the somewhat crippled papacy. On September 3, 1816, Pope Pius VII sent the letter

"Magno et acerbo" to the archbishop of Mohileff. In it he said,

> We were overcome with great and bitter sorrow when We
> learned that a pernicious plan, by no means the first, had been
> undertaken, whereby the most sacred books of the Bible are
> being spread everywhere in every vernacular tongue, with
> new interpretations which are contrary to the wholesome
> rules of the Church, and are skillfully turned into a distorted
> sense. For, from one of the versions of this sort already pre-
> sented to Us we notice that such a danger exists against sanc-
> tity of purer doctrine, so that the faithful might easily drink
> a deadly poison from those fountains from which they should
> drain "waters of saving wisdom" (Ecclus. 15:3). . . .
>
> For you should have kept before your eyes the warnings
> which Our predecessors have constantly given, namely, that, if
> the sacred books are permitted everywhere without discrimi-
> nation in the vulgar tongue, more damage will arise from this
> than advantage. Furthermore, the Roman Church, accepting
> only the Vulgate edition according to the well-known pre-
> scription . . . of the Council of Trent, disapproves the versions
> in other tongues and permits only those which are edited with
> the explanations carefully chosen from writings of the Fathers
> and Catholic Doctors, so that so great a treasure may not be
> exposed to the corruptions of novelties, and so that the Church,
> spread throughout the world, may be "of one tongue and of
> the same speech" (Gen. 11:1).[34]

UNAVAILING EFFORTS

The efforts of Pius VII to stem the tide were unavailing. The various Bible societies then and now have magnificently fulfilled the pre-

diction of John: "In the sight of their foes they [God's two witnesses] went up to heaven in a cloud" (Rev. 11:12).

"And at that hour there was a great earthquake, and a tenth of the city fell; seven thousand people were killed in the earthquake, and the rest were terrified and gave glory to the God of heaven" (Rev. 11:13). The same earthquake is spoken of at the time of the sounding of the seventh trumpet, at which time the "temple in heaven was opened" (Rev. 11:19). The earthquake occurred *after* a great message had been given to the world, represented by the Word of God being exalted to heaven in the sight of its foes (Rev. 11:12). It appears that, historically speaking, the earthquake has reference to the bitter experience of Revelation 10:10. This was the great disappointment of those who expected Christ to return to earth on October 22, 1844. The earthquake seems to symbolize the earth-shaking events of 1844 and the immediate results.

Note the parallel between Revelation 10 and 11 and Ezekiel 2:8–3:21. Ezekiel was instructed to eat a scroll (Ezek. 3:1, 2). It was sweet (3:3), but following an earthquake (3:12, 13), there was bitterness (3:14). In this case the earthquake was caused by the movement of the living creatures (heaven's angels) and the wheels beside them. God's providential intervention in the life of Israel, and specifically in the ministry of Ezekiel to his rebellious people, resulted in great disappointment and consternation for the prophet. He was "overwhelmed among them seven days" (3:15). Then came the renewed commission to take a message of warning to the people (3:16–21).

The symbolism in Ezekiel bears a striking similarity to that in Revelation 10 and 11. John was told to eat a scroll. It was sweet in his mouth but bitter in his stomach (Rev. 10:8–10). This event occurred after God's two witnesses (His Word) had been exalted for all to see following the destructive work of the French Revolution (Rev.

11:12). Then came the "great earthquake" (verse 13). As the earthquake in Ezekiel 3 represented the intervention of heavenly angels in the affairs of Israel, so the earthquake of Revelation 11:13 resulted from a special message given by God and conveyed by the holy ones who "stand before the Lord of the earth" (Rev. 11:4). The events surrounding 1844 were earthshaking. Many people rejected the message of the soon coming of Christ, and a huge number rejected the message of the commencement of the pre-Advent judgment. The professed people of God experienced a great shaking. Many lost their faith in the nearness of the Advent, but others held on to their faith and "gave glory to the God of heaven" (Rev. 11:13).

"And a tenth of the city fell" (Rev. 11:13). What city is referred to here? In the immediate context we read of "the great city which is allegorically called Sodom and Egypt, where their Lord was crucified" (Rev. 11:8). As we have seen, this great city is a symbol of France between 1793 and 1797. In a broader sense, "the great city" of Revelation 11:13 represents the kingdom of Satan, which was responsible for the devastating attack on the Bible in revolutionary France and responsible for all the antichristian movements in history. The book of Revelation symbolizes this great city as antitypical Babylon (cf. Rev. 16:19; 17:18; 18:10, 16–21).

It seems evident that the city, a tenth of which is said to have fallen because of the earthquake, is the kingdom of Satan. Revelation 14:8 tells us: "Fallen, fallen is Babylon the great, she who made all nations drink the wine of her impure passion." Before and after 1844, the first angel's message of Revelation 14:6, 7, stating that "the hour of his judgment has come," was rejected by many people. The result was a partial fall of Babylon, represented by those churches that veered toward worldly mores and turned a blind eye to the message of the soon coming of Christ. "Seven thousand people were killed in the earthquake" (Rev. 11:13)—in the sense that many lost their faith in the soon appearing of Christ and reverted to their worldly lifestyles.

"The rest were terrified and gave glory to the God of heaven" (Rev. 11:13). While many people rejected the message of Christ's soon coming, others responded positively and gave glory to God because their redemption was drawing near. They were "terrified" in the sense of being startled (Greek: *emphobos*)—moved to reverence and respect for the Lord who was soon to appear.[35]

In summary, it can be said that, considered historically, Revelation 11:2–13 traces in symbolic, prophetic language the events that led up to the measuring of God's temple and people in the pre-Advent judgment (Rev. 11:1). Those events were the 1,260 years of papal ecclesiastical supremacy, the French Revolution, and the denigration of Scripture followed by its exaltation in the late eighteenth and nineteenth centuries, which resulted in the preaching of Christ's soon coming and the dramatic events surrounding 1844.

---

1. See Maxwell, *God Cares,* 2:303, 304; Stefanovic, *Revelation of Jesus Christ,* 341.

2. Ellen G. White, *The Spirit of Prophecy* (Battle Creek, MI: Review and Herald®, 1884), 4:188.

3. Ibid. David E. Aune comments: "The two witnesses can be construed as representing the OT and the NT (an ancient view held by Tyconius, Primasius, Beatus, and Bede)." He adds, "With regard to the symbolic significance of the two witnesses, it is relatively clear that they represent the witness of the people of God in a godless world and that they, like their Lord, will ultimately triumph over suffering and death." *Revelation 6–16,* 602, 603. Jacques B. Doukhan sees Moses as representing the Old Testament and Elijah as representing the New Testament. He writes: "When we consider the Judeo-Christian background of Yohanan, we realize that the allusions to Moses and Elijah are no coincidence. It strongly evokes the two revelations of God received by the early Christians—the so-called Old and New Testaments. The two witnesses are both here present and play a part in the prophetic process. The dual reference brings out the relevance of the whole Bible, emphasizing the complementarity of, and the need for, the two

testimonies." *Secrets of Revelation,* 95, 96.

4. White, *The Great Controversy,* 267.

5. The "two lampstands" of Revelation 11:4 are not a reference to the seven-branched candlestick, the *menorah.* The seven-branched candlestick represented God's people into whose hearts the Holy Spirit is poured so that the light of God's love can shine forth (Zech. 4).

6. White, *Testimonies to Ministers,* 510.

7. S. M. Jackson, ed., *The New Schaff-Herzog Encyclopedia of Religious Knowledge* (Grand Rapids, MI: Baker Book House, 1963), 2:85, 86.

8. White, *The Great Controversy,* 267, 268.

9. The Greek verb is *telēsōsin.* It's the third person plural, first aorist subjunctive active of *teleō.* On the significance of the aorist without the augment, see Dana and Mantey, *A Manual Grammar of the Greek New Testament,* 193; J. H. Moulton, ed., *A Grammar of the New Testament Greek,* vol. 3, *Syntax,* Nigel Turner, ed. (Edinburgh: T. & T. Clark, 1963). Turner writes: "Clauses with _παν [_pan], _ταν [_tan], _ς _ν [_σ_η]. . . . With Aor[ist] Subj[unctive] (1) Most commonly of a definite action taking place in the future but concluded before the action of the main verb. Thus the main verb is usually fut[ure] ind[icative], but it may be imper[ative]." Ibid., 112. In Rev. 11:7, the main verb is future, *poiēsei.*

10. White, *The Great Controversy,* 268, 269.

11. For a detailed discussion of the status of religion in revolutionary France, see A. Aulard, *Christianity and the French Revolution* (London: Ernest Benn Limited, 1927); Adrien Dansette, *Religious History of Modern France* (New York: Herder and Herder, 1961); Christopher Dawson, *The Gods of Revolution* (New York: New York University Press, 1972); John McManners, *The French Revolution and the Church* (New York: Harper and Row, 1969); Burdette C. Poland, *French Protestantism and the French Revolution: A Study in Church and State, Thought and Religion, 1685–1815* (Princeton, NJ: Princeton University Press, 1957); Aimé Guillon de Montléon, *Memoires pour servir histoire de la ville de Lyon pendant la Révolution* (*History of the City of Lyon During the French Revolution*) (Paris: Baudoin, 1824), vol. 2; E. L. Higgins, *The French Revolution as Told by Contemporaries* (Boston: Houghton Mifflin, 1938); Maxwell, *God Cares,* 2:280–292; White, "The Bible and the French Revolution," chapter 15 in *The Great Controversy.*

12. Jackson, ed., *The New Schaff-Herzog Encyclopedia,* 2:386.

13. Aulard, *Christianity and the French Revolution,* 102.

14. Ibid., 103.

15. Ibid.

16. Ibid., 104.

17. Dansette, *Religious History of Modern France,* 1:94, 95.

18. Ibid., 1:95.

19. Aulard, *Christianity and the French Revolution,* 108, 109.

20. Ibid., 124.

21. Ibid., 130.

22. White, *The Great Controversy,* 269–271.

23. Jackson, ed., *The New Schaff-Herzog Encyclopedia,* 4:387, 388.

24. Ibid., 388. See also John Adolphus, *The History of France From the Year 1790 to the Peace Concluded at Amiens in 1802* (London: George Kearsley, 1803), 2:316–319.

25. White, *The Great Controversy,* 287.

26. David E. Aune comments: "The ascension of the two witnesses on a cloud before onlookers represents a miraculous divine rescue. The destruction of a tenth of the city and death of seven thousand inhabitants by a great earthquake result in the survivors giving glory to the God of heaven, language that suggests their conversion." *Revelation 6–16,* 52B:632.

27. John Dillenberger and Claude Welch, *Protestant Christianity Interpreted Through Its Development* (New York: Charles Scribner's Sons, 1954), 166. See also Kenneth S. Latourette, *A History of the Expansion of Christianity: The Great Century,* vols. IV–VII (New York: Harper, 1941, 1943, 1944, 1945).

28. Dillenberger and Welch, *Protestant Christianity,* 172, 173.

29. Ibid., 173.

30. Jackson, ed., *The New Schaff-Herzog Encyclopedia,* 2:88.

31. Ibid., 88–93.

32. Ibid., 92.

33. White, *The Great Controversy,* 288.

34. Henry Denzinger, *The Sources of Catholic Dogma,* trans. Roy J. Deferrari (St. Louis, MO: B. Herder Book Co., 1954), 398, 399.

35. For a complete discussion of the events surrounding 1844, see Ellen G. White, *The Great Controversy,* chapters 21 and 22.

CHAPTER 13

THE END-TIME EXALTATION OF GOD'S TWO WITNESSES

We have observed so far that the trumpets have a dual application. Christ's casting the censer into the earth (Rev. 8:5) symbolizes the close of probation for ancient Israel in AD 34, and also the end-time close of probation that will occur shortly before He returns. Similarly, each of the trumpets has a dual application: first, to historical events after AD 34, and then to eschatological events after the end-time close of probation.

We have also observed that the measuring of God's temple and people after the close of probation (Rev. 11:1) takes place when God intervenes on behalf of His persecuted people and reveals supernatural events in the heavens. The righteous and wicked are measured at that time in the sense that it becomes apparent who will be saved and who will be lost.

Eschatologically, the events of Revelation 11:2–13 take us back to those of the third through the sixth trumpets—events that lead up to Christ's intervention on behalf of His people (Rev. 10). The court is not measured immediately (Rev. 11:2) before He comes because the significance of His sacrifice in the antitypical court (in other words, the earth, Calvary) has been rejected by the lost inhabitants of earth.

The true gospel has no meaning for them, and no further hope is offered them.[1]

The trampling of the holy city by earth's nations for forty-two months of prophetic time (1,260 literal years) was a type of the events of the fourth through the sixth trumpets after the end-time close of probation. Just as spiritual and theological darkness almost prevailed during the medieval period, so, after Satan's impersonation of Christ (third trumpet), there will be almost universal spiritual and theological darkness (fourth trumpet). God's law will be denigrated and the Sabbath will be rejected, replaced by Sunday. False doctrine dictated by ecclesiastical and governmental commands will be substituted for God's two witnesses, the Old and New Testaments. The Protestant principle that the Bible and the Bible alone is the rule of our faith and practice will be almost universally set aside, and any who dare to uphold it will be regarded as partisans with those who are the cause of the world's woes.[2] As the law of God was despised during the French Revolution, so will it be when darkness envelops almost the whole world. Those who, like the faithful in medieval times and during the French Revolution, cling to the Word of God will be despised and persecuted.

This will be what's called "the time of Jacob's trouble"—the time during which evil demons and their human counterparts seek to destroy first the faith and then the persons of those who have committed themselves to God (fifth trumpet). The sixth trumpet warns of the final attack Satan and lost humankind make on the people of God. Then comes the sixth plague (Rev. 16:12), the drying up of the river Euphrates—when those who are lost withdraw their support for antitypical Babylon.

God's two witnesses

In the period from the sounding of the fourth trumpet (Rev. 8:12) through to the metaphorical drying up of the river Euphrates after the sixth trumpet, the Word of God will be replaced by the veneration of Satan and the exaltation of his counterfeit day of worship by the majority of the world.[3] As during the period of papal supremacy a satanic substitute religion replaced the religion of the Bible for most people in Western Europe, so in this period after probation's close the final act in the drama of deception is remarkably successful with the lost and unbelieving world.

But the darkness will not be complete, for "the people of God will not be misled."[4] Just as God had His faithful ones during the period of papal supremacy, so after the close of probation the faithful remnant refuse to be deluded.

During this period, which has been characterized as earth's darkest midnight, the power of God's Word will be evident by the fulfillment of its warnings and threatenings upon the wicked who have finally rejected Bible truth. God rains the plagues upon the wicked (Rev. 16) "because they refused to love the truth and so be saved" (2 Thess. 2:10). As the Word of God warned, the strong delusion caused by the "man of lawlessness" (2 Thess. 2:3–11) ends for the lost in suffering and retribution. In this sense the two witnesses have the power to produce fire "to consume their foes" (cf. Rev. 16:8, 9 with 11:5). They also "have power to shut the sky, that no rain may fall during the days of their prophesying" (Rev. 11:6). "They have power over the waters to turn them into blood" (Rev. 11:6; cf. the second and third plagues, Rev. 16:3–7). And they have the power to produce the seven last plagues. The predictions of Revelation 16 will be dramatically fulfilled when God's Word is "clothed in sackcloth" after the close of probation.[5]

THE BEAST'S ATTACK

The attack of revolutionary France on the Bible for three and a half years (1793–1797) was a historical type of the final attack of the unbelieving peoples of earth upon God's truth and His people. The people of France saw that the papacy was the prime cause of their suffering, and when they rejected the papal church, they rejected the Bible too. Like their spiritual predecessors, the people who live in the end time blame their sufferings on the people of God and the message they regard as dear.

Satan, working through antitypical Babylon (the papacy, apostate Protestantism, and spiritism), is "the beast that ascends from the bottomless pit" (Rev. 11:7). He stirs up the lost to pass a death decree and to attack the people of God and their faith (cf. Rev. 13:15). For a short period immediately before the Advent, it seems to the faithful that they have been left to perish.[6] This time, from the beginning of the death movement until the date set for it to be carried out,[7] is represented by the three and a half years during which the Bible was denigrated in France. During this period, the lost will exult over the people of God and try to destroy them and the truth they represent (Rev. 11:9, 10).

> To human sight it will appear that the people of God must soon seal their testimony with their blood as did the martyrs before them. They themselves begin to fear that the Lord has left them to fall by the hand of their enemies. It is a time of fearful agony. Day and night they cry unto God for deliverance. The wicked exult, and the jeering cry is heard: "Where now is your faith? Why does not God deliver you out of our hands if you are indeed His people?" But the waiting ones remember Jesus dying upon Calvary's cross and the chief priests and rulers

shouting in mockery: "He saved others; Himself He cannot save. If He be the King of Israel, let Him now come down from the cross, and we will believe Him." Matthew 27:42. Like Jacob, all are wrestling with God. Their countenances express their internal struggle. Paleness sits upon every face. Yet they cease not their earnest intercession.[8]

When the protection of human laws shall be withdrawn from those who honor the law of God, there will be, in different lands, a simultaneous movement for their destruction. As the time appointed in the decree draws near, the people will conspire to root out the hated sect. It will be determined to strike in one night a decisive blow, which shall utterly silence the voice of dissent and reproof.[9]

Eventually, though, the lost will see that they have been deceived by the church-state union (Babylon, Rev. 17; 18) that is Satan's masterpiece of deception. "When the voice of God turns the captivity of His people, there is a terrible awakening of those who have lost all in the great conflict of life."[10] When thus finally awakened to a realization of their lost state, the wicked turn against antitypical Babylon, and a terrible slaughter follows, similar to that seen in France during the Revolution when hundreds of priests were massacred or forced to flee, and the pope was taken prisoner. The events that marked the end of the period of papal ecclesiastical supremacy in France are a type of the events that mark the fall of Babylon when God's voice turns the captivity of His people.

The metaphorical drying up of the river Euphrates (Rev. 16:12), which prepares the way for the coming of Christ, was typified by the events leading up to 1798, which made possible the experience of those who looked with longing anticipation for Jesus to come in 1844. As Sodom and Egypt symbolize the people of France who rejected both the papal church and the Bible, so, in their end-time application, Sodom and Egypt represent the lost peoples of earth who reject both Satan's counterfeit—antitypical Babylon—and God's truth.

THE RESCUE

> But after the three and a half days a breath of life from God entered them, and they stood up on their feet, and great fear fell on those who saw them. Then they heard a loud voice from heaven saying to them, "Come up hither!" And in the sight of their foes they went up to heaven in a cloud. And at that hour there was a great earthquake, and a tenth of the city fell; seven thousand people were killed in the earthquake, and the rest were terrified and gave glory to the God of heaven (Rev. 11:11–13).

These events are dramatized on pages 635 to 640 of Ellen White's *The Great Controversy*. The wicked are about to destroy the people of God, when, suddenly, a dense blackness shrouds the earth. Then a rainbow with "overpowering brightness" appears in the heavens and seems to surround the praying people of God. The rainbow, the symbol of God's covenant, arouses great fear in the angry multitudes, who have been bent on destroying the faithful. The people of God, however, view the rainbow with joy. Looking toward heaven, they "see the glory of God and the Son of man seated upon His throne" and rejoice at God's miraculous intervention on their behalf. Then the faithful and the rebellious hear the voice of God announcing, "It is done" (Rev. 16:17). His voice creates a mighty earthquake, greater than any the world has ever witnessed.

> The firmament appears to open and shut. The glory from the throne of God seems flashing through. The mountains shake like a reed in the wind, and ragged rocks are scattered on every side. There is a roar as of a coming tempest. The sea is lashed into fury. There is heard the shriek of a hurricane like the voice of demons upon a mission of destruction. The whole earth heaves and swells like the waves of the sea. Its surface is breaking up. Its very foundations seem to be giving way. Mountain chains are sinking. Inhabited islands disappear. The seaports that have become like Sodom for wickedness are swallowed up by the angry waters. Babylon the great has come in remembrance before God, "to give unto her the cup of the wine of the fierceness of His wrath." Great hailstones, every one "about the weight of a talent," are doing their work of destruction. Verses 19, 21. The proudest cities of the earth are laid low. The lordly palaces, upon which the world's great men have lavished their wealth in order to glorify themselves, are crumbling to ruin before their eyes. Prison walls are rent asunder, and God's people, who have been held in bondage for their faith, are set free.[11]

Then occurs the partial resurrection (cf. Dan. 12:2; Matt. 26:64). Those who have died believing in the third angel's message, those who crucified Christ, and the most violent opposers of His truth and His people will be raised to see the final events of earth's history and to witness Christ's second coming.

In the midst of the cataclysmic events on earth and in the heavens, the wicked hear mysterious and awful voices declaring their ultimate doom. The false teachers who led out in the movement to destroy those who were honoring the commandments of God are, at this time, made especially aware of their lost condition.

> Demons acknowledge the deity of Christ and tremble before His power, while men are supplicating for mercy and groveling in abject terror. . . . Through a rift in the clouds there beams a star whose brilliancy is increased fourfold in contrast with the darkness. It speaks hope and joy to the faithful, but severity and wrath to the transgressors of God's law.[12]

God's faithful ones now rejoice in their newfound security. God has intervened on their behalf. They have been delivered from evil demons and their human counterparts. Faith, hope, and love have replaced their anxiety and fear, and they praise God in the words of Scripture: "God is our refuge and strength, a very present help in trouble. Therefore will not we fear, though the earth be removed, and though the mountains be carried into the midst of the sea; though the waters thereof roar and be troubled, though the mountains shake with the swelling thereof" (Ps. 46:1–3, KJV).

"Then there appears against the sky a hand holding two tables of stone folded together."[13]

God's law appears in the heavens, the law that was proclaimed from Sinai and that was faithfully observed by His believing people throughout history. The saved and the lost read the inspired words. Thus is fulfilled the prediction: "In the sight of their foes they [God's two witnesses] went up to heaven in a cloud" (Rev. 11:12). "Memory is aroused, the darkness of superstition and heresy is swept from every mind, and God's ten words, brief, comprehensive, and authoritative, are presented to the view of all the inhabitants of earth."[14]

The lost are overwhelmed with horror and despair. They have rejected God's law, the very law that now appears in the heavens before them, and they have despised and attacked those who faithfully observed it. They have followed Satan's demand that they profane the Sabbath day and observe his counterfeit day. Now they realize how wrong they have been. "Too late they see that the Sabbath of the fourth commandment is the seal of the living God."[15] They realize that they have been fighting against God and following religious teachers who professed to be leading them to heaven, but in fact were leading them to eternal destruction.

The saved hear the voice of God announcing the day and hour of Jesus' coming, and soon there appears "in the east a small black cloud, about half the size of a man's hand."[16] The faithful rejoice because they know that this is Jesus, the antitypical Cyrus, finally coming with all the holy angels to deliver them from this sin-cursed earth. But the wicked tremble with fear and foreboding as they contemplate their inevitable doom.

The end of time as we know it has finally come.

---

1. See White, *The Great Controversy,* 639, 640.
2. Ibid., 614.
3. Ibid., 624, 625.
4. Ibid., 625.
5. See ibid., 627–629.
6. Ibid., 630, 631.
7. Ibid., 635.
8. Ibid., 630.
9. Ibid., 635.
10. Ibid., 654.
11. Ibid., 637.
12. Ibid., 638.
13. Ibid., 639.

14. Ibid.
15. Ibid., 640.
16. Ibid.

CHAPTER 14

THE SEVENTH TRUMPET

We have seen that the trumpets are blown right after the historical and end-time closes of probation. Now the question arises, what is the end point for the historical trumpets and the eschatological trumpets?

The obvious answer is that the seventh trumpet announces the second coming of Christ. However, the Second Advent doesn't follow immediately after the seventh trumpet is blown; there are preliminary events that will occur first.

What are these events?

CHRIST'S REIGN

"Then the seventh angel blew his trumpet, and there were loud voices in heaven, saying, 'The kingdom of the world has become the kingdom of our Lord and of his Christ, and he shall reign for ever and ever' " (Rev. 11:15). There is a sense in which the kingdom of the world becomes Christ's during the pre-Advent judgment (Dan. 7:9–14). Daniel informs us that during this judgment, "to him [the "Son of man"; i.e., Christ] was given dominion and glory and kingdom, that all peoples, nations, and languages should serve him" (verse 14). But in the final analysis, the kingdom of the world becomes Christ's at His second advent—only then does the Lamb conquer the nations of earth and begin to reign as "Lord of lords and King of kings" (Rev. 17:14).

In Revelation 19, Christ is metaphorically depicted as coming on a white horse leading the armies of heaven:

> Then I saw heaven opened, and behold, a white horse! He who sat upon it is called Faithful and True, and in righteousness he judges and makes war. His eyes are like a flame of fire, and on his head are many diadems; and he has a name inscribed which no one knows but himself. He is clad in a robe dipped in blood, and the name by which he is called is The Word of God. And the armies of heaven, arrayed in fine linen, white and pure, followed him on white horses. From his mouth issues a sharp sword with which to smite the nations, and he will rule them with a rod of iron; he will tread the wine press of the fury of the wrath of God the Almighty. On his robe and on his thigh he has a name inscribed, King of kings and Lord of lords (Rev. 19:11–16).

We are, meanwhile, told:

> About His coming cluster the glories of that "restitution of all things, which God hath spoken by the mouth of all His holy prophets since the world began." Acts 3:21. Then the long-continued rule of evil shall be broken; "the kingdoms of this world" will become "the kingdoms of our Lord, and of His Christ; and He shall reign for ever and ever." Revelation 11:15. "The glory of the Lord shall be revealed, and all flesh

shall see it together." "The Lord God will cause righteousness and praise to spring forth before all nations." He shall be "for a crown of glory, and for a diadem of beauty, unto the residue of His people." Isaiah 40:5; 61:11; Isaiah 28:5.[1]

"The kingdoms of this world have not yet become the kingdoms of our Lord and of His Christ. Do not deceive yourselves; be wide awake and move rapidly, for the night cometh in which no man can work."[2]

"And the twenty-four elders who sit on their thrones before God fell on their faces and worshiped God, saying, 'We give thanks to thee, Lord God Almighty, who art and who wast, that thou hast taken thy great power and begun to reign' " (Rev. 11:16, 17). Christ's reign begins in the final eschatological sense at the Second Advent when the wicked are destroyed and the righteous are finally redeemed. Daniel spoke of the beginning of Christ's reign:

And in the days of those kings the God of heaven will set up a kingdom which shall never be destroyed, nor shall its sovereignty be left to another people. It shall break in pieces all these kingdoms and bring them to an end, and it shall stand for ever (Dan. 2:44).

Jesus also predicted the beginning of His eternal reign:

"Immediately after the tribulation of those days the sun will be darkened, and the moon will not give its light, and the stars will fall from heaven, and the powers of the heavens will be shaken; then will appear the sign of the Son of man in heaven, and then all the tribes of the earth will mourn, and they will see the Son of man coming on the clouds of heaven with power and great glory; and he will send out his angels with a loud trumpet call, and they will gather his elect from the four winds, from one end of heaven to the other" (Matt. 24:29–31).[3]

"The nations raged, but thy wrath came, and the time for the dead to be judged, for rewarding thy servants, the prophets and saints, and those who fear thy name, both small and great, and for destroying the destroyers of the earth" (Rev. 11:18). "The nations raged" takes us back in time to the period just before the Second Advent. "Thy wrath came" refers to the seven last plagues of Revelation 16, the ultimate manifestation of God's wrath, at least when Jesus appears (Rev. 6:12–17).

DEAD JUDGED

"The time for the dead to be judged" has a dual application. The pre-Advent judgment beginning in 1844 and continuing until the end-time close of probation is the time for the dead to be judged (Dan. 7:9–14; 8:14). But the ultimate time for the dead to be judged is at the Second Advent (2 Tim. 4:1, 8) and at the end of the millennium (Rev. 20:9–15). The time for the dead to be judged is the time "for rewarding thy servants." Rewards are given at "the resurrection of the just" (Luke 14:14; cf. John 5:28, 29; Acts 24:15; 1 Thess. 4:16–18; 1 Cor. 15:51–54). The time for the dead to be judged is the time "for destroying the destroyers of the earth." The wicked who are the destroyers of the earth are destroyed at the second coming of Jesus (2 Thess. 1:7, 8; 2:8; 2 Pet. 3:10; Ps. 94:1–3; Mic. 5:15; Rom. 12:19; Heb. 10:29–31).

Thus, considered as the culmination of a historical interpretation of the trumpets (in other words, from AD 34 to the end of history), the seventh trumpet (Rev. 11:15–19) covers the period from 1844 to the second coming of Jesus. The seventh trumpet begins to sound at the point of the proclamation "there should be time no longer [*chronos ouketi estai*]" (Rev. 10:6, KJV). The prophet wrote:

> The angel which I saw stand upon the sea and upon the earth lifted up his hand to heaven, and sware by him that liveth for ever and ever, who created heaven, and the things that therein are, and the earth, and the things that therein are, and the sea, and the things which are therein, that there should be time no longer: But in the days of the voice of the seventh angel, when he shall begin to sound, the mystery of God should be finished, as he hath declared to his servants the prophets (Rev. 10:5–7, KJV).

The proclamation that "there should be time no longer" marks the end of the time prophecies. But this is not the end of historical time. After that proclamation, John was told, "You must again prophesy about many peoples and nations and tongues and kings" (verse 11). None of the time prophecies extended beyond 1844, but the witness of the prophets continued after that date.

The seventh trumpet includes "the time for the dead to be judged, for rewarding thy servants, the prophets and saints, and those who fear thy name, both small and great, and for destroying the destroyers of the earth" (Rev. 11:18). The historical time for the dead to be judged is spelled out clearly in Bible prophecy. Daniel 7:9–14 describes the investigative judgment in heaven prior to the second coming of Jesus. God took His place on the throne in the heavenly court and was surrounded by myriads of heavenly beings. "The court sat in judgment, and the books were opened" (Dan. 7:10). Verse 22 indicates that this "judgment was given for the saints of the Most High"; hence, the pre-Advent judgment not only condemns the little horn power (verse 8), but also provides ultimate vindication for the people of God.

The historical time for the dead to be judged is also spoken of in Revelation 6:

> When he opened the fifth seal, I saw under the altar the souls of those who had been slain for the word of God and for the witness they had borne; they cried out with a loud voice, "O Sovereign Lord, holy and true, how long before thou wilt judge and avenge our blood on those who dwell upon the earth?" Then they were each given a white robe and told to rest a little longer, until the number of their fellow servants and their brethren should be complete, who were to be killed as they themselves had been (Rev. 6:9–11).

The altar represents the altar of burnt offering in the court of the sanctuary. The only place where Israelites were to offer sacrifices was at the altar of burnt offering (Lev. 17:1–8). In the offering of animal sacrifices, the excess blood was poured at the base of the altar of burnt offering (Lev. 4:7, 18, 25, 30). The blood represented life (Gen. 9:4; Lev. 17:10, 11; Deut. 12:23). The blood poured at the base of the altar symbolized the blood of Christ (Ps. 22:14; Isa. 53:12) and the blood of faithful martyrs (Phil. 3:10).

Though the martyrs lie asleep in their graves, their blood cries out to God for justice and vindication, as the blood of Abel cried out from the ground (Gen. 4:10). Then they are given white robes that represent vindication in the heavenly pre-Advent judgment. This is a fulfillment of Daniel 7:22: "Judgment was given in favor of the holy ones of the Most High" (JPS). They are told to "rest a little while longer" (Rev. 6:11). They are soon to be awakened from their sleep at the coming of Jesus (1 Cor. 15:51–54).

THE LIVING

What happens to living believers before the vindicated dead are raised? Translated literally from the Greek text, Revelation 6:11 says, "And a white robe was given to each of them, and it was said to them that they should rest yet a little time, until also their fellow servants and their brethren, who are about to be killed as they were, might be made complete." Note that the verb *to number* does not occur in the Greek text, nor is the making up of a number a necessary connotation of the Greek verb (*pleroō*). This verb means "to make full," "to fill," "to fulfill," "to complete," "to finish something already begun," and so "to perfect." The New Testament often uses this verb in contexts that mean God's will is to be perfectly fulfilled in and by believers who are filled with the Holy Spirit. (See Rom. 8:4; 2 Cor. 10:5, 6; Gal. 5:14; Eph. 3:19; 5:18; Phil. 1:9–11; Col. 2:10; 2 Thess. 1:11; Rev. 3:2.) After the judgment of the dead, they are told to rest a little while until their fellow believers who are living are made complete in Christ, which happens when He bestows upon them the gift of His righteousness (Rev. 19:7, 8).

Revelation 6:9–11 indicates that the historical time for the dead to be judged is followed by the Lord making their living brethren and sisters spiritually complete in Christ so that they, too, can be finally vindicated in the heavenly pre-Advent judgment.

THE TEMPLE IN HEAVEN

"Then God's temple in heaven was opened, and the ark of his

covenant was seen within his temple; and there were flashes of lightning, voices, peals of thunder, an earthquake, and heavy hail" (Rev. 11:19). When considered in terms of the historical interpretation of the trumpets, Revelation 11:19 refers to the beginning of the antitypical day of atonement in 1844, at which time the Most Holy Place ministry of Christ began. Only on the Day of Atonement did the high priest enter the Most Holy Place of the earthly sanctuary (Lev. 16:2, 29–34). With the eye of faith, the people followed the high priest as he entered into the presence of God to minister on their behalf. Just so it must be for God's people today.

"The temple of God was opened in heaven, and there was seen in His temple the ark of His testament." Revelation 11:19. The ark of God's testament is in the holy of holies, the second apartment of the sanctuary. In the ministration of the earthly tabernacle, which served "unto the example and shadow of heavenly things," this apartment was opened only upon the great Day of Atonement for the cleansing of the sanctuary. Therefore the announcement that the temple of God was opened in heaven and the ark of His testament was seen points to the opening of the most holy place of the heavenly sanctuary in 1844 as Christ entered there to perform the closing work of the atonement. Those who by faith followed their great High Priest as He entered upon His ministry in the most holy place, beheld the ark of His testament. As they had studied the subject of the sanctuary they had come to understand the Saviour's change of ministration, and they saw that He was now officiating before the ark of God, pleading His blood in behalf of sinners.

The ark in the tabernacle on earth contained the two tables of stone, upon which were inscribed the precepts of the law of God. The ark was merely a receptacle for the tables of the law, and the presence of the divine precepts gave to it its value and sacredness. When the temple of God was opened in heaven, the ark of His testament was seen. Within the holy of holies, in the sanctuary in heaven, the divine law is sacredly enshrined—the law that was spoken by God Himself amid the thunders of Sinai and written with His own finger on the tables of stone.

The law of God in the sanctuary in heaven is the great original, of which the precepts inscribed upon the tables of stone and recorded by Moses in the Pentateuch were an unerring transcript. Those who arrived at an understanding of this important point were thus led to see the sacred, unchanging character of the divine law.[4]

When the seventh trumpet is considered as the culmination of the eschatological interpretation of the trumpets (in other words, from the close of probation to the end of time), it refers to the period beginning immediately before the Second Advent and extending to the final destruction of the wicked at the end of the millennium (Rev. 11:15, 18; 20:7–15). The seventh trumpet parallels the seventh plague:

The seventh angel poured his bowl into the air, and a loud voice came out of the temple, from the throne, saying, "It is done!" And there were flashes of lightning, voices, peals of thunder, and a great earthquake such as had never been since men were on the earth, so great was that earthquake. The great city was split into three parts, and the cities of the nations fell, and God remembered great Babylon, to make her drain the cup of the fury of his wrath. And every island fled away, and no mountains were to be found; and great hailstones, heavy as a hundred-weight, dropped on men from heaven, till men cursed God for the plague of the hail, so fearful was that plague (Rev. 16:17–21; cf. 11:13).

In this eschatological interpretation, Revelation 11:19 refers to the opening of the heavenly temple just before the Second Advent to reveal God's law to the inhabitants of earth. It also refers to the final revelation of His law to the saved and the lost in the judgment scene at the end of the millennium.

"And He [Christ] gave unto Moses, when He had made an end of communicating with him upon Mount Sinai, two tables of testimony, tables of stone, written by the finger of God." Nothing written on those tables could be blotted out. The precious record of the law was placed in the ark of the testament and is still there, safely hidden from the human family. But in God's appointed time He will bring forth these tables of stone to be a testimony to all the world against the disregard of His commandments and against the idolatrous worship of a counterfeit Sabbath. . . .

There are abundant evidences of the immutability of God's law. It was written with the finger of God, never to be obliterated, never to be destroyed. The tables of stone are hidden by God, to be produced in the great judgment day, just as He wrote them. . . .

When the judgment shall sit, and the books shall be opened, and every man shall be judged according to the things written in the books, then the tables of stone, hidden by God until that day, will be presented before the world as the standard of righteousness. Then men and women will see that the prerequisite of their salvation is obedience to the perfect law of God. None will find excuse for sin. By the righteous principles of that law, men will receive their sentence of life or of death.[5]

When God's temple in heaven is opened, what a triumphant time that will be for all who have been faithful and true! In the temple will be seen the ark of the testament in which were placed the two tables of stone, on which are written God's law. These tables of stone will be brought forth from their hiding place, and on them will be seen the Ten Commandments engraved by the finger of God. These tables of stone now lying in the ark of the testament will be a convincing testimony to the truth and binding claims of God's law. . . .

Sacrilegious minds and hearts have thought they were mighty enough to change the times and laws of Jehovah; but safe in the archives of heaven, in the ark of God, are the original commandments, written upon the two tables of stone. No potentate of earth has power to draw forth those tables from their sacred hiding place beneath the mercy seat.[6]

When God intervenes on behalf of His people, they look up and see the tokens of their deliverance and praise God in the words of Psalm 46:1–3:

God is our refuge and strength,
    a very present help in trouble.
Therefore we will not fear though the earth should change,
    though the mountains shake in the heart of the sea;
Though its waters roar and foam,
    though the mountains tremble with its tumult.

While these words of holy trust ascend to God, the clouds sweep back, and the starry heavens are seen, unspeakably glorious in contrast with the black and angry firmament on either side. The glory of the celestial city streams from the gates ajar. Then there appears against the sky a hand holding two tables of stone folded together. Says the prophet: "The heavens shall declare His righteousness: for God is judge Himself." Psalm 50:6. That holy law, God's righteousness, that amid thunder and flame was proclaimed from Sinai as the guide of life, is now revealed to men as the rule of judgment. The hand opens the tables, and there are seen the precepts of the Decalogue, traced as with a pen of fire. The words are so plain that all can read them. Memory is aroused, the darkness of superstition and heresy is swept from every mind, and God's ten words, brief, comprehensive, and authoritative, are presented to the view of all the inhabitants of the earth.[7]

[At the end of the millennium,] the whole wicked world stand arraigned at the bar of God on the charge of high treason against the government of heaven. They have none to plead their cause; they are without excuse; and the sentence of eternal death is pronounced against them. . . .

As if entranced, the wicked have looked upon the coronation of the Son of God. They see in His hands the tables of the divine law, the statutes which they have despised and transgressed. They witness the outburst of wonder, rapture, and adoration from the saved; and as the wave of melody sweeps over the multitudes without the city, all with one voice exclaim, "Great and marvelous are Thy works, Lord God Almighty; just and true are Thy ways, Thou King of saints" (Rev. 15:3); and, falling prostrate, they worship the Prince of life.[8]

The chart titled "The Dual Interpretation of the Trumpets" illustrates how the historical and end-time interpretations of the trumpets fit the prophetic portrayal of end-time events.

THE DUAL INTERPRETATION OF THE TRUMPETS

Historical Trumpets

| | | | | | | | End-time Trumpets | | | | | | |

First Trumpet · Second Trumpet · Third Trumpet · Fourth Trumpet · Fifth Trumpet · Sixth Trumpet · Seventh Trumpet · 1 · 2 · 3 · 4 · 5 · 6 · 7

AD 34 · AD 1844 · Close of Probation · Seven Last Plagues · Second Advent

By way of summary, we can say that the historical trumpets cover the period from the close of probation for Israel in AD 34 till the Second Advent, the seventh trumpet occupying the period from 1844 to the Second Advent. God's temple in heaven opened in 1844 in the sense that at that time, people arrived at a clear understanding of Christ's Most Holy Place ministry in the pre-Advent judgment.

Considered eschatologically, the seven trumpets reach from the end-time close of probation to the Second Advent. From this perspective, the seventh trumpet occupies the period from God's intervention on behalf of His persecuted people till the coming of Jesus. And God's temple in heaven is then opened in the ultimate sense— the Ten Commandment law being displayed in the heavens for the whole world to see. At that time God's faithful people rejoice because, by His grace, they have been obedient to the commandments. In contrast, the lost grieve; their condition is hopeless because they have chosen to reject God's sacred law.

---

1. White, *The Great Controversy*, 301.
2. Ellen G. White, *Counsels to Parents and Teachers* (Mountain View, CA: Pacific Press®, 1913), 414.
3. See White, *The Great Controversy*, 641–652.
4. White, *The Great Controversy*, 433, 434. See also *Seventh-day Adventist Bible Commentary*, 4:1139, 1152; White, *The Story of Redemption*, 379–381; White, *Early Writings*, 32, 33; White, *Testimonies for the Church*, 2:693.
5. *Seventh-day Adventist Bible Commentary*, 1:1109.
6. Ibid., 7:972.
7. White, *The Great Controversy*, 639.
8. Ibid., 668, 669.

CHAPTER 15
SUMMARY AND CONCLUSIONS

The first chapter of this book discusses the theme and structure of the book of Revelation. The theme is Christ's care for His faithful people through the ages, in the process of which He counteracts Satan's destructive work. Hence, the book of Revelation dwells largely on the great controversy between Christ and Satan. Christ is depicted as our heavenly Mediator and Judge, who, after conducting the pre-Advent judgment, returns in glory to translate His redeemed people to heaven and to punish unbelievers. Revelation presents the sweep of history in view of the end time.

Of the five approaches to Revelation, I have favored the philosophy of history interpretation, which recognizes history as cyclical and repetitive. My concern has been to allow the Bible to be its own expositor. Revelation's symbolism must be interpreted in the light of the use of similar symbolism throughout Scripture.

In terms of literary structure, Revelation can be regarded as a chiasm, the last section paralleling the first, the next-to-the-last section paralleling the second, the third section from the end paralleling the third, and the center of the book comprising its climax, its main point. Chapter 14 is the center of Revelation. It points out the character

God's people must have to inherit the heavenly kingdom and indicates that such character results from entering into the experience presented in the messages delivered by the three angels pictured in that chapter.

The story of the trumpets begins with Revelation 8:2–5, which chapter 2 of this book discussed.* We find in the Old Testament how trumpets were used in Israel: (1) they were blown as a call to worship; (2) they signaled the approaching judgment on the Day of Atonement; (3) they were a call for God's people to go to war against their enemies; (4) they warned that God's unfaithful people would be punished by their enemies; (5) they proclaimed that ungodly nations that were used to punish God's people would themselves suffer retribution for their unbelief; and (6) they announced the coming day of the Lord, a day of local calamity that was a type of the ultimate eschatological Day of the Lord.

In Revelation, the prophecy of the trumpets serves (1) to call God's professed people to repentance and genuine worship; (2) to warn of Satan's historical and end-time attacks against God's people; (3) to warn of the coming pre-Advent judgment that would conclude with the close of probation; and (4) to announce the approaching Day of the Lord—the second advent of Christ.

As I pointed out in chapter 2, the altar of Revelation 8:3 represents the altar of incense in heaven upon which Christ is offering incense, the merits of His intercession mingling with the prayers of His people. In Scripture, incense is a symbol of prayer and of Christ's intercession. Christ's casting the censer to the earth (Rev. 8:5), then, represents the close of probation—the point beyond which God's

---

* Revelation 8:1 describes the opening of the seventh seal, so that verse belongs with the prophecy of the seals. Note also that the seven angels who were given the seven trumpets appear again in Revelation—see Rev. 15:6–8; 16:1; 17:1; 21:9.

mercy no longer pleads for His people; the point before which all people have decided whether or not they will serve God. The trumpets are given to the seven angels before Christ's intercessory ministry ends (Rev. 8:2), but they don't blow them until He casts the censer to the earth (Rev. 8:6). Thus, the sounding of the trumpets occurs after the close of probation.

There was a historical close of probation for the Israelite nation in AD 34—the end point of Daniel's seventy-week prophecy (Dan. 9:24–27). Hence, by the historical interpretation, the trumpets sound after a close of probation. There is also an end-time close of probation at the conclusion of the pre-Advent judgment (see also Rev. 7:1–3; 15:5–8; 22:11, 12). The trumpets sound after this event too. The historical trumpets are types or examples of events that will occur between the end-time close of probation and the second coming of Jesus.

FIRST TRUMPET

When the first trumpet sounds, "hail and fire, mixed with blood . . . fell on the earth; and a third of the earth was burnt up, and a third of the trees were burnt up, and all the green grass was burnt up" (Rev. 8:7). Hail, fire, and blood are symbols used in three main ways in Scripture: (1) to denote God's punishment of His enemies who are also enemies of His people; (2) to represent God's judgments on His own unfaithful people; and (3) in warnings of the judgments that will be poured out just before and during the second coming of Christ and at the end of the millennium.

Sometimes, in Scripture, the *earth* is used as a symbol of all the peoples of the world, while at other times it represents Israel, God's professed people. And sometimes *trees* represent God's professed people, while at other times they denote the leaders of His people.

The *burning* of trees symbolizes judgments upon God's unfaithful people. *Green grass* may represent the inhabitants of the earth or the people of God, whether faithful or unfaithful. The use of a fraction— the *third* of the earth and the trees—indicates that the destruction isn't universal, while the designation *all* the green grass suggests all the unfaithful people who live in the third of the earth that is under attack.

Applying the symbolism to the historical situation after the probationary period given to the ancient Israelite nation expired, I have concluded that the first trumpet refers to the destruction of Jerusalem and the temple in AD 70. This destruction was a type of the devil-inspired attack upon the professed people of God after the end-time close of probation. As in the destruction of Jerusalem, the faithful will be sheltered, while those who had once been believers but who have apostatized and aren't ready for the close of probation will suffer at the hands of their devil-inspired enemies.

SECOND TRUMPET

The second trumpet brings to view "a great mountain, burning with fire" that is thrown into the sea, resulting in "a third of the sea" becoming blood, and "a third of the living creatures in the sea" dying, and "a third of the ships" being destroyed (Rev. 8:8, 9).

In Scripture, a mountain often represents a nation or power. The fall of the Neo-Babylonian Empire is depicted as a great mountain being cast into the sea. Likewise, the nations that succeeded Babylon were ultimately destroyed because of their unfaithfulness to the Lord. The Roman Empire is referred to in Scripture as Babylon, and the fall of Rome is predicted in Daniel and Revelation.

I have concluded that, historically, the second trumpet refers to the decline and fall of the Roman Empire. Eschatologically, the second trumpet predicts that the secular authority that undergirds the end-time false religious system will be torn away. Earth's superpowers will collapse as did the Roman Empire. National apostasy will result in national ruin.

Third trumpet

The third trumpet (Rev. 8:10, 11) depicts "a great star" named Wormwood falling from heaven and polluting "the rivers and fountains of water." "A third of the waters became wormwood, and many men died of the water, because it was made bitter."

In the fifth chapter of this book, I have identified the star as Satan, who, with his demons, was cast out of heaven (Rev. 12). Satan, "blazing like a torch," provides a counterfeit to the light of Christ that is reflected through His Word and His people. "Rivers and fountains of water" refer to the love and truth God extends to humanity. He is "the fountain of living waters" (Jer. 2:13). Wormword (*apsinthos*) is a bitter herb, so it is an appropriate symbol of Satan.

Historically, in the period of Pergamum (AD 313–538; Rev. 2:12–17), Satan was successful in mingling truth with pagan error, which resulted in spiritual apostasy. It was during this period that the papacy rose to ecclesiastical predominance. The church experienced four major developments during this time: (1) the establishment of the monarchical episcopate; (2) the rise to primacy of the Roman episcopate; (3) the acceptance of theological dogmas in which Greek and pagan concepts were mingled with Christian truth; and (4) the growth of the medieval church-state union. These developments produced the compromised, fallen church of the Middle Ages.

Eschatologically, after the close of probation, Satan will launch a great final attack on God's truth. The crowning act of his efforts will be his impersonation of Christ. He will appear in various places on earth as though he is the Christ, and he will promote unbiblical teachings as though they are truth. He will exonerate Sunday worship and condemn those who are keeping holy the seventh-day Sabbath. But this almost overmastering delusion will not deceive the true people of God. Satan's effort will be to confirm his followers in their erroneous beliefs and to induce God's sealed people to forsake their faith and align themselves under his banner. But God's people will successfully resist his temptations.

FOURTH TRUMPET

The fourth trumpet (Rev. 8:12), dealt with in chapter 6, speaks of a third of the sun, moon, and stars being struck with darkness; "a third of the day was kept from shining, and likewise a third of the night."

The darkness of this trumpet is the direct result of Satan's pollution of Christian truth, described in the third trumpet. In Scripture, the sun sometimes represents God Himself and the spiritual light that emanates from Him. The sun also symbolizes Christ and His righteousness, heaven's angels, the light that comes from faithful leaders of the people, God's faithful people themselves, and in some instances false deities. The darkening of the sun, moon, and stars may refer to God's judgments upon those who have rejected His truth. The result is withdrawal of His divine favor, followed by the destruction that is the inevitable result of His leaving.

Historically, the fourth trumpet spells out the tragic result of the third one. The rise of the papacy in the period of Pergamum (AD 313–538) resulted in the darkness of the medieval period, symbolized by the church of Thyatira (AD 538–1517; Rev. 2:18–29). In this period, the church-state union was involved in the suppression of divine enlightenment, and consequently spiritual darkness blanketed so-called Christian Europe. The little horn power of Daniel 7 was successful at engendering theological and spiritual darkness.

Eschatologically, after the close of probation, Satan's impersonation of Christ, brought to view by the third trumpet, will result in almost universal spiritual and theological darkness under the fourth trumpet, and the masses of earth will unite under the banner of the prince of darkness himself. False doctrines and practices will be accepted by the multitudes of earth, and the greatest spiritual darkness of human history will result.

Fifth trumpet

The fifth trumpet (Rev. 9:1–12) describes the evil activities of "a star fallen from heaven to earth" who releases smoke from "the shaft of the bottomless pit." From this smoke emerge locusts that have the power of scorpions. They torture humans for a period of five months. But they are not permitted to harm those who have the seal of God. Some who are tortured will long to die, but "death will fly from them." These locusts that have the power of scorpions look like cavalry soldiers.

I believe the star fallen from heaven pictured in chapter 7 represents Satan. The bottomless pit represents the realm of the devil and his demons. Satan is identified as "Abaddon" and "Apollyon," meaning the destroyer (Rev. 9:11). He *is* the ultimate destroyer. The smoke that he releases upon the earth symbolizes spiritual confusion that results in the destruction of the unfaithful.

In Scripture, locusts may refer to a literal plague of insects, or they may denote destroying nations. The scorpions are symbols of the evil spirits whom Satan leads. The "grass of the earth," "green growth," and trees (Rev. 9:4) represent the people who are tortured—but not killed—by these demons. Those who have the seal of God and who are protected from these scorpions are those who have received both the initial seal of the Holy Spirit (Eph. 1:13, 14) and the end-time seal of God referred to in Revelation 7 and 14. The mention of the seal of God points us to an end-time application of this prophecy.

Historically, the power that tortured the Byzantine Empire and threatened the West for five prophetic months (or 150 literal years) was the empire of the Ottoman Turks. Their first attack on the Byzantine Empire was the Battle of Bapheum on July 27, 1299. This date marks the beginning of the 150 years of the fifth trumpet. This prophetic period ended on July 27, 1449, which marks the beginning of the period represented by the sixth trumpet.

The smoke from the bottomless pit symbolizes the teachings that were accepted by the Ottoman Turks—teachings that motivated them to fight the so-called infidels. Revelation 9:7–10 notes the appearance of the Ottoman cavalry.

Eschatologically, the greatest time of trouble this world has ever witnessed will occur after the close of probation. Demonic and human forces of evil will torment the professed people of God for an unspecified period of time. Those who are sealed will suffer as Satan endeavors to discourage them with the thought of their past sins and their lost condition, but they won't succumb to his deceptions. Those erstwhile believers who have not made the necessary spiritual preparation will suffer most intensely, wishing they could die because they are the focus of the exultant attacks of Satan and of the humans whom Satan controls.

This period is referred to in Scripture as the time of Jacob's trouble. As Jacob wrestled with Christ and gained the victory, so during this troublous period of the end time, God's faithful, sealed people will plead with Him and will refuse to give in to the discouragement and despair with which Satan wishes to overcome them.

History repeats itself. The Ottoman Turks are types of the demons who will torture the professed people of God after the end-time close of probation.

Sixth trumpet

The sixth trumpet (Rev. 9:13–21), dealt with in chapter 8 of this book, is a continuation of the fifth. It begins with the voice of Christ commanding the release of "the four angels bound at the great river Euphrates." In Scripture, the Euphrates is used as a symbol of the judgments upon unfaithful Israel and upon her pagan enemies. Revelation 9:14 seems to be announcing the coming judgments of God, who allows evil powers to attack and destroy the apostate peoples of earth. God allows humans to be punished and destroyed by the forces of evil because they have rejected His love, preferring idolatry, murder, sorcery, immorality, and theft (verses 20, 21). The four angels released at the river Euphrates may be regarded as the four main sultanates of the Ottoman Empire, located at Aleppo, Iconium, Damascus, and Baghdad.

Historically, the sixth trumpet began to sound on July 27, 1449. It stated that an antichristian power would persecute professed Christians for 391 years and fifteen days—a period that ended on August 11, 1840. On that very day the Ottoman Turks, who had grabbed control of the lands that stretched from Persia to Austria, formally accepted the suzerainty of Europe's great powers. (Rev. 9:17–19 describes the appearance of the Ottoman forces and alludes to their use of firearms.)

Eschatologically, the sixth trumpet describes the final great attack on the professed people of God after the close of probation and shortly before the intervention of Christ on behalf of His people. Evil spirits and humans who have rejected God will unite in a concerted, worldwide effort to wipe out God's last-day church. The Euphrates is a symbol of those end-time peoples who support antitypical Babylon. The professed people of God who have capitulated to its demands suffer most intensely; many will be wiped out, either by evil forces or by the plagues poured out by God.

The eschatological application of the sixth trumpet refers to Satan's final attack upon the professed people of God just prior to the second coming of Jesus. When the sixth trumpet is sounded, the sixth angel symbolically releases "the four angels who are bound at the great river Euphrates" (Rev. 9:14). These destroying angels (verse 15) represent the evil spirits who are responsible for motivating antitypical Babylon to make a final attack on the professed people of God.

The sixth plague (Rev. 16:12) presents the drying up of the river Euphrates as God's counteracting work, designed to protect His people from the work of Satan under the sixth trumpet. It counteracts the evil spirits by drying up the waters of the river. The peoples of earth will become disabused of Babylon's claims and will turn against their former religious and political leaders. The sixth trumpet is the work of Babylon; the sixth plague is Babylon's collapse, which is brought about by divine intervention immediately before the second coming of Jesus.

Revelation 16:13–16 parallels the sixth trumpet. These verses outline the work of Satan in uniting the forces of spiritualism, the papacy, and apostate Protestantism in preparation for the final clash with Christ. Satan will unite the world under his command in preparation for Armageddon (verse 16). But he will be frustrated by the metaphorical drying up of the river—because of Christ's intervention, lost human beings will realize that they have been deceived, and they will turn against their papal and apostate Protestant leaders.

Revelation 10 is part of the parenthetical section between the sixth and seventh trumpets (Rev. 10:1–11:14). Historically, chapter 10 contains Christ's announcement that there will be prophetic time no longer (Rev. 10:6), that no time prophecy extends beyond the beginning of the pre-Advent judgment (October 22, 1844). Christ is represented by the "mighty angel" whose presence spans earth and sea and who holds a little book open in His hand. The little book, once closed, is now open—which suggests that it was closed in the sense of not being understood and now is open in the sense of being understood.

Scripture mentions two books that were closed for a while but were to be opened eventually. The first is the book of Daniel, the end-time passages of which were not to be understood until the time of the end, which began in 1798 (Dan. 12:4–9). Historically speaking, the little book in the hand of Christ (Rev. 10:2) represents the book of Daniel. The last time prophecy of Daniel, in chapter 8:14, ended in 1844. Hence, Christ's proclamation that there shall be time no longer refers to the end of prophetic time prophecies in 1844.

John was told to take the little book and eat it; "it will be bitter to your stomach, but sweet as honey in your mouth" (Rev. 10:9). John ate the scroll, and, as he had been told, it was a sweet-bitter experience. The sweetness he tasted symbolizes the sweet experience of the Adventists who, with a new understanding of Daniel after 1840, proclaimed the second coming of Christ in 1844. But when He didn't return on the day they had expected Him, they were bitterly disappointed. Then the Adventists were told that they must prophesy again to "many peoples and nations and tongues and kings" (Rev. 10:11).

Considered eschatologically, Revelation 10 depicts Christ's intervention on behalf of His persecuted people when Satan and his followers launch their final, climactic attack upon them. Events in the heavens at that time will reveal Christ's protection of His faithful ones and will terrify those who have been pursuing them.

Christ's proclamation that time shall be no longer means that He is about to return to this earth to redeem the faithful and destroy the wicked. The little book in Christ's hand symbolizes the scroll of Revelation 5 that cannot be opened until the last seal is broken at Christ's second advent. This book of Revelation 5 contains the verdict of the heavenly court. As understanding of the book of Daniel gradually grew after 1798, so the verdict of the heavenly court will be partially known when the plagues are poured out upon the wicked, but not fully known until Jesus returns.

God's people went through a sweet-bitter experience in 1844; so will His people who live just before Jesus does return. His intervention for His people just before the Advent brings them great joy, but their rejoicing is mingled with the bitter sorrow of seeing so many people lost and the earth enveloped in turmoil and destruction.

As the early Adventists were told to prophesy again to and about the nations of earth, so the end-time believers will be privileged to prophesy for eternity to the multitudes in unfallen worlds. Their testimony of the love and saving grace of the Lord Jesus Christ as revealed by the cross will be a major influence in preventing the rise of sin again. "Affliction will not rise up a second time" (Nah. 1:9, NKJV).

Revelation 11:1 records God's instruction to the author of the book. John says, "Then I was given a measuring rod like a staff, and I was told: 'Rise and measure the temple of God and the altar and those who worship there.' " Since this is a continuation of chapter 10, we can conclude that the message to be proclaimed to the nations after 1844 is the truth that God's temple and His people are to be measured. The measuring of the temple points to the restoration of the truth regarding the heavenly sanctuary and its cleansing in the pre-Advent judgment (Dan. 7:9–14; 8:14; cf. Lev. 16). Prophecy informs us that the antitypical day of atonement, the pre-Advent judgment, began in 1844. In this judgment, God's heavenly sanctuary is cleansed of the record of the pardoned sins of God's faithful people, and the decision is made as to who will be saved and who will be lost. That's why both the heavenly temple and God's earthly people are measured.

Considered eschatologically, Revelation 11:1 refers to the carrying out of the decisions of the heavenly court after the close of probation. God's faithful people are finally vindicated, and the unfaithful face eternal loss. As the Neo-Babylonians were measured (judged) by God as worthy of death (Dan. 5:26), so those who have failed to receive and serve Christ as Savior and Lord will be judged as worthy of eternal death (Rom. 6:23). But those who have been vindicated in the pre-Advent judgment are measured in the sense of being judged worthy of receiving an eternal reward.

Revelation 11:2–13 traces in symbolic language the events that led up to the measuring of God's temple and people in the pre-Advent judgment (Rev. 11:1). Those events were the 1,260 years of papal ecclesiastical supremacy, the French Revolution, and the rejection of Scripture—but also the following exaltation of the Bible in the late eighteenth and the nineteenth centuries. The result was that the pervasive preaching in the nineteenth century of Christ's soon coming was followed by the dramatic events surrounding 1844.

God's "two witnesses" are the Old and New Testaments. They prophesied "clothed in sackcloth" during the period of papal supremacy in the sense that the papal church kept Scripture from the laity and depreciated Christ's heavenly, High-Priestly ministry by emphasizing an earthly ministry and priesthood. When God's two witnesses were finishing their testimony (Rev. 11:7), Satan attacked them violently through the French Revolution. For three-and-a-half years, 1793–1797, Bible Christianity was rejected in France, along with the papal religion (Rev. 11:8–10). But after that period it was accepted again, the great missionary movement began, and numerous Bible societies were established; they promoted the dissemination of the Scriptures worldwide. Thus verses 11 and 12 of Revelation 11 were fulfilled. Then followed the earth-shaking events surrounding 1844, in which many lost their faith, while others—their understanding increased—continued to proclaim the certainty of Christ's advent.

Eschatologically, the events of Revelation 11:2–13 take us back to the events of the third through the sixth trumpets, events that lead up to Christ's intervention on behalf of His people (Rev. 10) and the measuring of the temple and the people (Rev. 11:1). The court is not measured immediately before Christ comes (Rev. 11:2) because the lost have rejected the significance of Christ's sacrifice in the antitypical court (i.e., the earth, Calvary). The true biblical gospel means nothing to them, and no further hope is offered them.

The nations' trampling of the Holy City for forty-two months of prophetic time (1,260 literal years) was a type of the events of the third through the sixth trumpets after the close of probation. Satan's impersonation of Christ (third trumpet) results in the darkness of the fourth trumpet, which was typified by the spiritual darkness of the medieval period. God's Word will be denigrated; it will prophesy again "clothed in sackcloth" (Rev. 11:2, 3). But the power of God's two witnesses will be manifested in the pouring out of the seven last plagues (Rev. 11:5, 6).

Toward the end of the period of global spiritual darkness, there will be a final attempt to destroy those who honor God's Word and His law (Rev. 11:7–10). A death decree will be passed upon God's faithful people, but Christ will intervene at the time of their greatest need. Then the wicked will realize that they have been deceived. They will launch an attack upon their former spiritual leaders, and great destruction will follow. At that time, evidences of God's care for His Word and His people will appear in the sky. The law of God will also be displayed there (cf. Rev. 11:11, 12), and there will be a great earthquake. Some people will be killed and some will melt with fear, but those who are saved will rejoice that their redemption has come at last (Rev. 11:13).

SEVENTH TRUMPET

Like the trumpets before it, the seventh trumpet (Rev. 11:15–19) has meaning both historically and eschatologically. Historically, "the kingdom of the world" is becoming "the kingdom of our Lord and of his Christ" (Rev. 11:15) during the pre-Advent judgment that runs from 1844 till the close of probation. This is the historical "time for the dead to be judged" (Rev. 11:18). "God's temple in heaven was opened, and the ark of his covenant was seen within his temple" (Rev. 11:19) at the beginning of the pre-Advent judgment in 1844 (Dan. 7:9–14; 8:14). When God's people at that time understood the significance of Christ's heavenly sanctuary mediation and judgment, they entered with Christ into the Most Holy Place of the heavenly sanctuary by faith and accepted His saving mercy and the claims of His law contained in the ark of the covenant in heaven. They committed themselves to examining their hearts and becoming thoroughly right with their Lord during the antitypical day of atonement. God's faithful ones today continue to enjoy that spiritual experience.

Eschatologically, "the kingdom of the world" becomes "the kingdom of our Lord and of his Christ" (Rev. 11:15) at the second coming of

Christ. It is then that He takes His "great power" and begins to reign (Rev. 11:17). This is the ultimate "time for the dead to be judged, for rewarding thy servants, the prophets and saints . . . and for destroying the destroyers of the earth" (Rev. 11:18). This is the time of the executive judgment, when the decisions of the heavenly court are applied to both the saved and the lost. Immediately before Christ returns, "God's temple in heaven" is "opened, and the ark of his covenant" is "seen within his temple." Saved and lost will look up and see the tables of God's law displayed in the sky. Amid the reeling of the earth and in the midst of the final, cataclysmic events, all the surviving inhabitants of earth will be confronted by the authority of God's law. Then those saved by grace will rejoice that they accepted the power to obey God's law, and the lost will mourn that they turned their backs on God's saving mercy, scorning the demands of His law and refusing to be bound by it.

God's Word reveals to us the saving message of the cross and leaves us in no doubt as to the nature of future events. How can we ever reject such great salvation and close our eyes to the wonderful future the Lord has for us? How can we fail to heed the warnings the Bible contains of the calamitous events this world is about to witness and the ultimate fate of those who turn from the love of Christ?

Nominal Christian faith will never do. Claiming to be a Christian and convincing ourselves that our eternal salvation is secure while we are cherishing sin or ignoring the claims of Christ's law moves us down the path that leads to eternal ruin. Jesus said, "If you love me, you will keep my commandments" (John 14:15). Do you love Him enough to do what His Word asks of you? Do you love Him enough to turn your back on the world with its allurements and devote yourself every day to the service of Christ and of others? Do you love Him enough to pray and search His Word until you know for sure that you are in His merciful hands for eternity, and that nothing is separating you from fellowship with Him?

> Cast all your anxieties on him, for he cares about you. Be sober, be watchful. Your adversary the devil prowls around like a roaring lion, seeking some one to devour. Resist him, firm in your faith, knowing that the same experience of suffering is required of your brotherhood throughout the world. And after you have suffered a little while, the God of all grace, who has called you to his eternal glory in Christ, will himself restore, establish, and strengthen you. To him be the dominion for ever and ever. Amen (1 Pet. 5:7–11).

THE HISTORICAL AND END-TIME INTERPRETATIONS OF THE TRUMPETS
Revelation 8:2–11:19

HISTORICAL INTERPRETATION

Trump 1	Trump 2	Trump 3	Trump 4	Trump 5	Trump 6	Interlude	Trump 7
Fall of Jerusalem AD 70	Fall of Roman Empire	Rise of papacy AD 313–538	Dark Ages papal supremacy	Ottoman Empire 1299–1449	Ottoman Empire 1449–1840	Advent message disappointment 1840–1844	Investigative judgment 1844–End

ESCHATOLOGICAL INTERPRETATION

Trump 1	Trump 2	Trump 3	Trump 4	Trump 5	Trump 6	Interlude	Trump 7
Satan's attack on the church Rev. 8:7	Fall of the superpowers Rev. 8:8, 9	Satan impersonates Christ Rev. 8:10, 11	Spiritual darkness loyalty to Satan Rev. 8:12	Time of Jacob's trouble Rev. 9:1–12	Final attack on God's people Rev. 9:13–21	Voice of God "It is done." Rev. 10:1–11:14	Wicked punished temple opened law in sky Rev. 11:15–19

Bibliography

Anderson, Roy Allan. *Unfolding Daniel's Prophecies.* Mountain View, CA: Pacific Press®, 1975.

Andrews, John N. *The Three Messages of Revelation XIV, 6-12, Particularly the Third Angel's Message, and Two-Horned Beast.* Battle Creek, MI: Review and Herald®, 1892.

Aulard, A. *Christianity and the French Revolution.* London: Ernest Benn, 1927.

Aune, David E. *Revelation 6–16.* Word Biblical Commentary, vol. 52B. Nashville: Thomas Nelson, 1998.

Adolphus, John. *The History of France From the Year 1790 to the Peace Concluded at Amiens in 1802.* London: George Kearsley, 1803.

Arndt, William F., and Wilbur F. Gingrich. *A Greek-English Lexicon of the New Testament and Other Early Christian Literature,* 4th ed. Cambridge: University Press, 1957.

Baldinger, Albert H. *Preaching From Revelation.* Grand Rapids, MI: Zondervan, 1960.

Barclay, William. *The Revelation of John.* 2 vols. Philadelphia: Westminster Press, 1959.

Barnhouse, Donald G. *Revelation: An Expository Commentary.* Grand Rapids, MI: Zondervan, 1971.

Barr, David L. *Tales of the End: A Narrative Commentary on the Book of Revelation.* Santa Rosa, CA: Polebridge Press, 1998.

Beasley-Murray, G. R. *The Book of Revelation.* Grand Rapids, MI: Eerdmans, 1974.

Blass, Friedrich, and A. Debrunner. *A Greek Grammar of the New Testament and Other Early Christian Literature.* Chicago: University of Chicago Press, 1961.

Brown, Francis, S. R. Driver, and Charles A. Briggs. *A Hebrew and English Lexicon of the Old Testament.* Oxford: Clarendon Press, 1952.

Buis, Harry. *The Book of Revelation.* Philadelphia: Presbyterian and Reformed Publishing Co., 1960.

Bury, J. B. *History of the Later Roman Empire.* 2 vols. New York: Dover, 1958.

Buttrick, George Arthur, ed. *The Interpreter's Dictionary of the Bible.* 4 vols. New York: Abingdon, 1962.

Caird, G. B. *The Revelation of St. John the Divine.* New York: Harper and Row, 1966.

Charles, R. H. *A Critical and Exegetical Commentary on the Revelation of St. John.* 2 vols. Edinburgh: T. & T. Clark, 1920, 1970, 1971.

Criswell, W. A. *Expository Sermons on Revelation.* 5 vols. Grand Rapids, MI: Zondervan, 1962–1966.

Cross, F. L., ed. *The Oxford Dictionary of the Christian Church.* London: Oxford University Press, 1958.

Dana, H. E. and Julius R. Mantey. *A Manual Grammar of the Greek New Testament.* New York: Macmillan, 1927, 1960.

Dansette, Adrien. *Religious History of Modern France.* New York: Herder and Herder, 1961.

Dawson, Christopher. *The Gods of Revolution.* New York: New York University Press, 1972.

Bibliography

Denzinger, Henry. *The Sources of Catholic Dogma,* Roy Deferrari, trans. St. Louis, MO: B. Herder, 1954.

Dillenberger, John, and Claude Welch. *Protestant Christianity Interpreted Through Its Development.* New York: Charles Scribner's Sons, 1954.

Doukhan, Jacques B. *Secrets of Revelation.* Hagerstown, MD: Review and Herald®, 2002.

Ezell, Douglas. *Revelations on Revelation: New Sounds From Old Symbols.* Waco, TX: Word Books, 1977.

Farrer, Austin. *The Revelation of St. John the Divine.* Oxford: Clarendon Press, 1964.

Ford, J. Massyngberde. *Revelation, The Anchor Bible.* Vol. 38. Garden City, NY: Doubleday, 1975.

Froom, LeRoy. *The Conditionalist Faith of Our Fathers.* 2 vols. Washington, DC: Review and Herald®, 1965, 1966.

_____. *The Prophetic Faith of Our Fathers.* 4 vols. Washington, DC: Review and Herald®, 1950–54.

Gane, Erwin R. *You Ask, God Answers.* Ukiah, CA: Orion Publishing, 1998.

_____. *Heaven's Open Door.* Boise, ID: Pacific Press®, 1989.

Gane, Roy. *Altar Call.* Berrien Springs, MI: Diadem, 1999.

———. *Leviticus, Numbers: The NIV Application Commentary.* Grand Rapids, MI: Zondervan, 2004.

Gibbon, Edward. *The Decline and Fall of the Roman Empire.* 6 vols. New York: Dutton, 1910.

Glasson, T. F. *The Revelation of John.* Cambridge: University Press, 1965.

Hendriksen, W. *More Than Conquerors.* Grand Rapids, MI: Baker, 1965.

Higgins, E. L. *The French Revolution as Told by Contemporaries.* Boston: Houghton Mifflin, 1938.

Horn, Siegfried H., and Lynn H. Wood. *The Chronology of Ezra 7.* Washington, DC: Review and Herald®, 1953.

İnalcık, Halil. *The Ottoman Empire: The Classical Age 1300–1600.* London: Weidenfeld and Nicolson, 1973.

The Interpreter's Dictionary of the Bible. New York: Abingdon Press, 1962.

Jackson, S. M., ed. *The New Schaff-Herzog Encyclopedia of Religious Knowledge.* 14 vols. Grand Rapids, MI: Baker, 1963.

Kiddle, Martin. *The Revelation of St. John.* New York: Harper & Row, 1940.

Kuyper, Abraham. *The Revelation of St. John.* Grand Rapids, MI: Eerdmans, 1935, 1963.

Ladd, George Eldon. *A Commentary on the Revelation of John.* Grand Rapids, MI: Eerdmans, 1972.

Latourette, Kenneth S. *A History of the Expansion of Christianity.* 7 vols. New York: Harper, 1937–1971.

Lenski, Richard C. H. *The Interpretation of St. John's Revelation.* Minneapolis, MN: Augsburg, 1943.

Lewis, Bernard, ed. *Islam and the Arab World: Faith, People, Culture.* New York: American Heritage, 1976.

Litch, Josiah. "Dissertation on the Fall of the Ottoman Empire: The 11th of August, 1840," *Second Advent Tracts,* no. XI, 1841.

Loane, Marcus. *They Overcame: An Exposition of the First Three Chapters of Revelation.* Grand Rapids, MI: Baker, 1971.

McManners, John. *The French Revolution and the Church.* New York: Harper and Row, 1969.

Maxwell, C. Mervyn. *God Cares.* 2 vols. Boise, ID: Pacific Press®, 1981, 1985.

Montgomery, James A. *A Critical and Exegetical Commentary on the Book of Daniel.* Edinburgh: T. & T. Clark, 1927.

BIBLIOGRAPHY

De Montléon, Aimé Guillon. *Memoires pour servir histoire de la ville de Lyon pendant la Révolution (History of the City of Lyon During the French Revolution).* Paris: Baudoin, 1824.

Morris, Leon. *The Revelation of St. John.* Grand Rapids, MI: Eerdmans, 1969.

Mosheim, J. L. *Institutes of Ecclesiastical History, Ancient and Modern.* 4 vols. London: Longmans, 1845.

Moulton, J. H., ed. *A Grammar of New Testament Greek.* Vol. 3, *Syntax,* Nigel Turner, ed. Edinburgh: T & T. Clark, 1963.

Mounce, Robert H. *The Book of Revelation. The New International Commentary on the New Testament.* Grand Rapids, MI: Eerdmans, 1977.

Moyise, Steve. *Studies in the Book of Revelation.* New York: T. & T. Clark, 2001.

Neufeld, Don F., and Julia Neuffer, eds. *Seventh-day Adventist Bible Students' Source Book.* Washington, DC: Review and Herald®, 1962.

Nichol, Francis. D., ed. *Seventh-day Adventist Bible Commentary.* 7 vols. Washington, DC: Review and Herald®, 1953–1957.

Pack, Frank. *Revelation.* 2 vols. Austin, TX: Sweet Publishing Company, 1965.

Paulien, Jon. *Decoding Revelation's Trumpets.* Berrien Springs, MI: Andrews University Press, 1987.

Peake, Arthur. *The Revelation of John.* London: Primitive Methodist Publishing House, 1910.

Poland, Burdette C. *French Protestantism and the French Revolution: A Study in Church and State, Thought and Religion, 1685–1815.* Princeton, NJ: Princeton University Press, 1957.

Sale, George, ed. and trans. *The Koran or Alcoran of Mohammed.* London: Frederick Warne, 1734, 1736.

Schaff, Philip. *History of the Christian Church*. 8 vols. Grand Rapids, MI: Eerdmans, 1907, 1966.

Scott, Walter. *Exposition of the Revelation of Jesus Christ*. Westwood, NJ: Fleming H. Revell, 1968.

Seiss, J. A. *The Apocalypse: Lectures on the Book of Revelation*. Grand Rapids, MI: Zondervan, 1900, 1974.

De Sélincourt, Aubrey, trans. *Herodotus, the Histories*. Baltimore, MD: Penguin, 1954.

Shea, William. *Selected Studies on Prophetic Interpretation,* Daniel and Revelation Committee Series. Vol. 1. Washington, DC: Review and Herald®, 1982.

Smith, Uriah. *The Prophecies of Daniel and the Revelation*. Nashville: Southern Publishing Association, 1944.

Strand, Kenneth A. "An Overlooked Old Testament Background to Revelation 11:1," *Andrews University Seminary Studies* 22 (1984): 317–325.

———. *Interpreting the Book of Revelation*. Ann Arbor, MI: Ann Arbor Publishers, 1976.

Strand, Kenneth A., ed. *The Sabbath in Scripture and History*. Washington, DC: Review and Herald®, 1982.

Stefanovic, Ranko. *Revelation of Jesus Christ*. Berrien Springs, MI: Andrews University Press, 2002.

Summers, Ray. *Worthy Is the Lamb: An Interpretation of Revelation*. Nashville: Broadman, 1951.

Swete, Henry Barclay. *The Apocalypse of St. John*. Grand Rapids, MI: Eerdmans, 1968.

Tanakh: the Holy Scriptures. The New JPS Translation According to the Traditional Hebrew Text. New York: Jewish Publication Society, 1985.

Thiele, Edwin R. *Outline Studies in Revelation*. Angwin, CA: Pacific Union College, 1980.

Trevor, George. *Rome: From the Fall of the Western Empire.* London: Religious Tract Society, 1868.

Unruh, Ulrike. "Daniel Five: Who Was Belshazzar?" in *Studies in the Book of Daniel,* http://dedication.www3.50megs.com/dan/belshazzar.html.

Walvoord, John F. *Daniel, the Key to Prophetic Revelation.* Chicago: Moody Press, 1971.

White, Ellen G. *The Acts of the Apostles.* Mountain View, CA: Pacific Press®, 1911.

_____. *Christ's Object Lessons.* Battle Creek, MI: Review and Herald®, 1900.

_____. *Counsels to Parents and Teachers.* Mountain View, CA: Pacific Press®, 1913.

_____. *The Desire of Ages.* Mountain View, CA: Pacific Press®, 1898, 1940.

_____. *Early Writings.* Battle Creek, MI: Review and Herald®, 1882.

_____. *Education.* Mountain View, CA: Pacific Press®, 1903.

_____. *The Great Controversy.* Mountain View, CA: Pacific Press®, 1911.

_____. *Life Sketches.* Mountain View, CA: Pacific Press®, 1915, 1943.

_____. *Maranatha: The Lord Is Coming.* Washington, DC: Review and Herald®, 1976.

_____. *Patriarchs and Prophets.* Mountain View, CA: Pacific Press®, 1890.

_____. *Selected Messages.* 3 vols. Washington, DC: Review and Herald®, 1958, 1980.

_____. *The Spirit of Prophecy.* 4 vols. Battle Creek, MI: Review and Herald®, 1884.

_____. *Testimonies for the Church.* 9 vols. Mountain View, CA:

Pacific Press®, 1948.

_____. *Testimonies to Ministers and Gospel Workers.* Mountain View, CA: Pacific Press®, 1923.

Wood, Leon. *A Commentary on Daniel.* Grand Rapids, MI: Zondervan, 1973.

Yeager, Randolph O. *The Renaissance New Testament.* 18 vols. Bowling Green, KY: Renaissance Press, 1976.